2016

THE BEST OF
COUNTRY COOKING

Taste of Home

For other *Taste of Home* books and products,
visit ShopTasteofHome.com.

SAVOR THE VERY BEST OF COUNTRY COMFORT

It doesn't get any better than sharing a hearty meal while creating memories with loved ones, and *The Best of Country Cooking* will help you do both! Whether you're searching for enticing appetizers, family-friendly main dishes, go-to slow cooker options or sweet treats, you'll find what you need for any occasion right here. All the recipes come from home cooks just like you, meaning they've passed the "This is delicious!" test time and again.

Dig in to the following features (and many more):

Contest-Winning Favorites

When you see the blue ribbon icon next to a recipe, you know it's a good one because it placed in a *Taste of Home* contest! Serve one of these stunners at your next gathering to a chorus of accolades.

Cooking for Two

No need to do math when you're cooking for just the two of you! This special chapter has scaled-down recipes perfect for small households. From main dishes to sides and even breakfast staples, you're always covered without unwanted leftovers.

Dazzling Desserts

There's nothing more welcoming and comforting than homemade desserts. Get ready for any bridal shower, bake sale or birthday party after looking through this chapter. You'll soon be spreading joy by the dozen!

Bring everyone together for some home-cooked love. You can't go wrong when you turn to *The Best of Country Cooking* for mealtime inspiration.

■ **EDITORIAL**
Editor-in-Chief **Catherine Cassidy**
Creative Director **Howard Greenberg**
Editorial Operations Director **Kerri Balliet**

Managing Editor/Print & Digital Books **Mark Hagen**
Associate Creative Director **Edwin Robles Jr.**

Associate Editors **Molly Jasinski, Julie Kuczynski**
Layout Designer **Catherine Fletcher**
Editorial Production Manager **Dena Ahlers**
Editorial Production Coordinator **Jill Banks**
Copy Chief **Deb Warlaumont Mulvey**
Copy Editor **Chris McLaughlin**
Contributing Copy Editors **Valerie Phillips, Kristin Sutter**
Editorial Intern **Michael Welch**

Food Editors **Gina Nistico; James Schend; Peggy Woodward, RDN**
Recipe Editors **Sue Ryon (lead), Mary King, Irene Yeh**
Business Analyst, Content Tools **Amanda Harmatys**
Content Operations Manager **Shannon Stroud**
Editorial Services Administrator **Marie Brannon**

Test Kitchen & Food Styling Manager **Sarah Thompson**
Test Cooks **Nicholas Iverson (lead), Matthew Hass, Lauren Knoelke**
Food Stylists **Kathryn Conrad (lead), Shannon Roum, Leah Rekau**
Prep Cooks **Bethany Van Jacobson (lead), Megumi Garcia, Melissa Hansen**
Culinary Team Assistant **Megan Behr**

Photography Director **Stephanie Marchese**
Photographers **Dan Roberts, Jim Wieland**
Photographer/Set Stylist **Grace Natoli Sheldon**
Set Stylists **Melissa Franco, Stacey Genaw, Dee Dee Jacq**

Editorial Business Manager **Kristy Martin**
Editorial Business Associate **Samantha Lea Stoeger**

Editor, *Taste of Home* **Jeanne Ambrose**
Associate Creative Director, *Taste of Home* **Erin Burns**
Art Director, *Taste of Home* **Kristin Bowker**

■ **BUSINESS**
Vice President, Group Publisher **Kirsten Marchioli**
Publisher, *Taste of Home* **Donna Lindskog**
General Manager, Taste of Home Cooking School **Erin Puariea**

■ **TRUSTED MEDIA BRANDS, INC.**
President and Chief Executive Officer **Bonnie Kintzer**
Chief Financial Officer/Chief Operating Officer **Howard Halligan**
Chief Revenue Officer **Richard Sutton**
Chief Marketing Officer **Alec Casey**
Chief Digital Officer **Vince Errico**
Chief Technology Officer **Aneel Tejwaney**
Senior Vice President, Global HR & Communications **Phyllis E. Gebhardt, SPHR; SHRM-SCP**
Vice President, Digital Content & Audience Development **Diane Dragan**
Vice President, Brand Marketing **Beth Gorry**
Vice President, Financial Planning & Analysis **William Houston**
Publishing Director, Books **Debra Polansky**
Vice President, Consumer Marketing Planning **Jim Woods**

© 2016 RDA Enthusiast Brands, LLC
1610 N. 2nd St., Suite 102
Milwaukee, WI 53212-3906

International Standard Book Number:
978-1-61765-524-1

International Standard Serial Number:
1097-8321

Component Number: 117000046H

All Rights Reserved.

Taste of Home is a registered trademark of RDA Enthusiast Brands, LLC.

Printed in China

1 3 5 7 9 10 8 6 4 2

PICTURED ON THE FRONT COVER Black Bean 'n' Pumpkin Chili (p. 132), Chocolate Brownie Waffle Sundaes (p. 176), Ravishing Radish Salad (p. 53) and Homey Mac & Cheese (p. 78).

PICTURED ON THE BACK COVER Herbed Dinner Rolls (p. 64), Berry-Apple-Rhubarb Pie (p. 167) and Crumb-Coated Chicken & Blackberry Salsa (p. 118).

CONTENTS

SNACKS & BEVERAGES

When you need an afternoon pick-me-up, a refreshing sipper or a weekend nibble, these tasty bites and drinks are here for you. Choose savory or sweet treats—or a little of both. You can't go wrong!

Shrimp & Feta Cucumber Rounds

I love the contrasting tastes and textures of these rounds. Each bite balances the refreshing burst and crunch of cucumber with the rich flavor of the filling.

—DONNA POCHODAY-STELMACH
MORRISTOWN, NJ

START TO FINISH: 30 MIN.
MAKES: ABOUT 3 DOZEN

- 1 **package (8 ounces) cream cheese, softened**
- 1¼ **cups (5 ounces) crumbled feta cheese**
- 2 **teaspoons snipped fresh dill**
- ¼ **teaspoon salt**
- ¼ **teaspoon chili powder**
- ⅛ **teaspoon pepper**
- ⅔ **cup peeled and deveined cooked small shrimp (about 6 ounces), chopped**
- ¼ **cup finely chopped roasted sweet red pepper**
- 2 **large English cucumbers, cut into ½-inch slices**
  Fresh dill sprigs or additional chopped roasted sweet red peppers, optional

In a large bowl, beat the first six ingredients until blended. Stir in shrimp and red pepper. Place about 2 teaspoons shrimp mixture on each cucumber slice. Refrigerate until serving. If desired, top with dill or red peppers before serving.

Contest Winner

Berry Smoothies

Smooth out the morning rush with a boost of berries. It's tart, tangy and sweet enough so you won't need to add any extra sugar to this delightful beverage.

—ELISABETH LARSEN PLEASANT GROVE, UT

START TO FINISH: 5 MIN.
MAKES: 5 SERVINGS

- 2 **cups cranberry juice**
- 2 **containers (6 ounces each) raspberry yogurt**
- 1 **cup frozen unsweetened raspberries**
- 1 **cup frozen unsweetened blueberries**
- 8 **ice cubes**

In a blender, combine all ingredients; cover and process for 30-45 seconds or until blended. Pour into chilled glasses; serve immediately.

FREEZE FRESH BERRIES

If you want to freeze berries straight from your garden or farmers market, you can keep them frozen for up to 1 year. Wash berries, then blot dry and place in a single layer on a pan. Freeze until firm, then transfer to a heavy-duty resealable bag.

Meatball Sliders

You can make the meatballs ahead of time and keep them warm in a slow cooker or on the stovetop.

—**HILARY BREINHOLT** GLENWOOD, UT

PREP: 15 MIN. • **BAKE:** 25 MIN.
MAKES: 16 SERVINGS

- 1½ **pounds bulk Italian sausage**
- 16 **cubes part-skim mozzarella cheese (about 8 ounces)**
- 1 **jar (24 ounces) spaghetti sauce**
- 1 **jar (8.1 ounces) prepared pesto**
- 16 **dinner rolls, split and toasted**

1. Divide sausage into 16 portions. Shape each portion around a cube of cheese. Place on a greased rack in a shallow baking pan. Bake at 350° for 25-30 minutes or until meat is no longer pink. Remove meatballs to paper towels to drain.

2. In a large saucepan, combine spaghetti sauce and pesto; bring just to a boil over medium heat, stirring occasionally. Add the meatballs; heat through, stirring gently. Serve on rolls.

Spicy Pumpkin Fritters

Fall flavors shine in these little bites. Cut back on the chili powder and pepper flakes if you prefer a little less spice. You can also try using curry powder instead.

—**TRISHA KRUSE** EAGLE, ID

PREP: 10 MIN. • **COOK:** 5 MIN./BATCH
MAKES: ABOUT 3 DOZEN

- 1½ **cups all-purpose flour**
- 2 **teaspoons baking powder**
- 1¼ **teaspoons salt**
- ¾ **teaspoon chili powder**
- ½ **teaspoon onion powder**
- ¼ **teaspoon crushed red pepper flakes**
- 2 **large eggs**
- 1 **can (15 ounces) solid-pack pumpkin**
- ½ **cup 2% milk**
- 2 **tablespoons butter, melted**
  Oil for deep-fat frying
  Chipotle mayonnaise, optional

1. In a large bowl, whisk the first six ingredients. In another bowl, whisk eggs, pumpkin, milk and melted butter until blended. Add to dry ingredients, stirring just until moistened.

2. In an electric skillet or deep fryer, heat oil to 375°. Drop the batter by tablespoonfuls, a few at a time, into hot oil. Fry 1½-2 minutes on each side or until golden brown. Drain on paper towels. Serve warm. If desired, serve with chipotle mayonnaise.

Loaded Baked Potato Dip

I never thought of using waffle-cut fries as a scoop for dip until a friend of mine did at a baby shower. They're ideal for my cheesy bacon and chive dip, which tastes just like a baked potato topper.
—**BETSY KING** DULUTH, MN

START TO FINISH: 10 MIN. • **MAKES:** 2½ CUPS

- 2 cups (16 ounces) sour cream
- 2 cups (8 ounces) shredded cheddar cheese
- 8 center-cut bacon or turkey bacon strips, chopped and cooked
- ⅓ cup minced fresh chives
- 2 teaspoons Louisiana-style hot sauce
  Hot cooked waffle-cut fries

In a small bowl, mix the first five ingredients until blended; refrigerate until serving. Serve with waffle fries.

Contest Winner

Creamy Lemon Milk Shakes

Several recipes inspired the combination of ingredients I use in these shakes. They're so refreshing, especially on a warm day!
—**CAROL GILLESPIE** CHAMBERSBURG, PA

START TO FINISH: 10 MIN. • **MAKES:** 4 SERVINGS

- 2 tablespoons crushed lemon drop candies
- 1 teaspoon sugar
- ½ small lemon, cut into six slices, divided
- ½ cup 2% milk
- 2 cups vanilla ice cream
- 2 cups lemon sorbet
- 3 ounces cream cheese, softened
- 2 teaspoons grated lemon peel
- ½ teaspoon vanilla extract

1. In a shallow dish, mix crushed lemon drops and sugar. Using 1 or 2 lemon slices, moisten the rims of four glasses; dip rims into candy mixture.
2. Place remaining ingredients in a blender; cover and process until smooth. Pour into prepared glasses; serve immediately with remaining lemon slices.

1½ cups (6 ounces) shredded cheddar cheese, divided
5 ounces Canadian bacon, chopped
1½ cups (6 ounces) shredded part-skim mozzarella cheese
Marinara sauce

1. Unroll breadsticks into a greased 15x10x1-in. baking pan. Press onto the bottom and up the sides of pan; pinch seams to seal. Bake at 350° for 6-8 minutes or until set.
2. Meanwhile, in a large skillet, saute mushrooms, peppers, onion and 1 teaspoon Italian seasoning in 2 teaspoons oil until crisp-tender; drain.
3. Brush crust with remaining oil. Sprinkle with ¾ cup cheddar cheese; top with vegetable mixture and Canadian bacon. Combine mozzarella cheese and remaining cheddar cheese; sprinkle over top. Sprinkle with the remaining Italian seasoning.
4. Bake for 20-25 minutes or until cheese is melted and crust is golden brown. Serve with marinara sauce.
FREEZE OPTION *Bake crust as directed, add toppings and cool. Securely wrap and freeze unbaked pizza. To use, unwrap the pizza; bake as directed, increasing time as necessary.*

Apple and Peanut Butter Stackers

The best way to get kids interested in cooking and eating right is to let them help. Sliced apple "sandwiches" are one fun way to pique their interest and kitchen creativity.
—SHIRLEY WARREN THIENSVILLE, WI

START TO FINISH: 10 MIN. • **MAKES:** 6 SERVINGS

2 medium apples
⅓ cup chunky peanut butter
Optional fillings: granola, miniature semisweet chocolate chips and M&M's minis

Core apples. Cut each apple crosswise into six slices. Spread peanut butter over six slices; sprinkle with fillings of your choice. Top with remaining apple slices.

Breadstick Pizza

Make any day fun-day with a hassle-free, yummy homemade pizza featuring refrigerated breadsticks as the crust. Feeding kids? Slice pieces into small strips and let them dip each strip into marinara sauce. They'll love it!
—MARY HANKINS KANSAS CITY, MO

PREP: 25 MIN. • **BAKE:** 20 MIN. • **MAKES:** 12 SERVINGS

2 tubes (11 ounces each) refrigerated breadsticks
½ pound sliced fresh mushrooms
2 medium green peppers, chopped
1 medium onion, chopped
1½ teaspoons Italian seasoning, divided
4 teaspoons olive oil, divided

Hazelnut Mocha Coffee

I make this frosty coffee drink for special occasions. You can prepare the chocolate mixture a couple days in advance. When you're ready to serve it, simply brew the coffee and whip the chocolate.

—**MARY LEVERETTE** COLUMBIA, SC

PREP: 5 MIN. • **COOK:** 10 MIN. + CHILLING
MAKES: 6 SERVINGS

- 4 ounces semisweet chocolate, chopped
- 1 cup heavy whipping cream
- ⅓ cup sugar
- ½ teaspoon ground cinnamon
- 2 tablespoons hazelnut liqueur
- 4½ cups hot brewed coffee
  Sweetened whipped cream, optional

1. Place chocolate in a small bowl. In a small saucepan, bring cream just to a boil. Add sugar and cinnamon; cook and stir until sugar is dissolved. Pour over chocolate; stir with a whisk until smooth. Stir in liqueur.

2. Cool to room temperature, stirring occasionally. Refrigerate, covered, until cold. Beat just until soft peaks form, about 15 seconds (do not overbeat). For each serving, spoon ¼ cup into mugs. Top with ¾ cup coffee; stir to dissolve. Top with whipped cream if desired.

Layered Ranch Dip

I found something similar to this in a cookbook for kids. It looked like a winner, so I decided to create my own slightly more grown-up version.

—**PEGGY ROOS** MINNEAPOLIS, MN

PREP: 10 MIN. • **MAKES:** 8 SERVINGS

- 2 cups (16 ounces) sour cream
- 1 envelope ranch salad dressing mix
- 1 medium tomato, chopped
- 1 can (4 ounces) chopped green chilies, drained
- 1 can (2¼ ounces) sliced ripe olives, drained
- ¼ cup finely chopped red onion
- 1 cup (4 ounces) shredded Monterey Jack cheese
  Corn chips or tortilla chips

In a small bowl, mix sour cream and dressing mix; spread into a large shallow dish. Layer with the tomato, green chilies, olives, onion and cheese. Refrigerate until serving. Serve with chips.

Gingered Sweet & Spicy Hot Wings

My hot wings are a foolproof way to curry a little favor with my loved ones. They lick their fingers to get every bit of the sweet (orange marmalade) and hot (Sriracha) flavors that come bursting through along with every bite.

—JENNIFER LOCKLIN CYPRESS, TX

PREP: 15 MIN. + MARINATING
BAKE: 35 MIN. • **MAKES:** ABOUT 3 DOZEN

- 1 cup orange marmalade
- ½ cup minced fresh cilantro
- ½ cup Sriracha Asian hot chili sauce
- ½ cup reduced-sodium soy sauce
- ¼ cup lime juice
- ¼ cup rice vinegar
- ¼ cup ketchup
- ¼ cup honey
- 4 garlic cloves, minced
- 1 tablespoon minced fresh gingerroot
- 1 tablespoon grated lime peel
- 1 tablespoon sesame oil
- 1 teaspoon salt
- 1 teaspoon pepper
- 4 pounds chicken wingettes and drumettes

1. In a large resealable plastic bag, combine the first 14 ingredients. Add chicken; seal bag and turn to coat. Refrigerate contents 8 hours or overnight.

2. Preheat oven to 375°. Drain chicken, discarding marinade. Transfer chicken to two greased 15x10x1-in. baking pans. Bake 35-45 minutes or until juices run clear.

Contest Winner

CHEESE, PLEASE!

Yes, bring on the cheese! From well-loved favorites, such as cheddar and Parmesan, to less-familiar flavors, such as Jarlsberg and goat cheese, you'll want to dig into these cheesy options.

Fun-Do Fondue

Fondues are a hit at our gatherings. The younger crowd dips bread cubes, and the adults go for the pears. Veggies such as celery, cucumbers and bell peppers work, too.
—**JUDY BATSON** TAMPA, FL

START TO FINISH: 20 MIN. • **MAKES:** 3 CUPS

- 2 **cups (8 ounces) shredded Jarlsberg cheese**
- ½ **cup shredded Swiss cheese**
- ¼ **cup all-purpose flour**
- ½ **teaspoon ground mustard**
- ½ **teaspoon freshly ground pepper**
- 1 **cup heavy whipping cream**
- 1 **cup reduced-sodium chicken broth**
- 1 **tablespoon honey**
- 1 **teaspoon lemon juice**
  Cubed French bread, sliced pears and assorted fresh vegetables

1. In a small bowl, combine the first five ingredients; toss to combine. In a saucepan, combine cream, broth and honey; bring just to a boil, stirring occasionally. Reduce heat to medium-low. Add ½ cup cheese mixture; stir constantly until almost completely melted. Continue adding cheese, ½ cup at a time, allowing cheese to almost melt completely between additions. Continue stirring until thickened and smooth. Stir in lemon juice.

2. Transfer mixture to a heated fondue pot; keep fondue bubbling gently. Serve with bread, pears and vegetables for dipping. If fondue becomes too thick, stir in a little additional broth.

Grilled Cheese & Tomato Flatbreads

This recipe is like taking a grilled pizza and a cheesy flatbread and combining them into one. It's a great appetizer or main dish.
—**TINA MIRILOVICH** JOHNSTOWN, PA

PREP: 30 MIN. • **GRILL:** 5 MIN.
MAKES: 2 FLATBREADS (12 SERVINGS EACH)

- 1 **package (8 ounces) cream cheese, softened**
- ⅔ **cup grated Parmesan cheese, divided**
- 2 **tablespoons minced fresh parsley, divided**
- 1 **tablespoon minced chives**
- 2 **garlic cloves, minced**
- ½ **teaspoon minced fresh thyme**
- ¼ **teaspoon salt**
- ¼ **teaspoon pepper**
- 1 **tube (13.8 ounces) refrigerated pizza crust**
- 2 **tablespoons olive oil**
- 3 **medium tomatoes, thinly sliced**

1. In a small bowl, beat the cream cheese, ⅓ cup Parmesan cheese, 1 tablespoon parsley, chives, garlic, thyme, salt and pepper until blended.

2. Unroll pizza crust and cut in half. On a lightly floured surface, roll out each portion into a 12x6-in. rectangle; brush each side with oil. Grill, covered, over medium heat for 1-2 minutes or until bottoms are lightly browned. Remove from the grill.

3. Spread grilled sides with cheese mixture. Sprinkle with remaining Parmesan cheese; top with tomatoes. Return to the grill. Cover and cook for 2-3 minutes or until crust is lightly browned and cheese is melted, rotating halfway through cooking to ensure an evenly browned crust. Sprinkle with remaining parsley.

2. In an electric skillet or deep fryer, heat oil to 375°. Fry noodles in batches for 1-2 minutes or until golden brown, turning once. Drain on paper towels. Immediately sprinkle with cheese mixture.

3. For dip, in a large skillet, cook sausage over medium heat 4-6 minutes or until no longer pink, breaking into fine crumbles. Stir in ricotta, spaghetti sauce, garlic and other seasonings; bring to a boil. Reduce heat; simmer, uncovered, 5 minutes or until slightly thickened, stirring occasionally.

4. Transfer to a 1-qt. microwave-safe dish. Sprinkle with Italian cheese. Microwave, covered, on high for 45-60 seconds or until cheese is melted. Serve with lasagna chips.

Herbed Goat Cheese Baguette Slices

This special snack is guaranteed to wow guests. It takes just moments to whip up the herb-infused goat cheese spread.

—TASTE OF HOME TEST KITCHEN

PREP: 15 MIN. + CHILLING • **MAKES:** 4 SERVINGS

    2   ounces fresh goat cheese
    1   teaspoon minced fresh parsley
    ¾   teaspoon minced fresh rosemary
    ¼   teaspoon minced garlic
        Dash salt
        Dash coarsely ground pepper
    8   slices French bread baguette (¼ inch thick)
    1   plum tomato, cut into eight thin slices
        Additional coarsely ground pepper, optional

1. In a small bowl, combine the cheese, parsley, rosemary, garlic, salt and pepper; roll into a 3-in. log. Cover log and refrigerate for at least 1 hour.

2. Spread over bread; top with tomato slices. Sprinkle with additional pepper if desired.

Lasagna Dip

My idea for lasagna noodle chips turned out great, and they're truly out-of-this-world crispy. On top of that, the dip actually tastes like rich, cheesy lasagna.

—LINDA CIFUENTES MAHOMET, IL

PREP: 25 MIN. • **COOK:** 15 MIN. • **MAKES:** 3 CUPS DIP (36 CHIPS)

    6   uncooked lasagna noodles
    2   tablespoons grated Parmesan cheese
    2   tablespoons Italian seasoning
    ½   teaspoon garlic powder
        Oil for deep-fat frying
DIP
    ½   pound bulk Italian sausage
    2   cups whole-milk ricotta cheese
    1   cup spaghetti sauce
    2   garlic cloves, minced
    1   teaspoon dried basil
    1   teaspoon dried oregano
    ½   teaspoon salt
    ½   teaspoon pepper
    ½   cup shredded Italian cheese blend

1. Cook lasagna noodles according to package directions; drain. Cut noodles into 2-in. pieces; prick each piece several times with a fork. Mix Parmesan cheese, Italian seasoning and garlic powder.

Mini BLT Appetizers

Five simple ingredients is all it takes to impress friends and family with this tasty app. I love to make these as much as I love to share them.

—**NICK BERG** MILWAUKEE, WI

START TO FINISH: 30 MIN.
MAKES: ABOUT 2½ DOZEN

- 30 cherry tomatoes
- ¾ cup reduced-fat mayonnaise
- 2 Bibb or Boston lettuce leaves, torn into 1-inch pieces
- ¼ cup salad croutons, broken into pieces
- 3 bacon strips, cooked and crumbled
  Coarsely ground pepper

1. Cut a thin slice off the top of each tomato. Scoop out and discard pulp; invert tomatoes on paper towels to drain. Pipe mayonnaise into tomatoes.
2. Top each with a piece of rolled up lettuce, croutons and bacon. Sprinkle with pepper. Cover and refrigerate up to 1 hour.

Garbanzo-Stuffed Mini Peppers

Pretty mini peppers are naturally sized for a two-bite snack. They have all the crunch of a pita chip, but offer a fresh twist.

—**CHRISTINE HANOVER** LEWISTON, CA

START TO FINISH: 20 MIN.
MAKES: 32 APPETIZERS

- 1 teaspoon cumin seeds
- 1 can (15 ounces) garbanzo beans or chickpeas, rinsed and drained
- ¼ cup fresh cilantro leaves
- 3 tablespoons water
- 3 tablespoons cider vinegar
- ¼ teaspoon salt
- 16 miniature sweet peppers, halved lengthwise
  Additional fresh cilantro leaves

1. In a dry small skillet, toast cumin seeds over medium heat 1-2 minutes or until aromatic, stirring frequently. Transfer to a food processor. Add garbanzo beans, cilantro, water, vinegar and salt; pulse until blended.
2. Spoon into pepper halves. Top with additional cilantro. Refrigerate until serving.

Refreshing Beer Margaritas

I'm always excited to introduce someone to this drink. It's a great summertime cocktail, and it's easy to double or triple the recipe for larger get-togethers.

—**ARIANNE BARNETT** KANSAS CITY, MO

START TO FINISH: 5 MIN.
MAKES: 6 SERVINGS

- Lime slices and kosher salt, optional
- 2 bottles (12 ounces each) beer
- 1 can (12 ounces) frozen limeade concentrate, thawed
- ¾ cup tequila
- ¼ cup sweet and sour mix
  Ice cubes
- **GARNISH**
  Lime slices

1. If desired, use lime slices to moisten the rims of six margarita or cocktail glasses. Sprinkle salt on a plate; hold each glass upside down and dip rims into salt. Discard salt remaining on plate.
2. In a pitcher, combine the beer, concentrate, tequila and sweet and sour mix. Serve in prepared glasses over ice. Garnish with lime slices.

Apple Cider Smash

A smash is a fruity and chilled cocktail. Those apples you bought from the orchard make this drink a real hit.

—**MOFFAT FRAZIER** NEW YORK, NY

START TO FINISH: 20 MIN.
MAKES: 16 SERVINGS

- 2 cups finely chopped Gala or other red apples (about 2 small)
- 2 cups finely chopped Granny Smith apples (about 2 small)
- 2½ cups bourbon
- ⅔ cup apple brandy
- 4 teaspoons lemon juice
  Ice cubes
- 5⅓ cups chilled sparkling apple cider

1. In a bowl, toss apples to combine. In a small pitcher, mix the bourbon, brandy and lemon juice.
2. To serve, fill each of 16 rocks glasses halfway with ice. To each glass, add ¼ cup of the apple mixture and 3 tablespoons bourbon mixture; top each with ⅓ cup cider.

Nuts and Seeds Trail Mix

My party mix combines seeds, nuts, fruit and dark chocolate, and it's one I enjoy sharing with my family.

—**KRISTIN RIMKUS** SNOHOMISH, WA

START TO FINISH: 5 MIN. • **MAKES:** 5 CUPS

- 1 cup salted pumpkin seeds or pepitas
- 1 cup unblanched almonds
- 1 cup unsalted sunflower kernels
- 1 cup walnut halves
- 1 cup dried apricots
- 1 cup dark chocolate chips

Place all ingredients in a large bowl; toss to combine. Store in an airtight container.

Contest Winner

Spiced-Pumpkin Coffee Shakes

The winter holidays are my favorite time of year, and this spiced pumpkin drink is one reason I love the season so much. If you don't have a coffee maker, it's OK to use instant coffee—just make it stronger.

—**KATHIE PEREZ** EAST PEORIA, IL

PREP: 15 MIN. + CHILLING
MAKES: 6 SERVINGS

- 2 cups whole milk
- ½ cup canned pumpkin
- 2 tablespoons sugar
- 1 teaspoon pumpkin pie spice
- 1 cup strong brewed coffee
- 3 teaspoons vanilla extract
- 4 cups vanilla ice cream
- 1 cup crushed ice
  Sweetened whipped cream and additional pumpkin pie spice

1. In a small saucepan, heat milk, pumpkin, sugar and pie spice until bubbles form around sides of pan and sugar is dissolved. Transfer to a bowl; stir in coffee and vanilla. Refrigerate, covered, several hours or overnight.
2. Place milk mixture, ice cream and ice in a blender; cover and process until blended. Serve immediately with whipped cream; sprinkle with additional pie spice.

Sage & Prosciutto Pinwheels

I came up with the recipe because I can make the savory rolls ahead and keep them in the freezer, then slice and bake as needed. They're perfect for when you're entertaining guests.
—**KATE DAMPIER** QUAIL VALLEY, CA

START TO FINISH: 30 MIN. • **MAKES:** 3 DOZEN

- 1 package (17.3 ounces) frozen puff pastry, thawed
- ¼ cup honey mustard
- 1 cup (4 ounces) shredded Gruyere or Swiss cheese
- 8 thin slices prosciutto or deli ham, chopped
- 2 tablespoons chopped fresh sage

1. Preheat oven to 400°. Unfold one pastry sheet. Spread 2 tablespoons mustard to within ½ in. of edges. Sprinkle with ½ cup cheese; top with half each of the chopped prosciutto and sage. Roll up jelly-roll style. Using a serrated knife, cut roll crosswise into 18 slices.
2. Place cut side down on a greased baking sheet. Repeat with remaining ingredients. Bake 12-15 minutes or until golden brown. Serve warm.
FREEZE OPTION *Cover and freeze unbaked rolls on a waxed paper-lined baking sheet until firm. Transfer to resealable plastic freezer bags; return to freezer. To use, let rolls stand at room temperature 10 minutes. Cut and bake pinwheels as directed, increasing time as necessary.*

Date Shake

This shake has a lovely, mild date taste. We recommend using the larger, more flavorful Medjool dates for the best results.
—*TASTE OF HOME* TEST KITCHEN

START TO FINISH: 10 MIN. • **MAKES:** 4 SERVINGS

- ⅔ cup chopped dates
- ¼ cup water
- 3 cups vanilla ice cream
- 1 cup 2% milk

1. In a microwave-safe dish, combine dates and water; microwave, covered, on high for 30-45 seconds or until dates are softened. Cool completely.
2. Place date mixture in a blender; cover and pulse until pureed. Add ice cream and milk; cover and process until blended. Serve immediately.

Barbecue Glazed Meatballs

Stock your freezer with these meatballs and you'll always have something on hand for unexpected guests. We even like to eat these as a main dish with rice or noodles on busy weeknights.

—ANNA FINLEY COLUMBIA, MO

PREP: 30 MIN. • **BAKE:** 15 MIN./BATCH • **MAKES:** 8 DOZEN

- 2 cups quick-cooking oats
- 1 can (12 ounces) fat-free evaporated milk
- 1 small onion, finely chopped
- 2 teaspoons garlic powder
- 2 teaspoons chili powder
- 3 pounds lean ground beef (90% lean)

SAUCE

- 2½ cups ketchup
- 1 small onion, finely chopped
- ⅓ cup packed brown sugar
- 2 teaspoons liquid smoke, optional
- 1¼ teaspoons chili powder
- ¾ teaspoon garlic powder

1. Preheat oven to 400°. In a large bowl, combine the first five ingredients. Add beef; mix lightly but thoroughly. Shape into 1-in. balls.

2. Place the meatballs on greased racks in shallow baking pans. Bake 15-20 minutes or until cooked through. Drain on paper towels.

3. In a Dutch oven, combine sauce ingredients. Bring to a boil over medium heat, stirring constantly. Reduce heat; simmer, uncovered, 2-3 minutes or until slightly thickened. Add meatballs; heat through, stirring gently.

FREEZE OPTION *Freeze cooled meatball mixture in freezer containers. To use, partially thaw in refrigerator overnight. Microwave, covered, on high in a microwave-safe dish until heated through, gently stirring and adding a little water if necessary.*

Chicken Chili Wonton Bites

Everyone needs an easy appetizer recipe that's also sure to please. Wonton wrappers filled with chicken and spices make these bites crunchy, simple to serve—and delightful to eat!

—HEIDI JOBE CARROLLTON, GA

START TO FINISH: 30 MIN. • **MAKES:** 3 DOZEN

- 36 wonton wrappers
- ½ cup buttermilk ranch salad dressing
- 1 envelope reduced-sodium chili seasoning mix
- 1½ cups shredded rotisserie chicken
- 1 cup (4 ounces) shredded sharp cheddar cheese
  Sour cream and sliced green onions, optional

1. Preheat oven to 350°. Press wonton wrappers into greased miniature muffin cups. Bake 4-6 minutes or until lightly browned.

2. In a small bowl, mix salad dressing and seasoning mix; add chicken and toss to coat. Spoon 1 tablespoon filling into each wonton cup. Sprinkle with the cheese.

3. Bake 8-10 minutes longer or until heated through and wrappers are golden brown. Serve warm. If desired, top with sour cream and green onions before serving.

Basil White Bean Dip

We're big fans of hummus, but my son is allergic. I came up with a similar dip that uses cannellini beans, and it's turned out to be a great alternative.

—**ERIN BOSCO** CARLTON, WA

START TO FINISH: 15 MIN.
MAKES: 6 SERVINGS

- 1 **can (15 ounces) white kidney or cannellini beans, rinsed and drained**
- 2 **tablespoons lemon juice**
- 1 **garlic clove, halved**
- ½ **teaspoon salt**
- ⅛ **teaspoon pepper**
- ¼ **cup olive oil**
- 1 **plum tomato, seeded and chopped**
- ⅔ **cup loosely packed basil leaves, coarsely chopped**
  Baked pita chips

Place the first five ingredients in a food processor; pulse until beans are coarsely chopped. Add oil; process until blended. Add the tomato and basil; pulse to combine. Serve with pita chips.

Contest Winner

Savory BLT Cheesecake

Did you know that cheesecake could be savory instead of sweet? Tomato and green onions give a flavor of gazpacho to the creamy, rich filling. This is a flexible recipe, so experiment with other cheese in place of the Gruyere. Then add olives, crab meat, cooked mushrooms—or just about anything that strikes your fancy.

—**JONI HILTON** ROCKLIN, CA

PREP: 35 MIN. • **BAKE:** 45 MIN. + CHILLING
MAKES: 24 SERVINGS

- ¾ **cup dry bread crumbs**
- ½ **cup grated Parmesan cheese**
- 3 **tablespoons butter, melted**

FILLING

- 4 **packages (8 ounces each) cream cheese, softened**
- ½ **cup heavy whipping cream**
- 1½ **cups crumbled cooked bacon**
- 1 **cup oil-packed sun-dried tomatoes, patted dry and chopped**
- 1 **cup (4 ounces) shredded Gruyere or Swiss cheese**
- 2 **green onions, sliced**
- 1 **teaspoon freshly ground pepper**
- 4 **eggs, lightly beaten**
  Optional toppings: shredded iceberg lettuce, chopped cherry tomatoes and additional crumbled cooked bacon
  Assorted crackers, optional

1. Preheat oven to 325°. Place a greased 9-in. springform pan on a double thickness of heavy-duty foil (about 18 in. square). Securely wrap foil around pan.

2. In a small bowl, combine the bread crumbs, Parmesan cheese and butter. Press onto the bottom of prepared pan. Place pan on a baking sheet. Bake 12 minutes. Cool on a wire rack.

3. In a large bowl, beat cream cheese and cream until smooth. Beat in the bacon, tomatoes, Gruyere cheese, onions and pepper. Add eggs; beat on low speed just until combined. Pour over crust. Place springform pan in a large baking pan; add 1 in. of boiling water to larger pan.

4. Bake 45-55 minutes or until the center is just set and top appears dull. Remove springform pan from water bath; remove foil. Cool cheesecake on a wire rack 10 minutes; loosen edges from pan with a knife. Cool 1 hour longer. Refrigerate overnight.

5. Remove rim from pan. Serve cheesecake with toppings and crackers if desired.

Sparkling White Grape Punch

White cranberry juice adds a touch of tartness to this punch. For a light blush tone, use regular cranberry juice.

—JULIE STERCHI CAMPBELLSVILLE, KY

START TO FINISH: 10 MIN.
MAKES: 24 SERVINGS (¾ CUP)

- 1 bottle (64 ounces) white grape juice, chilled
- 1½ cups white cranberry juice, chilled
- 2 liters lemon-lime soda, chilled
  Seedless red or green grapes, optional

Just before serving, combine juices in a 5-qt. punch bowl. Stir in soda. Add grapes if desired.

Parm-Ranch Popcorn

Make ho-hum popcorn worthy of a carnival with a savory seasoning blend.

—*TASTE OF HOME* TEST KITCHEN

START TO FINISH: 10 MIN.
MAKES: 3½ QUARTS

- ¼ cup grated Parmesan cheese
- 2 tablespoons ranch salad dressing mix
- 1 teaspoon dried parsley
- ¼ teaspoon onion powder
- ⅓ cup butter
- 3½ quarts popped popcorn

Combine Parmesan cheese, dressing mix, parsley and onion powder. Melt butter; drizzle over popcorn and toss. Sprinkle with cheese mixture; toss.

Ham & Potato Salad Sandwiches

These little sandwiches with colorful layers of toppings are super simple to pull together. This classic version originated in a deli in Prague, where they're a really popular winter party food.

—**CARA MCDONALD** WINTER PARK, CO

START TO FINISH: 15 MIN.
MAKES: 6 SERVINGS

- 1½ cups deli potato salad
- 6 diagonally cut French bread baguette slices (½ inch thick)
- 6 ounces fully cooked ham, thinly sliced
- 6 slices tomato
- 12 dill pickle slices
- 2 hard-cooked eggs, sliced
- 2 slices red onion, separated into rings

Spread ¼ cup potato salad on each baguette slice. Layer with ham, tomato, pickle, egg and onion.

SIDE DISHES & CONDIMENTS

Folks will be saying, "Pass me some of that!" when they spot these inviting dishes on your table. Turn here for the perfect side dishes and condiments to round out any meal.

Baked Parmesan Breaded Squash

Yellow summer squash crisps beautifully when baked. You don't have to turn the pieces, but do keep an eye on them.

—DEBI MITCHELL FLOWER MOUND, TX

PREP: 20 MIN. • **BAKE:** 20 MIN.
MAKES: 6 SERVINGS

- 4 **cups thinly sliced yellow summer squash (3 medium)**
- 3 **tablespoons olive oil**
- ½ **teaspoon salt**
- ½ **teaspoon pepper**
- ⅛ **teaspoon cayenne pepper**
- ¾ **cup panko (Japanese) bread crumbs**
- ¾ **cup grated Parmesan cheese**

1. Preheat oven to 450°. Place squash in a large bowl. Add oil and seasonings; toss to coat.

2. In a shallow bowl, mix bread crumbs and cheese. Dip squash in crumb mixture to coat both sides, patting to help coating adhere. Place on parchment paper-lined baking sheets. Bake 20-25 minutes or until golden brown, rotating pans halfway through baking.

Contest Winner

Cilantro Blue Cheese Slaw

Serve this slaw as a side dish to any meal, or use it to complete your favorite fish taco recipe in place of lettuce and the usual toppings.

—CHRISTI DALTON HARTSVILLE, TN

START TO FINISH: 25 MIN.
MAKES: 8 SERVINGS

- 8 **cups shredded cabbage**
- 1 **small red onion, halved and thinly sliced**
- ⅓ **cup minced fresh cilantro**
- 1 **jalapeno pepper, seeded and minced**
- ¼ **cup crumbled blue cheese**
- ¼ **cup fat-free mayonnaise**
- ¼ **cup reduced-fat sour cream**
- 2 **tablespoons rice vinegar**
- 2 **tablespoons lime juice**
- 1 **garlic clove, minced**
- 1 **teaspoon sugar**
- 1 **teaspoon grated lime peel**
- ¾ **teaspoon salt**
- ½ **teaspoon coarsely ground pepper**

In a large bowl, combine the cabbage, onion, cilantro and jalapeno. In a small bowl, combine the remaining ingredients; pour over salad and toss to coat.

NOTE *Wear disposable gloves when cutting hot peppers; the oils can burn skin. Avoid touching your face.*

Lemon Pepper Roasted Broccoli

Transform fresh green broccoli into a tangy and tasty treat by roasting it with lemon juice and pepper. A sprinkle of almonds also adds a nice crunch.

—LIZ BELLVILLE HAVELOCK, NC

START TO FINISH: 25 MIN.
MAKES: 8 SERVINGS

- 1½ pounds fresh broccoli florets (about 12 cups)
- 2 tablespoons olive oil
- ½ teaspoon lemon juice
- ¼ teaspoon salt
- ¼ teaspoon coarsely ground pepper, divided
- ¼ cup chopped almonds
- 2 teaspoons grated lemon peel

1. Preheat oven to 450°. Place broccoli in a large bowl. Whisk oil, lemon juice, salt and ⅛ teaspoon pepper until blended; drizzle over broccoli and toss to coat. Transfer to a 15x10x1-in. baking pan.
2. Roast 10-15 minutes or until tender. Transfer to a serving dish. Sprinkle with almonds, lemon peel and remaining pepper; toss together to combine.

Braised & Creamy Vidalia Onions

In Georgia, where Vidalia onions are king, I make big batches of creamy onions to go along with grilled chicken and beef.

—ELAINE OPITZ MARIETTA, GA

PREP: 10 MIN. • **COOK:** 40 MIN.
MAKES: 6 SERVINGS

- 2 tablespoons butter
- 3 tablespoons honey
- 10 cups sliced Vidalia or other sweet onions (about 5 onions)
- ¼ cup chicken broth
- ½ teaspoon salt
- ⅛ teaspoon white pepper
- ⅛ teaspoon ground mace
- ½ cup heavy whipping cream

1. In a Dutch oven, melt butter over medium heat; stir in honey until blended. Add onions, broth and seasonings. Bring to a boil. Reduce heat; simmer, covered, 15-18 minutes or until onions are tender.
2. Cook, uncovered, over medium-high heat 15-20 minutes or until the liquid is almost evaporated, stirring occasionally. Stir in cream; cook 3-5 minutes longer or until sauce is thickened.

Oktoberfest Red Cabbage

Four generations of our family celebrate Oktoberfest. We love this tart-sweet cabbage and apple dish known as *rotkohl* because of its red color. Serve it with brats or roast pork.
—**DIANA LIKES** CHANDLER, AZ

PREP: 20 MIN. • **COOK:** 50 MIN. • **MAKES:** 6 SERVINGS

  3 tablespoons bacon drippings or canola oil
  1 small head red cabbage (about 1½ pounds), shredded
  2 medium tart apples, peeled and chopped
  1 cup water
  ¼ cup sugar
  ¾ teaspoon salt
  ¼ teaspoon pepper
  ⅛ teaspoon ground cloves
  ¼ cup white vinegar

1. In a Dutch oven, heat bacon drippings over medium heat. Add cabbage and apples; cook and stir 2-3 minutes. Stir in water, sugar, salt, pepper and cloves.
2. Bring to a boil. Reduce heat; simmer, covered, 40-45 minutes or until cabbage is tender, stirring occasionally. Stir in vinegar.

Marmalade Candied Carrots

Crisp-tender carrots have a citrusy flavor that's perfect for special occasions. This is my favorite carrot recipe.
—**HEATHER CLEMMONS** SUPPLY, NC

START TO FINISH: 30 MIN. • **MAKES:** 8 SERVINGS

  2 pounds fresh baby carrots
  ⅔ cup orange marmalade
  3 tablespoons brown sugar
  2 tablespoons butter
  ½ cup chopped pecans, toasted
  1 teaspoon rum extract

1. In a large saucepan, place steamer basket over 1 in. of water. Place carrots in basket. Bring water to a boil. Reduce heat to maintain a low boil; steam, covered, 12-15 minutes or until carrots are crisp-tender.
2. Meanwhile, in a small saucepan, combine marmalade, brown sugar and butter; cook and stir over medium heat until mixture is thickened and reduced to about ½ cup. Stir in pecans and extract.
3. Place carrots in a large bowl. Add marmalade mixture and toss gently to coat.

Contest Winner

Parsnips & Turnips au Gratin

You don't need potatoes to make a delicious au gratin dish! I sometimes substitute rutabaga for the turnips. This is a recipe to cherish in your collection.

—**PRISCILLA GILBERT** INDIAN HARBOUR BEACH, FL

PREP: 20 MIN. • **BAKE:** 15 MIN. • **MAKES:** 8 SERVINGS

- 1½ **pounds parsnips, peeled and sliced**
- 1¼ **pounds turnips, peeled and sliced**
- 1 **can (10¾ ounces) reduced-fat reduced-sodium condensed cream of celery soup, undiluted**
- 1 **cup fat-free milk**
- ½ **teaspoon pepper**
- 1 **cup (4 ounces) shredded sharp cheddar cheese**
- ½ **cup panko (Japanese) bread crumbs**
- 1 **tablespoon butter, melted**

1. Place parsnips and turnips in a large saucepan; cover with water. Bring to a boil. Reduce heat; simmer, uncovered, for 5-7 minutes or until crisp-tender.

2. Meanwhile, in a small saucepan, combine the soup, milk and pepper. Bring to a boil; reduce heat to low. Stir in cheese until melted. Drain vegetables; transfer to an 11x7-in. baking dish coated with cooking spray. Pour sauce over vegetables.

3. Combine bread crumbs and butter; sprinkle over top. Bake, uncovered, at 400° for 15-20 minutes or until vegetables are tender and crumbs are golden brown.

FREEZE OPTION *Cool unbaked casserole; cover and freeze. To use, partially thaw in refrigerator overnight. Remove from refrigerator 30 minutes before baking. Preheat oven to 375°. Bake casserole as directed, increasing time as necessary to heat through and for a thermometer inserted in center to read 165°.*

Smoky Grilled Corn on the Cob

We love corn and are always looking for new ways to enjoy it. I like to let the corn cool, cut it off the cob, then top it with butter and fresh cracked pepper. Save leftovers to include in salads or tacos.

—RACHEL KIRTLEY VICKSBURG, MI

PREP: 15 MIN. + SOAKING • **GRILL:** 25 MIN.
MAKES: 6 SERVINGS

- 6 medium ears sweet corn
- 2 tablespoons olive oil
- 1 teaspoon chili powder
- 1 teaspoon smoked paprika
- ½ teaspoon seasoned salt
- ⅛ teaspoon cayenne pepper

1. Carefully peel back corn husks to within 1 in. of bottoms; remove silk. Brush corn with oil. In a small bowl, combine remaining ingredients; sprinkle over corn. Rewrap corn in husks; secure with kitchen string. Place in a Dutch oven; cover with cold water. Soak 20 minutes; drain.
2. Grill corn, covered, over medium heat 25-30 minutes or until tender, turning often.

Thymed Zucchini Saute

Simple and flavorful, this recipe is a tasty way to use up all those zucchini taking over the garden. And it's ready in no time!

—BOBBY TAYLOR ULSTER PARK, NY

START TO FINISH: 15 MIN.
MAKES: 4 SERVINGS

- 1 tablespoon olive oil
- 1 pound medium zucchini, quartered lengthwise and halved
- ¼ cup finely chopped onion
- ½ vegetable bouillon cube, crushed
- 2 tablespoons minced fresh parsley
- 1 teaspoon minced fresh thyme or ¼ teaspoon dried thyme

In a large skillet, heat oil over medium-high heat. Add zucchini, onion and bouillon; cook and stir 4-5 minutes or until zucchini is crisp-tender. Sprinkle with herbs.
NOTE *This recipe was prepared with Knorr vegetable bouillon.*

Creamy Carrot Bake

Wondering what vegetable to serve for your next feast? Here's a special way of preparing and serving sliced fresh carrots.

—**SANDY O'NEAL** BOALSBURG, PA

PREP: 20 MIN. • **BAKE:** 25 MIN.
MAKES: 8 SERVINGS

- 2 pounds fresh carrots, thinly sliced
- ¼ cup butter, cubed
- ¼ cup finely chopped onion
- ¼ cup all-purpose flour
- ¼ teaspoon ground mustard
- 2 cups 2% milk
- 1 cup (4 ounces) shredded Monterey Jack cheese
- 1 cup (4 ounces) shredded sharp cheddar cheese
- 1 tablespoon prepared horseradish
- 1 teaspoon salt
- ½ teaspoon pepper
- ¼ teaspoon celery salt
- 1 cup soft bread crumbs
- 2 tablespoons butter, melted

1. Preheat oven to 350°. In a Dutch oven, bring 1 in. of water to a boil. Add carrots; cook, covered, 5-7 minutes or until crisp-tender. Drain; set aside.

2. In same pan, heat butter over medium heat. Add onion; cook and stir 1-2 minutes or until tender.

3. Stir in flour and mustard until blended; gradually whisk in milk. Bring to a boil, stirring constantly; cook and stir 1-2 minutes or until thickened. Add cheeses, horseradish and seasonings; cook and stir until cheese is melted. Stir in carrots.

4. Transfer to a greased 11x7-in. baking dish. In a small bowl, toss bread crumbs with melted butter; sprinkle over top. Bake, uncovered, 25-30 minutes or until heated through and bread crumbs are lightly browned.

NOTE *To make soft bread crumbs, tear bread into pieces and place in a food processor or blender. Cover and pulse until crumbs form. One slice of bread yields ½ to ¾ cup crumbs.*

Texas-Style BBQ Sauce

In the South, barbecue sauce must make all the right moves. For us, that includes ketchup, mustard and vinegar tang. To show off, there's a little sweet heat.

—**SANDY KLOCINSKI** SUMMERVILLE, SC

START TO FINISH: 25 MIN.
MAKES: 1¾ CUPS

- 1 tablespoon butter
- 1 small onion, chopped
- 2 garlic cloves, minced
- 1 cup ketchup
- ¼ cup packed brown sugar
- ¼ cup lemon juice
- 2 tablespoons apple cider vinegar
- 2 tablespoons tomato paste
- 1 tablespoon yellow mustard
- 1 tablespoon Worcestershire sauce
- 2 teaspoons chili powder

In a large saucepan, heat butter over medium heat. Add onion; cook and stir 2-3 minutes or until tender. Add garlic; cook 1 minute longer. Stir in remaining ingredients; bring to a boil. Reduce heat; simmer, uncovered, 15-20 minutes to allow flavors to blend.

PLENTIFUL POTATOES

Mashed, cut into fries or layered in a casserole—no matter how you slice 'em, potatoes perfectly pair up with just about any main dish. Serve these taters alongside your next meal.

Contest Winner

Au Gratin Potato Pancakes

Family and friends say these savory pancakes are among the best they've ever tasted. They go especially well with barbecued ribs or chicken, but you can substitute them for almost any potato dish.

—**CATHY HALL** LYNDHURST, VA

START TO FINISH: 25 MIN. • **MAKES:** 8 POTATO PANCAKES

- 2 cups mashed potatoes (without added milk and butter)
- 1 egg, lightly beaten
- 1 tablespoon minced chives
- 1 teaspoon minced fresh parsley
- ¾ teaspoon salt
- ⅛ teaspoon dried minced garlic
- ⅛ teaspoon pepper
  Dash dried rosemary, crushed
- ½ cup shredded sharp cheddar cheese
- 4 tablespoons canola oil, divided

1. In a large bowl, combine the first eight ingredients. Stir in the cheese.

2. Heat 2 tablespoons oil in a large nonstick skillet over medium heat. Drop batter by ¼ cupfuls into oil; press lightly to flatten. Cook in batches for 2-3 minutes on each side or until golden brown, using remaining oil as needed. Drain on paper towels.

Oh-So-Good Creamy Mashed Potatoes

Yukon Golds are great for mashed potatoes because of their buttery flavor and low moisture content. They easily absorb the warm milk or melted butter you add to your spuds.

—**BRITTANY JACKSON** SEYMOUR, WI

PREP: 20 MIN. • **COOK:** 25 MIN.
MAKES: 18 SERVINGS (¾ CUP EACH)

- 8 large Yukon Gold potatoes, peeled and quartered (about 6 pounds)
- 2 teaspoons salt
- 2½ cups 2% milk
- ½ cup butter, cubed
- 3 teaspoons garlic salt
- 1 teaspoon pepper
- ¼ cup sour cream
  Additional 2% milk, optional
  Chopped fresh parsley

1. Place potatoes and salt in a stockpot; add water to cover. Bring to a boil. Reduce heat; cook, uncovered, for 20-25 minutes or until potatoes are tender. Meanwhile, in a large saucepan, heat milk, butter, garlic salt and pepper over medium heat until butter is melted.

2. Drain potatoes, then shake over low heat for 1-2 minutes to dry. Mash potatoes with a potato masher or beat with a mixer; gradually add milk mixture. Stir in sour cream. Stir in additional milk to thin if desired. Sprinkle with parsley.

Potato Kugel

Alternate grating the potatoes and onions, and the potatoes will stay nice and white. This is the recipe to impress everyone.
—**ELLEN RUZINSKY** YORKTOWN HEIGHTS, NY

PREP: 20 MIN. • **BAKE:** 40 MIN. • **MAKES:** 12 SERVINGS

- 2 **large eggs**
- ¼ **cup matzo meal**
- 2 **teaspoons kosher salt**
  Dash pepper
- 6 **large potatoes (about 4¾ pounds), peeled**
- 1 **large onion, cut into 6 wedges**
- ¼ **cup canola oil**

1. Preheat oven to 375°. In a large bowl, whisk eggs, matzo meal, salt and pepper.
2. In a food processor fitted with the grating attachment, alternately grate potatoes and onion. Add to egg mixture; toss to coat. In a small saucepan, heat oil over medium heat until warmed. Stir into potato mixture. Transfer to a greased 13x9-in. baking dish. Bake 40-50 minutes or until golden brown.

Parmesan & Garlic Fries

The addition of Parmesan cheese and fresh garlic takes this side dish from ordinary to irresistible.
—*TASTE OF HOME* TEST KITCHEN

START TO FINISH: 20 MIN. • **MAKES:** 5 SERVINGS

- 5 **cups frozen french-fried potatoes**
- 2 **tablespoons olive oil**
- 3 **to 4 garlic cloves, minced**
- ¼ **teaspoon salt**
- ¼ **cup grated Parmesan cheese**

1. Preheat oven to 450°. Place potatoes in a large bowl. Mix oil, garlic and salt; toss with potatoes. Arrange in a single layer on a large baking sheet.
2. Bake 15-20 minutes or until golden brown, stirring once. Sprinkle with cheese; toss lightly. Serve immediately.

DIY GRATED PARMESAN

Want to grate your own Parmesan cheese? Buy some fresh cheese, then grate using the finest section on your grating tool. If you prefer a less hands-on approach, simply cut the cheese into 1-inch cubes and process 1 cup of cubes at a time on high in a blender or food processor until cheese is finely grated.

Roasted Green Beans with Lemon & Walnuts

I first tasted roasted green beans in a Chinese restaurant and fell in love with the texture and flavor. This is my own take, and it's always a big hit at our table.

—LILY JULOW LAWRENCEVILLE, GA

START TO FINISH: 25 MIN.
MAKES: 8 SERVINGS

- 2 **pounds fresh green beans, trimmed**
- 2 **shallots, thinly sliced**
- 6 **garlic cloves, crushed**
- 2 **tablespoons olive oil**
- ¾ **teaspoon salt**
- ¼ **teaspoon pepper**
- 2 **teaspoons grated lemon peel**
- ½ **cup chopped walnuts, toasted**

1. Preheat oven to 425°. In a large bowl, combine green beans, shallots and garlic; drizzle with oil and sprinkle with salt and pepper. Transfer to two 15x10x1-in. baking pans coated with cooking spray.

2. Roast 15-20 minutes or until tender and lightly browned, stirring occasionally. Remove from oven; stir in 1 teaspoon lemon peel. Sprinkle with the walnuts and remaining lemon peel.

NOTE *To toast nuts, bake in a shallow pan in a 350° oven for 5-10 minutes or cook in a skillet over low heat until lightly browned, stirring occasionally.*

Thyme-Roasted Vegetables

The smell of our house while this dish bakes calls everyone to dinner. Normally, it serves 10, but if you're like my husband you might find yourself wanting to double up on servings.

—JASMINE ROSE CRYSTAL LAKE, IL

PREP: 25 MIN. • **BAKE:** 45 MIN.
MAKES: 10 SERVINGS (¾ CUP EACH)

- 2 **pounds red potatoes, cubed (about 9 cups)**
- 3 **cups sliced sweet onions (about 1½ large)**
- 3 **medium carrots, sliced**
- ½ **pound medium fresh mushrooms, halved**
- 1 **large sweet red pepper, cut into 1½-inch pieces**
- 1 **large sweet yellow pepper, cut into 1½-inch pieces**
- 2 **tablespoons butter, melted**
- 2 **tablespoons olive oil**
- 1 **tablespoon minced fresh thyme or 1 teaspoon dried thyme**
- 1 **teaspoon salt**
- ¼ **teaspoon pepper**

1. Preheat oven to 400°. In a large bowl, combine vegetables. Add remaining ingredients; toss to coat.

2. Transfer to a 15x10x1-in. baking pan. Roast 45-50 minutes or until tender, stirring occasionally.

Calico Squash

I have a thriving country garden and try every recipe I find to use my squash. It's a pleasure to make this beautiful casserole for special meals.

—LUCILLE TERRY FRANKFORT, KY

PREP: 20 MIN. • **BAKE:** 30 MIN.
MAKES: 8 SERVINGS

- 2 **cups sliced yellow summer squash (¼ inch thick)**
- 1 **cup sliced zucchini (¼ inch thick)**
- 1 **medium onion, chopped**
- ¼ **cup sliced green onions**
- 1 **cup water**
- 1 **teaspoon salt, divided**
- 2 **cups crushed butter-flavored crackers**
- ½ **cup butter, melted**
- 1 **can (10¾ ounces) condensed cream of chicken soup, undiluted**
- 1 **can (8 ounces) sliced water chestnuts, drained**
- 1 **large carrot, shredded**
- ½ **cup mayonnaise**
- 1 **jar (2 ounces) diced pimientos, drained**
- 1 **teaspoon rubbed sage**
- ½ **teaspoon white pepper**
- 1 **cup (4 ounces) shredded sharp cheddar cheese**

1. In a large saucepan, combine the first five ingredients; add ½ teaspoon salt. Cover and cook until squash is tender, about 6 minutes. Drain well; set aside.

2. Combine crumbs and butter; spoon half into a greased shallow 1½-qt. baking dish. In a large bowl, combine the soup, water chestnuts, carrot, mayonnaise, pimientos, sage, pepper and remaining salt; fold in squash mixture. Spoon over crumbs in dish.

3. Sprinkle with cheese and the remaining crumb mixture. Bake, uncovered, at 350° for 30 minutes or until lightly browned.

Browned Butter Red Potatoes

I've been making my version of Dad's potatoes for years, and it goes great with any meal. Browning the butter gives the potatoes a rich and hearty taste.

—ANNE PAVELAK ENDICOTT, WA

START TO FINISH: 30 MIN.
MAKES: 12 SERVINGS (¾ CUP EACH)

- 16 **medium red potatoes (about 4 pounds), quartered**
- 1 **cup butter, cubed**
- 8 **garlic cloves, minced**
- 2 **teaspoons salt**
- 1 **teaspoon pepper**

1. Place potatoes in a Dutch oven; add water to cover. Bring to a boil. Reduce heat; cook, uncovered, 15-20 minutes or until tender.

2. Meanwhile, in a small heavy saucepan, melt butter over medium heat. Heat 5-7 minutes or until light golden brown, stirring constantly. Stir in garlic; cook 30 seconds longer or until butter is golden brown. Remove from heat.

3. Drain potatoes; transfer to a bowl. Sprinkle with salt and pepper. Drizzle with browned butter and toss to coat.

Contest Winner

Brussels Sprouts & Cauliflower Gratin

I decided to combine two of my favorite veggies for a family-friendly dish. Topped with crunchy panko bread crumbs and savory Italian cheeses, it's the kind of yummy casserole you want to serve at your next buffet.

—**PRISCILLA GILBERT** INDIAN HARBOUR BEACH, FL

PREP: 25 MIN. • **BAKE:** 30 MIN. • **MAKES:** 8 SERVINGS

- 4 **cups fresh caulifloweretes**
- 4 **cups fresh Brussels sprouts, quartered**
- 4 **bacon strips, chopped**
- 1 **large sweet onion, chopped**
- 4 **garlic cloves, minced**
- ¼ **cup all-purpose flour**
- 1½ **cups 2% milk**
- ⅔ **cup half-and-half cream**
- 1 **teaspoon salt**
- ¼ **teaspoon pepper**
- ½ **cup panko (Japanese) bread crumbs**
- ⅓ **cup grated Parmesan and Romano cheese blend**

1. Preheat the oven to 375°. Place the cauliflower and Brussels sprouts in a large saucepan and cover with water. Bring to a boil. Cover and cook 2-3 minutes or until crisp-tender; drain.

2. Meanwhile, in a large skillet, cook bacon over medium heat until crisp. Remove to paper towels with a slotted spoon; drain, reserving drippings. Saute onion and garlic in drippings until tender. Stir in flour until blended; gradually add the milk, cream, salt and pepper. Bring to a boil; cook and stir 2 minutes or until thickened.

3. Stir in cauliflower mixture and bacon. Transfer to a greased 2½-qt. baking dish. Cover and bake 15 minutes.

4. Combine bread crumbs and cheese blend. Uncover vegetables; sprinkle with bread crumb mixture. Bake, uncovered, 15-20 minutes or until golden brown.

Kathy's Herbed Corn

My husband and I agreed that the original recipe for this corn needed a little jazzing up, so I added thyme and cayenne pepper. Now fresh corn makes a regular appearance on our grill.

—**KATHY VONKORFF** NORTH COLLEGE HILL, OH

START TO FINISH: 30 MIN. • **MAKES:** 8 SERVINGS

- ½ **cup butter, softened**
- 2 **tablespoons minced fresh parsley**
- 2 **tablespoons minced fresh chives**
- 1 **teaspoon dried thyme**
- ½ **teaspoon salt**
- ½ **teaspoon cayenne pepper**
- 8 **ears sweet corn, husked**

1. In a small bowl, beat the first six ingredients until blended. Spread 1 tablespoon mixture over each ear of corn. Wrap ears individually in heavy-duty foil.

2. Grill corn, covered, over medium heat 10-15 minutes or until tender, turning occasionally. Open foil carefully to allow steam to escape.

Giblet Turkey Gravy

Gravy enhanced with giblets is traditional in our house. Try this hearty version that's seasoned with sage and a dash of wine.

—**JEFF LOCKE** ARMA, KS

START TO FINISH: 25 MIN.
MAKES: 16 SERVINGS (ABOUT ¼ CUP EACH)

- ¼ cup cornstarch
- 4 cups chicken stock, divided
- 1 tablespoon butter
- 1 tablespoon olive oil
  Giblets from 1 turkey, finely chopped
- ½ cup dry white wine or additional chicken stock
- 2 tablespoons minced fresh sage or 2 teaspoons dried sage leaves
- ¼ teaspoon salt
- ¼ teaspoon pepper

1. In a small bowl, mix cornstarch and ½ cup stock until smooth. In a large saucepan, heat butter and oil over medium-high heat. Add giblets; cook and stir 5-8 minutes or until browned.

2. Add wine and sage to pan; cook 3-5 minutes, stirring to loosen browned bits from pan. Add remaining stock; bring to a boil. Stir in cornstarch mixture; return to a boil. Reduce heat; simmer 3-5 minutes or until thickened to desired consistency, stirring occasionally. Stir in salt and pepper.

Zucchini Onion Pie

We have a lot of zucchini on hand when it's in season, and I often turn to this recipe to put the bounty to good use.

—**LUCIA JOHNSON** MASSENA, NY

START TO FINISH: 30 MIN. • **MAKES:** 6 SERVINGS

- 3 eggs
- 1 cup grated Parmesan cheese
- ½ cup canola oil
- 1 tablespoon minced fresh parsley
- 1 garlic clove, minced
- ¼ teaspoon salt
- ⅛ teaspoon pepper
- 3 cups sliced zucchini
- 1 cup biscuit/baking mix
- 1 small onion, chopped

In a large bowl, whisk the first seven ingredients. Stir in the zucchini, baking mix and onion. Pour into a greased 9-in. deep-dish pie plate. Bake at 350° for 25-35 minutes or until lightly browned.

Favorite Cheesy Potatoes

My kids, husband and nephews all love these potatoes. I make a large batch in disposable pans and serve them at get-togethers—the holidays aren't the same without them.
—**BRENDA SMITH** CURRAN, MI

PREP: 30 MIN. • **BAKE:** 45 MIN.
MAKES: 12 SERVINGS (⅔ CUP EACH)

- 3½ **pounds potatoes (about 7 medium), peeled and cut into ¾-inch cubes**
- 1 **can (10½ ounces) condensed cream of potato soup, undiluted**
- 1 **cup French onion dip**
- ¾ **cup 2% milk**
- ⅔ **cup sour cream**
- 1 **teaspoon minced fresh parsley**
- ¼ **teaspoon salt**
- ¼ **teaspoon pepper**
- 1 **package (16 ounces) process cheese (Velveeta), cubed**
  Additional minced fresh parsley

1. Preheat oven to 350°. Place the potatoes in a Dutch oven; add water to cover. Bring to a boil. Reduce heat; cook, uncovered, 8-12 minutes or until tender. Drain. Cool slightly.
2. In a large bowl, mix soup, onion dip, milk, sour cream, parsley, salt and pepper; gently fold in potatoes and cheese. Transfer mixture to a greased 13x9-in. baking dish.
3. Bake, covered, 30 minutes. Remove cover; bake dish 15-20 minutes longer or until heated through and cheese is melted. Just before serving, stir to combine and sprinkle with additional parsley. (The potatoes will thicken upon standing.)

FREEZE OPTION *Cover and freeze unbaked casserole. To use, partially thaw in refrigerator overnight. Remove from refrigerator 30 minutes before baking. Preheat oven to 350°. Cover casserole with foil; bake as directed, increasing covered time to 1¼-1½ hours or until heated through and a thermometer inserted in center reads 165°. Uncover; bake 15-20 minutes longer or until lightly browned. Just before serving, stir to combine and sprinkle with additional parsley.*

Contest Winner

Sweet Potato Delight

I serve this dish at least once a month—it's that popular! The fluffy texture and subtle orange flavor make it a standout.
—**MARLENE KROLL** CHICAGO, IL

PREP: 25 MIN. • **BAKE:** 30 MIN.
MAKES: 10 SERVINGS

- 4 **large sweet potatoes, peeled and quartered**
- ½ **cup orange marmalade**
- ½ **cup orange juice**
- ¼ **cup packed brown sugar**
- ½ **teaspoon almond extract**
- 3 **egg whites**
- ¼ **cup slivered almonds**

1. Place sweet potatoes in a Dutch oven; cover with water. Bring to a boil. Reduce heat; cover and cook for 15-20 minutes or just until tender. Drain potatoes; place in a large bowl and mash. Stir in orange marmalade, orange juice, brown sugar and extract. Cool slightly.
2. In a small bowl, beat egg whites until stiff peaks form. Fold into sweet potato mixture. Transfer to a 2½-qt. baking dish coated with cooking spray. Sprinkle with the almonds. Bake, uncovered, at 350° for 30-35 minutes or until a thermometer reads 160°.

Sweet & Spicy Pickled Red Seedless Grapes

Most people don't think about grapes when creating a canned pickle recipe. These grapes are a delicious surprise on an antipasto, pickle or cheese tray.

—**CHERYL PERRY** HERTFORD, NC

PREP: 35 MIN. • **PROCESS:** 10 MIN.
MAKES: 4 PINTS

- 5 cups seedless red grapes
- 4 jalapeno peppers, seeded and sliced
- 2 tablespoons minced fresh gingerroot
- 2 cinnamon sticks (3 inches), halved
- 4 whole star anise
- 2 teaspoons coriander seeds
- 2 teaspoons mustard seed
- 2 cups packed brown sugar
- 2 cups white wine vinegar
- 1 cup each water and dry red wine
- 1½ teaspoons canning salt

1. Pack grapes into four hot 1-pint jars to within 1½ in. of the top. Divide jalapenos, ginger, cinnamon, star anise, coriander seeds and mustard seed among jars.

2. In a large saucepan, combine brown sugar, vinegar, water, wine and canning salt. Bring to a boil; cook 15-18 minutes or until liquid is reduced to 3 cups.

3. Carefully ladle hot liquid over grape mixture, leaving ½-in. of headspace. Remove air bubbles and adjust headspace, if necessary, by adding hot liquid. Wipe rims. Center lids on jars; screw on bands until fingertip tight.

4. Place jars into canner, ensuring that they are completely covered with water. Bring to a boil; process for 10 minutes. Remove jars and cool.

NOTE *The processing time listed is for altitudes of 1,000 feet or less. For altitudes up to 3,000 feet, add 5 minutes; 6,000 feet, add 10 minutes; 8,000 feet, add 15 minutes; 10,000 feet, add 20 minutes.*

Pancetta Brioche Dressing

I crave this stuffing every year, and I suspect my guests do, too. It's usually gone before the turkey!

—**JAMIE BROWN-MILLER** NAPA, CA

PREP: 15 MIN. • **BAKE:** 25 MIN.
MAKES: 12 CUPS (¾ CUP EACH)

- 16 cups cubed Brioche bread (about 1¾ pounds)
- 2 cups diced red onions
- ¼ teaspoon kosher salt
- ⅛ teaspoon pepper
- 2 tablespoons olive oil
- 2 cups chopped radicchio
- 1½ cups chicken broth
- 5 ounces pancetta, diced
- 2 large eggs, lightly beaten
- 2 tablespoons minced fresh rosemary
- ¼ cup crumbled Roquefort or blue cheese

1. Spread bread cubes on a baking sheet. Bake at 400° for 6-8 minutes or until dried (do not brown); set aside.

2. Meanwhile, in a large skillet, cook the onions, salt and pepper in oil over medium-high heat until onions begin to brown. Stir in radicchio; remove from the heat.

3. In a large bowl, combine bread cubes, radicchio mixture, chicken broth, pancetta, eggs and rosemary; gently toss. Transfer to a greased 13x9-in. baking dish. Sprinkle with cheese. Bake, uncovered, at 400° for 25-30 minutes or until golden brown.

WHAT'S PANCETTA?

Sometimes known as "Italian bacon," pancetta is made from pork belly. But unlike bacon, it's cured, not smoked.

Broccoli with Garlic, Bacon & Parmesan

My approach to broccoli is to cook it slowly, which allows the garlic to blend with the smoky bacon. A few simple ingredients make this common vegetable uncommonly delectable.
—**ERIN CHILCOAT** CENTRAL ISLIP, NY

START TO FINISH: 30 MIN. • **MAKES:** 8 SERVINGS

- 1　teaspoon salt
- 2　bunches broccoli (about 3 pounds), stems removed, cut into florets
- 6　thick-sliced bacon strips, chopped
- 2　tablespoons olive oil
- 6　to 8 garlic cloves, thinly sliced
- ½　teaspoon crushed red pepper flakes
- ¼　cup shredded Parmesan cheese

1. Fill a 6-qt. stockpot two-thirds full with water; add salt and bring to a boil. In batches, add broccoli and cook 2-3 minutes or until broccoli turns bright green; remove with a slotted spoon.
2. In a large skillet, cook bacon over medium heat until crisp, stirring occasionally. Remove with a slotted spoon; drain on paper towels. Discard the drippings, reserving 1 tablespoon in pan.
3. Add oil to drippings; heat over medium heat. Add garlic and pepper flakes; cook and stir 2-3 minutes or until garlic is fragrant (do not allow to brown). Add broccoli; cook until broccoli is tender, stirring occasionally. Stir in bacon; sprinkle with cheese.

Beet and Sweet Potato Fries

Instead of offering traditional french fries, try these oven-baked root vegetables for a healthier and eye-pleasing twist.
—**MARIE RIZZIO** INTERLOCHEN, MI

PREP: 15 MIN. • **BAKE:** 20 MIN. • **MAKES:** 5 SERVINGS (½ CUP SAUCE)

- ½　cup reduced-fat mayonnaise
- 1　teaspoon pink peppercorns, crushed
- ½　teaspoon green peppercorns, crushed
- ½　teaspoon coarsely ground pepper, divided
- 1　large sweet potato (about 1 pound)
- 2　tablespoons olive oil, divided
- ½　teaspoon sea salt, divided
- 2　large fresh beets (about 1 pound)

1. In a small bowl, combine the mayonnaise, peppercorns and ¼ teaspoon ground pepper. Cover and refrigerate until serving.
2. Peel and cut sweet potato in half widthwise; cut each half into ½-in. strips. Place in a small bowl. Add 1 tablespoon oil, ¼ teaspoon salt and ⅛ teaspoon pepper; toss to coat. Spread onto a parchment paper-lined baking sheet.
3. Peel and cut beets in half; cut into ½-in. strips. Transfer to the same bowl; add the remaining oil, salt and pepper. Toss to coat. Spread onto another parchment paper-lined baking sheet.
4. Bake vegetables, uncovered, at 425° for 20-30 minutes or until tender, turning once. Serve with peppercorn mayonnaise.

Roasted Tomato Salsa

Our family's all-time favorite salsa, this recipe is the reason we grow a huge garden every summer. We make gallons of it and share with our neighbors. You might find yourself eating it right out of the bowl with a spoon.

—**DONNA KELLY** PROVO, UT

START TO FINISH: 25 MIN. • **MAKES:** 8 CUPS

- 12 **large tomatoes, halved and seeded, divided**
- 2 **tablespoons olive oil, divided**
- 1 **bunch fresh cilantro, trimmed**
- ¼ **cup lime juice**
- 4 **garlic cloves, peeled**
- 2 **teaspoons grated lime peel**
- 1 **large sweet yellow pepper, finely chopped**
- 6 **jalapeno peppers, minced**
- 12 **green onions, thinly sliced**
- 1 **tablespoon ground cumin**
- 1 **tablespoon smoked paprika**
- 1 **tablespoon ground chipotle pepper**
- 2 **teaspoons salt**
- ¼ **teaspoon Louisiana-style hot sauce**
  Tortilla chips

1. Arrange six tomatoes cut side down on a 15x10x1-in. baking pan; drizzle with 1 tablespoon oil. Broil 4 in. from the heat until the skin blisters, about 4 minutes. Cool slightly; drain well.

2. In a food processor, process uncooked and roasted tomatoes in batches until chunky. Transfer mixture to a large bowl.

3. Place the cilantro, lime juice, garlic, lime peel and remaining oil in the food processor. Cover and process until blended; add to tomatoes. Stir in the peppers, onions, cumin, paprika, chipotle pepper, salt and hot sauce. Let stand 1 hour to allow flavors to blend. Serve with chips.

NOTE *Wear disposable gloves when cutting hot peppers; the oils can burn skin. Avoid touching your face.*

Favorite Bread & Butter Pickles

I made these pickles while growing up and love them because they go with just about anything you can think of. Now, both of my children love them as much as I do. I think you will, too!

—**LINDA WEGER** ROBINSON, IL

PREP: 45 MIN. + STANDING • **PROCESS:** 10 MIN./BATCH
MAKES: 11 PINTS

- 20 **cups sliced cucumbers (about 12 medium)**
- 3 **cups sliced onions (about 4 medium)**
- 1 **medium sweet red pepper, sliced**
- 1 **medium green pepper, sliced**
- 3 **quarts ice water**
- ½ **cup canning salt**
- 6 **cups sugar**
- 6 **cups white vinegar**
- 3 **tablespoons mustard seed**
- 3 **teaspoons celery seed**
- 1½ **teaspoons ground turmeric**
- ¼ **teaspoon plus ⅛ teaspoon ground cloves**

1. Place cucumbers, onions and peppers in a large bowl. In another large bowl, mix ice water and salt; pour over vegetables. Let stand 3 hours.

2. Rinse vegetables and drain well. Pack vegetables into eleven hot 1-pint jars to within ½ in. of the top.

3. In a Dutch oven, bring sugar, vinegar, mustard seed, celery seed, turmeric and cloves to a boil. Carefully ladle hot liquid over vegetable mixture, leaving ½-in. headspace. Remove air bubbles and adjust headspace, if necessary, by adding hot liquid. Wipe rims. Center lids on jars; screw on bands until fingertip tight.

4. Place jars into canner, ensuring that they are completely covered with water. Bring to a boil; process for 10 minutes. Remove jars and cool.

NOTE *The processing time listed is for altitudes of 1,000 feet or less. For altitudes up to 3,000 feet, add 5 minutes; 6,000 feet, add 10 minutes; 8,000 feet, add 15 minutes; 10,000 feet, add 20 minutes.*

SOUPS, SALADS & SANDWICHES

This chapter offers up everything you love at your local diner—but with a very homemade twist! Take a bite of a scrumptious sandwich or salad paired with a hearty soup on the side. It'll be mealtime in no time!

Ruby Red Spinach Salads

I love the peppery bite of sliced fennel combined with Parmesan and grapefruit. Pomegranate seeds add vibrant color, a pleasant crunch and a dose of vitamin C.

—VERONICA CALLAGHAN

GLASTONBURY, CT

START TO FINISH: 20 MIN.
MAKES: 4 SERVINGS

- 3 tablespoons red grapefruit juice
- 1 tablespoon olive oil
- ½ teaspoon honey
- ¼ teaspoon kosher salt
- ⅛ teaspoon pepper
- 1 large fennel bulb
- 2 large red grapefruit, sectioned
- 1 cup fresh baby spinach
- ¼ cup shaved Romano cheese
- ½ cup pomegranate seeds

1. In a small bowl, whisk the first five ingredients. Remove fronds from fennel; set aside for garnish. Cut bulb into thin slices and coarsely chop the slices. In a large bowl, combine the chopped fennel, grapefruit and spinach. Drizzle dressing over salad; toss to coat.

2. Divide salad among four plates; sprinkle cheese and pomegranate seeds over salads. Garnish with the fennel fronds.

Roasted Tomato Soup

After we gather up all of the tomatoes from my mom's garden, we create this flavor-packed soup. Although it sounds like a lot of garlic, when it's roasted, the garlic becomes mellow and almost sweet.

—KAITLYN LERDAHL MADISON, WI

PREP: 25 MIN. • **COOK:** 40 MIN.
MAKES: 6 SERVINGS

- 15 large tomatoes (5 pounds), seeded and quartered
- ¼ cup plus 2 tablespoons canola oil, divided
- 8 garlic cloves, minced
- 1 large onion, chopped
- 2 cups water
- 1 teaspoon salt
- ½ teaspoon crushed red pepper flakes, optional
- ½ cup heavy whipping cream
  Fresh basil leaves, optional

1. Preheat oven to 400°. Place tomatoes in a greased 15x10x1-in. baking pan. Combine ¼ cup oil and garlic; drizzle over tomatoes. Toss to coat. Bake 15-20 minutes or until softened, stirring occasionally. Remove and discard skins.

2. Meanwhile, in a Dutch oven, saute the onion in remaining oil until tender. Add tomatoes, water, salt and, if desired, pepper flakes. Bring to a boil. Reduce heat; cover and simmer 30 minutes or until flavors are blended. Cool slightly.

3. In a blender, process soup in batches until smooth. Return to pan. Stir in cream and heat through; top with basil if desired.

FREEZE OPTION *Cool soup and transfer to freezer containers. Freeze up to 3 months. To use, thaw in the refrigerator overnight. Place in a large saucepan; heat through. Garnish with basil if desired.*

Contest Winner

Grilled Prosciutto-Cheddar Sandwiches with Onion Jam

April is National Grilled Cheese Month in honor of the gooey greatness that is toasted bread and melted cheese. For a modern version full of comfy farmhouse flavors, use raisin bread with onion jam, prosciutto and cheddar.

—SUSAN ANDRICHUK NEW YORK, NY

PREP: 1¼ HOURS • **COOK:** 5 MIN.
MAKES: 4 SANDWICHES
(½ CUP ONION JAM)

ONION JAM
- 2 large sweet onions, sliced
- 1 cup dry red wine
- 2 tablespoons honey
- 1 tablespoon red wine vinegar
- ¼ teaspoon crushed red pepper flakes
- ¼ teaspoon salt
- ¼ teaspoon pepper
- 4 teaspoons apricot preserves

SANDWICHES
- 8 slices cinnamon-raisin bread
- 8 thin slices prosciutto or deli ham
- 4 slices aged cheddar cheese
- 3 tablespoons butter, softened

1. For jam, place the onions and red wine in a large skillet; bring to a boil. Reduce heat; cover and simmer for 30 minutes. Stir in honey, vinegar, pepper flakes, salt and pepper. Simmer, uncovered, 30 minutes or until liquid is evaporated.
2. Stir in preserves; cook 3-5 minutes longer or until the onions are glazed. Remove from the heat; cool slightly.
3. Spread four bread slices with onion jam. Layer with prosciutto and cheese. Top with remaining bread. Butter outsides of sandwiches.
4. In a large skillet over medium heat, toast sandwiches for 2-3 minutes on each side or until golden brown and cheese is melted.

> **FREEZE HONEY?**
> I'm a beekeeper and often freeze honey to keep it from crystallizing. The low moisture content will keep the honey from freezing solid.
> —J.M. WEST BEND, WI

Dill Garden Salad

I love to cut up whatever fresh vegetables I have on hand and toss them with this delicious dressing and fresh dill. This salad appears on our table several times a week during the summer.

—BETHANY MARTIN MILTON, PA

START TO FINISH: 15 MIN.
MAKES: 6 SERVINGS

- 3 cups chopped English cucumbers
- 1 large tomato, seeded and cut into ½-inch pieces
- 1 small sweet red pepper, chopped
- 2 tablespoons chopped sweet onion
- 3 tablespoons reduced-fat mayonnaise
- 4 teaspoons olive oil
- 2 teaspoons sugar
- 2 teaspoons rice vinegar
- ½ teaspoon salt
- ¼ teaspoon garlic powder
- ¼ teaspoon pepper
- 2½ teaspoons snipped fresh dill

In a large bowl, combine cucumbers, tomato, red pepper and onion. In a small bowl, whisk mayonnaise, oil, sugar, vinegar, salt, garlic powder and pepper until blended. Stir in dill. Spoon dressing over salad; toss to coat.

Spicy Black Bean Soup

A splash of sherry enhances this hearty, easy-to-make soup. Want to turn down the heat? Remove the ribs and seeds from the jalapeno before dicing.

—**TIA MUSSER** HUDSON, IN

PREP: 25 MIN. • **COOK:** 40 MIN.
MAKES: 12 SERVINGS (¾ CUP EACH)

- 1 **large red onion, chopped**
- 1 **medium sweet red pepper, chopped**
- 1 **jalapeno pepper, seeded and minced**
- 2 **tablespoons olive oil**
- 3 **garlic cloves, minced**
- 3 **cans (15 ounces each) black beans, rinsed and drained**
- 3½ **cups vegetable broth**
- 1 **can (14½ ounces) diced tomatoes with mild green chilies, undrained**
- 1 **can (4 ounces) chopped green chilies**
- ⅓ **cup sherry or additional vegetable broth**
- 2 **tablespoons minced fresh cilantro**
- ½ **cup fat-free sour cream**
- ¼ **cup shredded cheddar cheese**

1. In a Dutch oven, saute onion and peppers in oil until tender. Add garlic; cook 1 minute longer.
2. Stir in the beans, broth, tomatoes and chopped green chilies. Bring to a boil. Reduce heat; simmer, uncovered, for 25 minutes. Add sherry and cilantro; cook 5 minutes longer.
3. Remove from the heat; cool slightly. Place half of soup in a blender; cover and process until pureed. Return to the pan and heat through. Top each serving with 2 teaspoons sour cream and 1 teaspoon cheese.
NOTE *Wear disposable gloves when cutting hot peppers; the oils can burn skin. Avoid touching your face.*

Contest Winner

Tomatoes with Buttermilk Vinaigrette

I like to make the most of tomatoes when they are in season and plentiful, and I love an old-fashioned homemade dressing with refreshing taste.

—**JUDITH FOREMAN** ALEXANDRIA, VA

START TO FINISH: 20 MIN. • **MAKES:** 12 SERVINGS (¾ CUP EACH)

- ¾ **cup buttermilk**
- ¼ **cup minced fresh tarragon**
- ¼ **cup white wine vinegar**
- 3 **tablespoons canola oil**
- 1½ **teaspoons sugar**
- ½ **teaspoon ground mustard**
- ¼ **teaspoon celery salt**
- ¼ **teaspoon pepper**
- 4 **pounds cherry tomatoes, halved**
- ⅓ **cup minced fresh chives**

1. In a small bowl, whisk the first eight ingredients until blended. Refrigerate, covered, until serving.
2. Just before serving, arrange tomatoes on a platter; drizzle with vinaigrette. Sprinkle with chives.

Steak House Burgers

When I asked my brothers to come over for a barbecue, they laughed. So I came up with this. They don't laugh anymore.
—**BONNIE GEAVARAS-BOOTZ** SCOTTSDALE, AZ

PREP: 25 MIN. • **GRILL:** 10 MIN. • **MAKES:** 4 SERVINGS

- 5 tablespoons mayonnaise
- 4½ teaspoons prepared horseradish
- ¼ cup shredded Parmesan cheese
- 3 tablespoons butter, softened, divided
- ½ teaspoon garlic powder
- 4 hamburger buns, split
- 1½ pounds ground beef
- ¼ cup steak sauce
- 4½ teaspoons onion soup mix
- 4 slices Swiss cheese
- 1½ pounds sliced fresh mushrooms
- 2 green onions, chopped
- ¼ cup french-fried onions
  Sliced tomato and lettuce, optional

1. In a small bowl, combine mayonnaise and horseradish; cover and refrigerate until serving. In another small bowl, combine Parmesan cheese, 1 tablespoon butter and garlic powder; spread over bun tops. Set aside.

2. In a large bowl, combine the beef, steak sauce and onion soup mix. Shape into four patties.

3. Moisten a paper towel with cooking oil; using long-handled tongs, lightly coat the grill rack. Grill burgers, covered, over medium heat or broil 4 in. from the heat for 4-5 minutes on each side or until a thermometer reads 160° and juices run clear.

4. Top with Swiss cheese; cover and grill 1-2 minutes longer or until cheese is melted. Place buns, cut side down, on grill for 1-2 minutes or until toasted.

5. Meanwhile, in a large skillet, saute mushrooms and green onions in remaining butter until tender. Serve burgers on buns; top with horseradish sauce, french-fried onions, mushroom mixture and, if desired, tomato and lettuce.

Halibut Chowder

I have a passion for cooking and entertaining. Several times a year I invite both my retired and current teaching friends to a dinner party with their spouses. I've served this halibut chowder at those parties, and it's a big hit.
—**TERESA LUECK** ONAMIA, MN

PREP: 25 MIN. • **COOK:** 30 MIN. • **MAKES:** 12 SERVINGS (3 QUARTS)

- 4 celery ribs, chopped
- 3 medium carrots, chopped
- 1 large onion, chopped
- ½ cup butter, cubed
- ½ cup all-purpose flour
- ¼ teaspoon white pepper
- 2 cups 2% milk
- 1 can (14½ ounces) chicken broth
- ¼ cup water
- 1 tablespoon chicken base
- 3 medium potatoes, peeled and chopped
- 1 can (15¼ ounces) whole kernel corn, drained
- 3 bay leaves
- 2 cups half-and-half cream
- 2 tablespoons lemon juice
- 1 pound halibut or other whitefish fillets, cut into 1-inch pieces
- 1 cup salad croutons
- ¾ cup grated Parmesan cheese
- ½ cup minced chives

1. In a large saucepan, saute the celery, carrots and onion in butter until tender. Stir in flour and pepper until blended; gradually add the milk, broth, water and chicken base. Bring to a boil; cook and stir for 2 minutes or until thickened.

2. Add the potatoes, corn and bay leaves. Return to a boil. Reduce heat; cover and simmer for 15-20 minutes or until potatoes are tender.

3. Stir in cream and lemon juice; return to a boil. Add halibut. Reduce heat; simmer, uncovered, for 7-11 minutes or until fish flakes easily with a fork. Discard bay leaves.

4. Garnish servings with croutons, cheese and chives.
NOTE *Look for chicken base near the broth and bouillon.*

Bloody Mary Soup with Beans

I love a good Bloody Mary, which inspired this recipe. The soup packs a punch, and it'll warm you right up on a chilly day.

—AMBER MASSEY ARGYLE, TX

PREP: 20 MIN. • **COOK:** 55 MIN.
MAKES: 16 SERVINGS (4 QUARTS)

- 1 tablespoon olive oil
- 1 large onion, chopped
- 2 celery ribs, chopped
- 1 large carrot, finely chopped
- 1 poblano pepper, seeded and chopped
- 3 garlic cloves, minced
- 1 carton (32 ounces) reduced-sodium chicken broth
- 1 can (28 ounces) crushed tomatoes
- 1 can (14½ ounces) fire-roasted diced tomatoes, undrained
- ¼ cup tomato paste
- 2 cans (15 ounces each) white kidney or cannellini beans, rinsed and drained
- ¼ cup vodka
- 2 tablespoons Worcestershire sauce
- ½ teaspoon sugar
- 2 tablespoons lemon juice
- 1 tablespoon prepared horseradish
- ½ teaspoon pepper
  Minced fresh parsley, celery ribs, lemon wedges and hot pepper sauce, optional

1. In a Dutch oven, heat oil over medium-high heat. Add onion, celery, carrot and poblano pepper; cook and stir 4-5 minutes or until crisp-tender. Add garlic; cook 1 minute longer.
2. Stir in the broth, tomatoes and tomato paste. Bring to a boil. Reduce heat; simmer, covered, 15 minutes. Add beans, vodka, Worcestershire sauce and sugar; return to a boil. Reduce heat; simmer, uncovered, 25-30 minutes or until vegetables are tender, stirring occasionally.
3. Stir in lemon juice, horseradish and pepper. If desired, sprinkle servings with parsley and serve with celery ribs, lemon wedges and pepper sauce.
NOTE *Wear disposable gloves when cutting hot peppers; the oils can burn skin. Avoid touching your face.*

Hero Pasta Salad

Hide this salad until serving time, or you might be surprised to find it gone! For variety, try adding kalamata olives, peppers or yellow tomatoes—there are so many possibilities.

—ANGELA LEINENBACH
MECHANICSVLLE, VA

PREP: 35 MIN. • **MAKES:** 4 SERVINGS

- 3 tablespoons olive oil
- 3 tablespoons balsamic vinegar
- 2 small garlic cloves, minced
- ⅛ teaspoon salt
- ⅛ teaspoon pepper

SALAD
- 2 cups uncooked spiral pasta
- 1 small red onion, halved and thinly sliced
- ¾ cup sliced pepperoncini
- 4 ounces cubed provolone cheese
- 2 ounces thinly sliced deli ham, cut into strips (⅔ cup)
- 2 ounces thinly sliced hard salami, cut into strips (⅔ cup)
- 5 cups shredded lettuce
- 1 large tomato, coarsely chopped
- ¾ cup cherry tomatoes, halved

1. In a small bowl, whisk the first five ingredients until blended. Cook pasta according to package directions. Drain pasta; rinse with cold water.
2. In a large bowl, combine onion, pepperoncini, cheese, meats and pasta. Just before serving, add lettuce and tomatoes. Drizzle with dressing; toss to coat.

Pea Soup with Mushroom Cream Sauce

Fresh garden peas combine with a hint of basil for a delightfully light spring soup. A special mushroom drizzle adds extra depth to this beautiful creation.

—**SALLY SIBTHORPE** SHELBY TOWNSHIP, MI

PREP: 25 MIN. • **COOK:** 15 MIN.
MAKES: 6 SERVINGS

- ½ **pound sliced baby portobello mushrooms, divided**
- 1 **tablespoon butter**
- ¼ **cup chopped onion**
- 1 **garlic clove, minced**
- ½ **cup half-and-half cream**
- 3 **tablespoons sherry or reduced-sodium chicken broth**
- 1 **tablespoon minced fresh thyme or 1 teaspoon dried thyme**
- ¾ **teaspoon salt, divided**
- 5 **cups fresh or frozen peas, divided**
- 3 **cups reduced-sodium chicken broth**
- 2 **tablespoons lemon juice**
- 4½ **teaspoons minced fresh basil or 1½ teaspoons dried basil**

1. Set aside 3 tablespoons mushrooms for garnish. In a large skillet, saute remaining mushrooms in butter until tender.
2. Add onion to skillet; saute until tender. Add garlic; cook 1 minute longer. Stir in the cream, sherry, thyme and ¼ teaspoon salt. Bring to a boil. Reduce the heat; simmer, uncovered, for 2 minutes. Cool slightly. Transfer to a blender; process until smooth. Set aside.
3. In a Dutch oven, combine 4½ cups peas, chicken broth and remaining salt. Bring to a boil. Reduce heat; simmer, uncovered, for 4 minutes or until the peas are tender. Stir in lemon juice and basil; heat through. Transfer to a blender; process in batches until blended.
4. Ladle soup into serving bowls; top with mushroom cream sauce. Garnish with reserved mushrooms and remaining peas.

Cookout Potato Salad

Instead of using all mayonnaise in this dressing, I mixed in plain yogurt. It lightens up the dish and gives it a welcome tang.

—**ANN HORNE** GREENWOOD, MS

PREP: 10 MIN. • **COOK:** 20 MIN. + CHILLING
MAKES: 6 SERVINGS

- 2 **pounds medium Yukon Gold potatoes, cut into ½-inch cubes**
- 1 **garlic clove, chopped**
- ½ **cup plain yogurt**
- 3 **tablespoons mayonnaise**
- 1 **tablespoon olive oil**
- 2 **teaspoons white wine vinegar**
- ¾ **teaspoon salt**
- ¼ **teaspoon pepper**
- 1 **tablespoon minced fresh parsley**
  Optional toppings: chopped hard-cooked eggs, blanched green beans and salad croutons

1. Place potatoes and garlic in a large saucepan and cover with water. Bring to a boil. Reduce the heat; cover and simmer for 13-18 minutes or until tender. Drain the potatoes; cool completely.
2. Place potatoes in a large bowl. In a small bowl, whisk the yogurt, mayonnaise, oil, vinegar, salt and pepper; pour over potatoes and toss to coat. Refrigerate, covered, until chilled. Sprinkle with parsley; serve with toppings if desired.

Contest Winner

HARVEST OF FLAVORS

When the temperatures cool and fall officially arrives, it's time to enjoy a bounty of autumnal produce. Highlight the best crops of the season with these cozy recipes.

Chicken & Apple Waffle Sandwiches

Waffles aren't just a breakfast item anymore! These fun sandwiches make a delicious dinner in no time.
—**DEBORAH WILLIAMS** PEORIA, AZ

START TO FINISH: 20 MIN. • **MAKES:** 4 SERVINGS

- 8 **frozen waffles, thawed**
- 3 **tablespoons mayonnaise**
- 8 **slices sharp cheddar cheese**
- ¾ **pound thinly sliced deli chicken**
- 1 **medium apple, thinly sliced**
- 2 **tablespoons butter, softened**

1. Spread four waffles with mayonnaise; top with half of the cheese. Layer with chicken, apple and remaining cheese. Top with remaining waffles. Spread outsides of sandwiches with butter.

2. Toast sandwiches in a large skillet over medium heat for 4-5 minutes on each side or until waffles are lightly browned and cheese is melted.

Turkey Sausage, Butternut & Kale Soup

Kale and butternut squash are two of my favorite fall veggies. This recipe combines them into a warm and comforting soup. If you love sweet potatoes, sub them for the squash.
—**LAURA KOCH** LINCOLN, NE

PREP: 20 MIN. • **COOK:** 30 MIN. • **MAKES:** 10 SERVINGS (2½ QUARTS)

- 1 **package (19½ ounces) Italian turkey sausage links, casings removed**
- 1 **medium butternut squash (about 3 pounds), peeled and cubed**
- 2 **cartons (32 ounces each) reduced-sodium chicken broth**
- 1 **bunch kale, trimmed and coarsely chopped (about 16 cups)**
- ½ **cup shaved Parmesan cheese**

1. In a stockpot, cook sausage over medium heat 8-10 minutes or until no longer pink, breaking into crumbles.

2. Add squash and broth; bring to a boil. Gradually stir in kale, allowing it to wilt slightly between additions. Return to a boil. Reduce heat; simmer, uncovered, 15-20 minutes or until vegetables are tender. Top servings with cheese.

Harvest Salad with Cherry Vinaigrette

Mixed greens and plenty of fresh foods make this salad so satisfying, and it's gorgeous to serve for special occasions.
—**JAYE BEELER** GRAND RAPIDS, MI

PREP: 10 MIN. • **BAKE:** 50 MIN. + COOLING
MAKES: 10 SERVINGS (1 CUP EACH)

- 3 medium fresh beets (about 1 pound)
- 1 package (5 ounces) spring mix salad greens
- 2 medium apples, thinly sliced
- 1 medium carrot, shredded
- ½ cup grape tomatoes, halved
- ½ cup yellow grape tomatoes or pear tomatoes, halved
- ½ cup garbanzo beans or chickpeas, rinsed and drained
- ½ cup coarsely chopped walnuts, toasted
- 4 thick-sliced bacon strips, cooked and crumbled

CHERRY VINAIGRETTE
- ½ cup tart cherry preserves
- 3 tablespoons olive oil
- 2 tablespoons red wine vinegar
- 2 teaspoons Dijon mustard
- 1 garlic clove, minced
- ¼ teaspoon salt
- ⅛ teaspoon pepper

1. Preheat oven to 400°. Scrub beets and trim tops to 1 in. Wrap in foil; place on a baking sheet. Bake 50-60 minutes or until tender. Remove foil; cool completely. Peel beets and cut into ½-in. pieces.
2. In a large bowl, combine salad greens, apples, carrot, tomatoes, beans, walnuts, bacon and cooled beets. In a small bowl, whisk vinaigrette ingredients until blended. Serve with salad.

Chicken and Sweet Potato Chili

Sweet potatoes and chicken make this chili a true meal in one bowl. Even though I enjoy it on its own, I sometimes spoon it over rice or quinoa.
—**BRYNN RADER** OLYMPIA, WA

PREP: 35 MIN. • **COOK:** 1½ HOURS
MAKES: 10 SERVINGS (3½ QUARTS)

- 1 medium onion, chopped
- 1 whole garlic bulb, cloves separated, peeled and minced
- 2 tablespoons olive oil
- 1 broiler/fryer chicken (3 to 4 pounds), cut up
- 2 cans (14½ ounces each) plus 1½ cups chicken broth, divided
- 1 tablespoon chili powder
- ¾ teaspoon salt
- ¼ teaspoon crushed red pepper flakes
- ¼ teaspoon pepper
- ½ cup quinoa, rinsed
- 3 medium sweet potatoes, peeled and cubed
- 2 cans (15 ounces each) black beans, rinsed and drained
- 2 cans (16 ounces each) kidney beans, rinsed and drained
- 1 can (14½ ounces) diced tomatoes, undrained

1. In a Dutch oven, saute onion and garlic in oil until tender. Add the chicken, 2 cans broth and seasonings. Bring to a boil. Reduce heat; cover and simmer for 1 hour or until chicken is tender.
2. Meanwhile, in a small saucepan, bring remaining broth to a boil. Add quinoa. Reduce heat; cover and simmer for 12-15 minutes or until liquid is absorbed. Remove from the heat; fluff with a fork. Set aside.
3. Remove the chicken; cool slightly. Strain the broth, reserving vegetables; skim fat from the broth. Return vegetables and broth to the Dutch oven; add the sweet potatoes, beans, tomatoes and cooked quinoa. Bring to a boil. Reduce heat; simmer for 15-20 minutes or until sweet potatoes are tender.
4. Meanwhile, remove the chicken from the bones; cut into bite-size pieces. Discard bones. Stir chicken into chili; heat through.
NOTE *Look for quinoa in the cereal, rice or organic food aisle.*

Vegetable Orzo Soup

This inviting soup is a perfect way to enjoy a rustic-style dish that's heavy on the veggies but light on the prep work. Hearty broth, protein-rich beans and a handful of orzo help fortify against the cold.
—*TASTE OF HOME* TEST KITCHEN

PREP: 15 MIN. • **COOK:** 25 MIN.
MAKES: 6 SERVINGS (2 QUARTS)

- 1   medium sweet yellow pepper, chopped
- 1   medium onion, chopped
- 2   teaspoons olive oil
- 3   garlic cloves, minced
- 1   jar (24 ounces) garden-style spaghetti sauce
- 1   package (16 ounces) frozen Italian vegetables
- 1   can (15 ounces) white kidney or cannellini beans, rinsed and drained
- 1   can (14½ ounces) chicken broth
- ½   pound small red potatoes, quartered
- 1   cup water
- ⅓   cup uncooked orzo pasta
- ½   teaspoon dried marjoram
- ½   teaspoon dried thyme

Saute pepper and onion in oil in a Dutch oven until tender. Add garlic; cook 1 minute longer. Stir in the remaining ingredients. Bring to a boil. Reduce heat; cover and simmer for 15-20 minutes or until potatoes and pasta are tender.

Contest Winner

Summer Chicken Salad with Raspberry Vinaigrette

This pretty, best-of-the-season salad is guaranteed to be a hit! It's piled high with fruits, chicken and greens, then drizzled with a tasty raspberry vinaigrette.
—**HEIDI FARNWORTH** RIVERTON, UT

START TO FINISH: 20 MIN.
MAKES: 6 SERVINGS

- 1   package (10 ounces) ready-to-serve salad greens
- 3½   cups cubed cooked chicken
- 1   cup fresh sugar snap peas
- 1   cup fresh blueberries
- 1   cup fresh raspberries
- 1   celery rib, thinly sliced
- ¼   cup olive oil
- 3   tablespoons balsamic vinegar
- 1   tablespoon seedless red raspberry preserves
- ½   teaspoon salt
- ½   teaspoon onion powder
- ½   teaspoon pepper
- ¼   cup slivered almonds, toasted

Place the salad greens, chicken, peas, berries and celery in a large bowl. In a small bowl, whisk the oil, vinegar, preserves, salt, onion powder and pepper. Drizzle over salad; toss gently to coat. Top with almonds.

Cheesy Chicken Subs

I've been part of the food services staff at a local university for a long time. One year we created this irresistible sandwich that thousands of students have enjoyed since.
—**JANE HOLLAR** VILAS, NC

START TO FINISH: 25 MIN.
MAKES: 4 SERVINGS

- 12 **ounces boneless skinless chicken breasts, cut into strips**
- 1 **envelope Parmesan Italian or Caesar salad dressing mix**
- 1 **cup sliced fresh mushrooms**
- ½ **cup sliced red onion**
- ¼ **cup olive oil**
- 4 **submarine buns, split and toasted**
- 4 **slices Swiss cheese**

1. Place chicken in a large bowl; sprinkle with salad dressing mix. In a large skillet, saute mushrooms and onion in oil for 3 minutes. Add chicken; saute for 6 minutes or until chicken is no longer pink.
2. Spoon mixture onto bun bottoms; top with cheese. Broil 4 in. from the heat for 4 minutes or until cheese is melted. Replace tops.

Fresh Fruit Combo

Whenever I take this eye-catching fruit salad to a party or gathering, people ask for the recipe. The blueberries and cherries give the salad its distinctive flavor.
—**JULIE STERCHI** CAMPBELLSVILLE, KY

START TO FINISH: 20 MIN.
MAKES: 14 SERVINGS

- 2 **cups cubed fresh pineapple**
- 2 **medium oranges, peeled and chopped**
- 3 **kiwifruit, peeled and sliced**
- 1 **cup sliced fresh strawberries**
- 1 **cup halved seedless red grapes**
- 2 **medium firm bananas, sliced**
- 1 **large red apple, cubed**
- 1 **cup fresh or frozen blueberries**
- 1 **cup fresh or canned pitted dark sweet cherries**

In a large bowl, combine the first five ingredients; refrigerate until serving. To serve, fold in bananas, apple, blueberries and cherries.

Contest Winner

PARTY-PERFECT BANANAS

To keep bananas in a fruit salad from turning brown, squeeze the juice of an orange, lemon or lime into a bowl, then slice the banana into the bowl. Stir gently to coat all sides of the banana slices before removing them with a slotted spoon just before adding to your salad.

Black-Eyed Pea Spinach Salad

Here's a Southern take on a classic spinach salad. The simple dressing is delicious, and the black-eyed peas and pecans give the salad some heft.

—**DEBBIE INGLE** WINFIELD, AL

START TO FINISH: 20 MIN. • **MAKES:** 16 SERVINGS (¾ CUP EACH)

- ¼ cup olive oil
- ¼ cup red wine vinegar
- 4 teaspoons Dijon mustard
- 1 teaspoon salt
- 1 teaspoon pepper
- 2 cans (15½ ounces each) black-eyed peas, rinsed and drained
- 3 medium tomatoes, seeded and chopped
- ½ cup thinly sliced red onion
- 1 package (9 ounces) fresh spinach
- ½ cup chopped pecans, toasted
- 6 bacon strips, cooked and crumbled

1. In a large bowl, whisk the first five ingredients. Stir in the black-eyed peas, tomatoes and onion. Cover and refrigerate until serving.

2. Place spinach and vegetable mixture in a large serving bowl; toss gently. Sprinkle with pecans and bacon.

Contest Winner

Ham & Brie Melts

Melty cheese, ham and apricot preserves offer a change of pace from the classic grilled cheese. These fast, crispy sandwiches remind me of baked Brie.

—**BONNIE BAHLER** ELLINGTON, CT

START TO FINISH: 20 MIN. • **MAKES:** 4 SERVINGS

- 8 slices multigrain bread
- ¼ cup apricot preserves, divided
- ½ pound sliced deli ham
- 1 round (8 ounces) Brie cheese, rind removed, sliced
- 3 tablespoons butter, softened

1. Spread four bread slices with half of the preserves. Layer with ham and cheese. Spread remaining bread with remaining preserves; place over cheese, preserves side down. Spread outsides of sandwiches with butter.

2. In a large skillet, toast sandwiches over medium heat 2-3 minutes on each side or until golden brown and cheese is melted.

Tortellini & Chicken Caesar Salad

My family loved this pasta salad right from the start, so these days I serve it a lot. When warm weather arrives, I grill the chicken as a special treat.
—**LEE REESE** ROLLA, MO

START TO FINISH: 25 MIN. • **MAKES:** 6 SERVINGS

- 1 package (20 ounces) refrigerated cheese tortellini
- 1 pound boneless skinless chicken breasts, cut into 1½-inch pieces
- ⅓ cup finely chopped onion
- 1 tablespoon olive oil
- 2 garlic cloves, minced
- ¾ teaspoon salt
- ¼ teaspoon pepper
- 1 package (10 ounces) hearts of romaine salad mix
- 1½ cups grape tomatoes
- 1 can (6½ ounces) sliced ripe olives, drained
- ¾ cup creamy Caesar salad dressing
- ¾ cup shredded Parmesan cheese
- 6 bacon strips, cooked and crumbled

1. Cook tortellini according to package directions. Drain; rinse with cold water.
2. Meanwhile, in a small bowl, combine chicken, onion, oil, garlic, salt and pepper; toss to coat. Heat a large skillet over medium-high heat. Add the chicken mixture; cook and stir 4-6 minutes or until chicken is no longer pink. Remove from heat.
3. In a large bowl, combine salad mix, tomatoes, olives, tortellini and chicken mixture. Drizzle with dressing; toss to coat. Sprinkle with cheese and bacon. Serve immediately.

Cheddar Cheese & Beer Soup

The taste of beer is subtle here, but it's just enough to complement the cheese. For a slightly sweeter version, you can use apple juice instead of beer.
—**HOLLY LEWIS** SWINK, CO

PREP: 15 MIN. • **COOK:** 25 MIN. • **MAKES:** 6 SERVINGS

- ¼ cup butter, cubed
- ¾ pound potatoes, peeled and chopped (about 2 cups)
- 4 celery ribs, chopped (about 2 cups)
- 2 medium onions, chopped (about 1½ cups)
- 2 medium carrots, sliced (about 1 cup)
- ½ cup all-purpose flour
- 1½ teaspoons salt
- 1 teaspoon ground mustard
- ⅛ teaspoon cayenne pepper
- 3 cups chicken stock
- 3 cups (12 ounces) shredded sharp cheddar cheese
- 2 cups 2% milk
- ½ cup beer or apple juice

1. In a 6-qt. stockpot, heat butter over medium-high heat. Add potatoes, celery, onions and carrots; cook and stir 5-7 minutes or until onions are tender.
2. Stir in flour, salt, mustard and cayenne until blended; gradually stir in stock. Bring to a boil, stirring occasionally. Reduce heat; simmer, uncovered, 10-12 minutes or until potatoes are tender. Add remaining ingredients; cook and stir until cheese is melted.

Warm Green Bean & Potato Salad

The combination of green beans and red potatoes, sometimes known as Green Beans Pierre, is one of my go-to side dishes. It's terrific with chicken.

—PRECI D'SILVA DUBAI, UAE

START TO FINISH: 30 MIN.
MAKES: 10 SERVINGS

- 1 pound small red potatoes, quartered
- ¼ cup olive oil
- 2 tablespoons white wine vinegar
- ½ teaspoon salt
- ⅛ teaspoon each garlic powder, ground mustard and pepper
- ⅛ teaspoon each dried basil, parsley flakes and tarragon
- 1 pound fresh green beans, cut into 2-inch pieces
- 2 medium tomatoes, coarsely chopped
- 2 tablespoons chopped onion

1. Place potatoes in a large saucepan; add water to cover. Bring to a boil. Cook, uncovered, for 10 minutes. Meanwhile, in a large bowl, whisk the oil, vinegar and seasonings.
2. Add green beans to potatoes; return to a boil. Cook 3-5 minutes longer or until the vegetables are tender. Drain; add to dressing and toss to coat. Stir in tomatoes and onion. Serve warm.

Contest Winner

Cheesy Corn Chowder

I've had this chowder recipe for more than 30 years, and the whole family really enjoys its cheesy corn taste. It makes a big pot, so it's perfect for entertaining.

—LOLA COMER MARYSVILLE, WA

PREP: 30 MIN. • **COOK:** 30 MIN.
MAKES: 15 SERVINGS (3¾ QUARTS)

- 6 bacon strips, chopped
- ¾ cup chopped sweet onion
- 2½ cups water
- 2½ cups cubed peeled potatoes
- 2 cups sliced fresh carrots
- 2 teaspoons chicken bouillon granules
- 3 cans (11 ounces each) gold and white corn, drained
- ½ teaspoon pepper
- 7 tablespoons all-purpose flour
- 5 cups 2% milk
- 3 cups (12 ounces) shredded cheddar cheese
- 1 cup cubed process cheese (Velveeta)

1. In a Dutch oven, cook the bacon and onion over medium heat until onion is tender. Add the water, potatoes, carrots and bouillon; bring to a boil. Reduce heat; cover and simmer for 15-20 minutes or until potatoes are tender.
2. Stir in corn and pepper. In a large bowl, whisk flour and milk until smooth; add to soup. Bring to a boil; cook and stir for 2 minutes or until thickened. Reduce heat. Add the cheeses; cook and stir until melted.

Ravishing Radish Salad

Showcase radishes in all their glory in this recipe. The unique, crunchy salad really complements grilled entrees.

—MAGGIE RUDDY ALTOONA, IA

PREP: 30 MIN. + CHILLING
MAKES: 6 SERVINGS

- 24 **radishes, quartered**
- 1 **teaspoon salt**
- 1 **teaspoon pepper**
- 6 **green onions, chopped**
- ½ **cup thinly sliced fennel bulb**
- 6 **fresh basil leaves, thinly sliced**
- ¼ **cup snipped fresh dill**
- ¼ **cup olive oil**
- 2 **tablespoons champagne vinegar**
- 2 **tablespoons honey**
- 2 **garlic cloves, minced**
- ½ **cup chopped walnuts, toasted**

1. Place radishes in a large bowl. Sprinkle with salt and pepper; toss to coat. Add the onions, fennel, basil and dill. In a small bowl, whisk the oil, vinegar, honey and garlic. Pour over salad and toss to coat.

2. Cover and refrigerate for at least 1 hour. Sprinkle with walnuts just before serving.

Contest Winner

Brown Rice Chutney Salad

A simple rice salad in a cafe inspired my idea of adding Indian spices and chutney to this dish. To fire things up, mix in a small amount of hot chili oil, tasting as you go.

—BROOKE MARTIN GREENFIELD, MN

PREP: 30 MIN. + CHILLING
MAKES: 8 SERVINGS

- 8 **cups cooked brown rice, cooled**
- 3 **medium carrots, shredded**
- ¾ **cup dried cranberries**
- 1 **small sweet red pepper, chopped**
- 3 **green onions, sliced**
- ½ **cup mango chutney**
- 3 **tablespoons olive oil**
- 2 **tablespoons red wine vinegar**
- 2 **teaspoons curry powder**
- ½ **teaspoon salt**
- ½ **teaspoon garam masala**
- 3 **cups fresh baby spinach, chopped if desired**
- 1 **medium apple, chopped**
- 1 **cup salted cashews**

1. In a large bowl, combine the first five ingredients. In a small bowl, whisk the chutney, oil, vinegar, curry powder, salt and garam masala. Pour over rice mixture; toss to coat. Refrigerate for several hours.

2. Just before serving, add spinach and apple; toss to combine. Sprinkle with cashews.

NOTE *Look for garam masala in the spice aisle.*

Greens with Homemade Croutons

A lively salad of fresh greens gets a nice boost from homemade croutons baked with tarragon, thyme and basil.

—**ANN BUSH** COLORADO CITY, CO

PREP: 25 MIN. • **BAKE:** 15 MIN. • **MAKES:** 4 SERVINGS

- 5 slices day-old French bread (½ inch thick), cubed
- ¼ cup unsalted butter, melted
- 2 teaspoons minced fresh tarragon
- 2 teaspoons minced fresh thyme
- 1 teaspoon minced fresh basil
- ¼ teaspoon onion powder
- ¼ teaspoon garlic salt

DRESSING
- 3 tablespoons canola oil
- 2 tablespoons lime juice
- 2 teaspoons sugar
- ¼ teaspoon salt
  Dash celery salt

SALAD
- 2 cups spring mix salad greens
- 2 cups torn romaine or fresh baby spinach
- ½ small cucumber, thinly sliced
- 1 cup cherry tomatoes, halved
- 1 green onion, thinly sliced

1. Preheat oven to 325°. Place bread cubes in a bowl. Drizzle with butter; toss lightly. Sprinkle with seasonings; toss to combine. Arrange in a single layer on an ungreased baking sheet. Bake 14-18 minutes or until golden brown, turning occasionally.

2. Meanwhile, in a small bowl, whisk the dressing ingredients. In a large bowl, combine salad ingredients. Just before serving, drizzle with dressing; toss to coat. Top with croutons.

Coleslaw with Poppy Seed Dressing

I love this salad because I can keep it in the fridge for a couple of days and it just gets better. It packs lots of flavor for very little effort. If you prefer raisins or dried cranberries, feel free to toss some in as well.

—**TRISHA KRUSE** EAGLE, ID

PREP: 20 MIN. + CHILLING • **MAKES:** 12 SERVINGS (¾ CUP EACH)

- ½ medium head cabbage, shredded (about 4½ cups)
- 6 large carrots, shredded (about 4½ cups)
- 8 green onions, chopped (about 1 cup)
- 1 cup fat-free poppy seed salad dressing
- ⅓ cup sunflower kernels

In a large bowl, combine cabbage, carrots and green onions. Drizzle with dressing; toss to coat. Refrigerate, covered, at least 1 hour. Just before serving, top with sunflower kernels.

Contest Winner

Pear Salad with Sesame Vinaigrette

After a recent party, I created this recipe using ingredients I had on hand: pears, mozzarella and salad greens. It's beautiful, has a good blend of textures and takes only 15 minutes to fix.

—JERRY BODFIELD TUCSON, AZ

START TO FINISH: 15 MIN. • **MAKES:** 6 SERVINGS

- 1 package (10 ounces) hearts of romaine salad mix
- 3 medium pears, sliced
- 8 ounces fresh mozzarella cheese, sliced
- ¾ cup sesame ginger vinaigrette
- 1 package (3¾ ounces) oven-roasted sliced almonds

Divide salad mix among six plates. Top with pears and cheese; drizzle with vinaigrette. Sprinkle with almonds.

Turkey Pitas with Creamy Slaw

Pack these pockets for school, work or a weekend picnic—or just enjoy them at home. You can even toss in some red bell pepper for added crunch.

—TASTE OF HOME TEST KITCHEN

START TO FINISH: 10 MIN. • **MAKES:** 4 SERVINGS

- 3 cups coleslaw mix
- ¼ cup golden raisins
- 3 tablespoons chopped red onion
- ⅓ cup reduced-fat mayonnaise
- 3 tablespoons mango chutney
- 8 pita pocket halves
- ½ pound sliced deli turkey
- 8 ready-to-serve fully cooked bacon strips, warmed
- 1 medium cucumber, thinly sliced

In a large bowl, combine coleslaw mix, raisins and onion. Add mayonnaise and chutney; toss to coat. Line pita halves with turkey, bacon and cucumber; fill with coleslaw mixture.

Chunky Beef & Vegetable Soup

Nothing cures winter woes like wonderful soup, including this beefy one I first cooked up on a snowy day. Serve with French bread or dinner rolls.

—BILLY HENSLEY MOUNT CARMEL, TN

PREP: 25 MIN. • **COOK:** 2¾ HOURS • **MAKES:** 8 SERVINGS (3 QUARTS)

- 1½ pounds beef stew meat, cut into ½-inch pieces
- 1 teaspoon salt, divided
- 1 teaspoon salt-free seasoning blend, divided
- ¾ teaspoon pepper, divided
- 2 tablespoons olive oil, divided
- 4 large carrots, sliced
- 1 large onion, chopped
- 1 medium sweet red pepper, chopped
- 1 medium green pepper, chopped
- 2 garlic cloves, minced
- 1 cup Burgundy wine or additional reduced-sodium beef broth
- 4 cups reduced-sodium beef broth
- 1 can (14½ ounces) diced tomatoes, undrained
- 2 tablespoons tomato paste
- 2 tablespoons Worcestershire sauce
- 1 bay leaf
- 4 medium potatoes (about 2 pounds), cut into ½-inch cubes

1. Sprinkle beef with ½ teaspoon each salt, seasoning blend and pepper. In a Dutch oven, heat 1 tablespoon oil over medium heat. Brown beef in batches. Remove from pan.

2. In the same pan, heat remaining oil over medium heat. Add carrots, onion and peppers; cook and stir until carrots are crisp-tender. Add garlic; cook 1 minute longer.

3. Add wine, stirring to loosen browned bits from pan. Stir in broth, tomatoes, tomato paste, Worcestershire sauce, bay leaf and remaining seasonings. Return beef to pan; bring to a boil. Reduce heat; simmer, covered, 2 hours.

4. Add potatoes; cook 30-40 minutes longer or until beef and potatoes are tender. Skim fat and discard bay leaf.

BREADS, ROLLS & MORE

Mmm! What else is there to say when freshly baked breads, muffins, buns and biscuits are pulled from the oven? If the aroma doesn't immediately attract a crowd, the beautiful baked results will!

Cherry-Pecan Cocoa Bread

Full of sweet cherries and nuts, this loaf has a mild cocoa flavor. It would be perfect to serve for breakfast, brunch or a mid-morning snack. Have a tall glass of milk at the ready!

—**MARGARET BEYERSDORF** KISSIMMEE, FL

PREP: 10 MIN. • **BAKE:** 3 HOURS
MAKES: 1 LOAF (1½ POUNDS, 16 SLICES)

- ⅔ cup warm whole milk (70° to 80°)
- ⅓ cup water (70° to 80°)
- 5 tablespoons butter, softened
- ⅓ cup packed brown sugar
- 1 teaspoon salt
- 3 cups bread flour
- 5 tablespoons baking cocoa
- 2¼ teaspoons active dry yeast
- ½ cup chopped pecans
- ½ cup dried cherries

1. In a bread machine pan, place the first eight ingredients in the order suggested by manufacturer. Select basic bread setting. Choose crust color and loaf size if available.

2. Check dough after 5 minutes of mixing; add 1 to 2 tablespoons of water or flour if needed. Just before the final kneading (your bread machine may audibly signal this), add the pecans and cherries. Bake according to bread machine directions.

Contest Winner

Pull-Apart Bacon Bread

I stumbled across this bread while looking for something different to take to a brunch. Boy, am I glad I did! Everyone asked for the recipe and couldn't believe it only called for five ingredients. It's also great for any informal get-together.

—**TRACI COLLINS** CHEYENNE, WY

PREP: 20 MIN. + RISING • **BAKE:** 20 MIN.
MAKES: 1 LOAF

- 12 bacon strips, diced
- 1 loaf (1 pound) frozen bread dough, thawed
- 2 tablespoons olive oil, divided
- 1 cup (4 ounces) shredded part-skim mozzarella cheese
- 1 envelope (1 ounce) ranch salad dressing mix

1. In a large skillet, cook the bacon over medium heat for 5 minutes or until partially cooked; drain on paper towels. Roll out dough to ½-in. thickness; brush with 1 tablespoon of oil. Cut into 1-in. pieces; place in a large bowl. Add the bacon, cheese, dressing mix and remaining oil; toss to coat.

2. Arrange pieces in a 9x5-in. oval on a greased baking sheet, layering as needed. Cover and let rise in a warm place for 30 minutes or until doubled.

3. Bake at 350° for 15 minutes. Cover with foil; bake 5-10 minutes longer or until golden brown.

Apple & Cheddar Mini Scones

Cheese and sage go well with apples, so why not with scones? These mini scones are an attractive, appealing size for an autumn brunch, tailgate or party.

—**SUE GRONHOLZ** BEAVER DAM, WI

PREP: 25 MIN. • **BAKE:** 10 MIN.
MAKES: 32 SCONES

- 3 **cups all-purpose flour**
- 3 **teaspoons baking powder**
- ½ **teaspoon salt**
- ½ **teaspoon baking soda**
- 1 **cup cold butter**
- 1 **large egg**
- ¾ **cup (6 ounces) vanilla yogurt**
- 3 **tablespoons 2% milk, divided**
- ⅓ **cup shredded peeled apple**
- ⅓ **cup shredded sharp cheddar cheese**
- 1 **tablespoon minced fresh sage**
- 1 **tablespoon sugar**

1. Preheat oven to 425°. In a large bowl, whisk flour, baking powder, salt and baking soda. Cut in butter until mixture resembles coarse crumbs. In another bowl, whisk egg, yogurt and 2 tablespoons milk; stir into the crumb mixture just until moistened. Stir in apple, cheese and sage.
2. Turn onto a lightly floured surface; knead gently 10 times. Divide dough in half; pat each portion into a 6-in. circle. Cut each circle into eight wedges; cut each wedge in half.
3. Transfer to parchment paper-lined baking sheets. Brush tops with the remaining milk; sprinkle with sugar. Bake 10-12 minutes or until golden brown. Serve warm.

FOR REGULAR-SIZE SCONES *Do not cut wedges in half. Bake as directed, increasing baking time to 12-14 minutes. Makes: 16 regular scones.*

Peanut Butter & Jam Muffins

It won't be hard to convince little ones to try bran muffins when PB&J are key ingredients. Delicious and easy to freeze, they make a fast and portable breakfast food or anytime snack.

—**JUDY VAN HEEK** CROFTON, NE

PREP: 20 MIN. • **BAKE:** 15 MIN.
MAKES: 1 DOZEN

- 1 **cup all-purpose flour**
- 1 **cup oat bran**
- ½ **cup packed brown sugar**
- 2 **teaspoons baking powder**
- ½ **teaspoon salt**
- ¼ **teaspoon baking soda**
- 1 **cup 2% milk**
- ½ **cup unsweetened applesauce**
- ⅓ **cup peanut butter**
- 1 **large egg white**
- 2 **tablespoons honey**
- ¼ **cup seedless strawberry jam**

1. In a large bowl, combine the flour, oat bran, brown sugar, baking powder, salt and baking soda. In a small bowl, beat the milk, applesauce, peanut butter, egg white and honey on low speed until smooth; stir into the dry ingredients just until moistened.
2. Fill greased or foil-lined muffin cups half full. Drop 1 teaspoon jam into the center of each muffin; cover with remaining batter.
3. Bake at 400° for 15-20 minutes or until a toothpick inserted in muffin comes out clean. Cool for 5 minutes before removing from pan to a wire rack. Serve warm.

Grandma's Biscuits

Homemade biscuits add a warm and comforting touch to any meal. My grandmother makes these tender biscuits to go with her seafood chowder.

—**MELISSA OBERNESSER** UTICA, NY

START TO FINISH: 25 MIN. • **MAKES:** 10 BISCUITS

- 2 **cups all-purpose flour**
- 3 **teaspoons baking powder**
- 1 **teaspoon salt**
- ⅓ **cup shortening**
- ⅔ **cup 2% milk**
- 1 **large egg, lightly beaten**

1. Preheat oven to 450°. In a large bowl, whisk flour, baking powder and salt. Cut in shortening until mixture resembles coarse crumbs. Add milk; stir just until moistened.

2. Turn onto a lightly floured surface; knead dough gently 8-10 times. Pat dough into a 10x4-in. rectangle. Cut the rectangle in half lengthwise; then cut crosswise to make ten squares.

3. Place 1 in. apart on an ungreased baking sheet; brush tops with egg. Bake 8-10 minutes or until golden brown. Serve biscuits warm.

Overnight Cinnamon Rolls

You can vary the fillings you put in these soft rolls so many fun ways, but make sure you keep the cinnamony flavor.

—**CHRIS O'CONNELL** SAN ANTONIO, TX

PREP: 35 MIN. + RISING • **BAKE:** 20 MIN. • **MAKES:** 2 DOZEN

- 2 **packages (¼ ounce each) active dry yeast**
- 1½ **cups warm water (110° to 115°)**
- 2 **large eggs**
- ½ **cup butter, softened**
- ½ **cup sugar**
- 2 **teaspoons salt**
- 5¾ to 6¼ **cups all-purpose flour**

CINNAMON FILLING
- 1 **cup packed brown sugar**
- 4 **teaspoons ground cinnamon**
- ½ **cup softened butter, divided**

GLAZE
- 2 **cups confectioners' sugar**
- ¼ **cup half-and-half cream**
- 2 **teaspoons vanilla extract**

1. In a small bowl, dissolve yeast in warm water. In a large bowl, combine eggs, butter, sugar, salt, yeast mixture and 3 cups flour; beat on medium speed until smooth. Stir in enough remaining flour to form a very soft dough (dough will be sticky). Do not knead. Cover with plastic wrap; refrigerate overnight.

2. In a small bowl, mix brown sugar and cinnamon. Turn dough onto a floured surface; divide dough in half. Roll one portion into an 18x12-in. rectangle. Spread with ¼ cup butter to within ½ in. of edges; sprinkle evenly with half of the brown sugar mixture.

3. Roll up jelly-roll style, starting with a long side; pinch seam to seal. Cut into 12 slices. Place in a greased 13x9-in. baking pan, cut side down. Repeat with remaining dough and filling.

4. Cover with kitchen towels; let rise in a warm place until doubled, about 1 hour. Preheat oven to 375°.

5. Bake 20-25 minutes or until lightly browned. In a small bowl, mix confectioners' sugar, cream and vanilla; spread over warm rolls.

Chocolate Banana Bran Muffins

So easy-to-make, these treats are healthy but still satisfy my chocolate-loving family. Stir in raisin bran instead of bran flakes for a little extra flavorful fun.

—**TRACY CHAPPELL** HAMIOTA, MB

START TO FINISH: 25 MIN. • **MAKES:** 1 DOZEN

- 1 **cup all-purpose flour**
- ½ **cup sugar**
- 2 **tablespoons baking cocoa**
- 1 **teaspoon baking powder**
- 1 **teaspoon baking soda**
- ½ **teaspoon salt**
- 1 **cup bran flakes**
- 2 **large eggs**
- 1 **cup mashed ripe bananas (about 2 medium)**
- ⅓ **cup canola oil**
- ¼ **cup buttermilk**

1. Preheat oven to 400°. In a large bowl, whisk the first six ingredients. Stir in bran flakes. In another bowl, whisk eggs, bananas, oil and buttermilk until blended. Add to flour mixture; stir just until moistened.

2. Fill foil-lined muffin cups three-fourths full. Bake for 12-14 minutes or until a toothpick inserted in center comes out clean. Cool 5 minutes before removing from pan to a wire rack. Serve warm.

Island Breezes Coffee Cake

Invite sunshine to brunch with a delightful make-ahead bread. You won't believe how simple it is.

—**DEBRA GOFORTH** NEWPORT, TN

PREP: 20 MIN. + CHILLING • **BAKE:** 35 MIN. + COOLING
MAKES: 12 SERVINGS

- ⅔ **cup packed brown sugar**
- ½ **cup flaked coconut, toasted**
- 1 **package (3.4 ounces) cook-and-serve coconut cream pudding mix**
- 20 **frozen bread dough dinner rolls**
- 1 **can (20 ounces) pineapple tidbits, drained**
- 1 **jar (3 ounces) macadamia nuts, coarsely chopped**
- ½ **cup butter, cubed**

1. In a small bowl, mix brown sugar, coconut and pudding mix. Place 10 rolls in a greased 10-in. fluted tube pan; layer with half of the sugar mixture, 1 cup pineapple tidbits, ⅓ cup macadamia nuts and ¼ cup butter. Repeat layers. Cover with plastic wrap and refrigerate overnight.

2. Remove pan from refrigerator about 1¾ hours before serving; let rise in a warm place until dough reaches the top of pan, about 1 hour.

3. Preheat oven to 350°. Remove plastic wrap. Bake coffee cake 35-40 minutes or until golden brown. (Cover loosely with foil if top browns too quickly.) Cool 10 minutes before inverting onto a serving plate; serve warm.

NOTE *To toast coconut, bake in a shallow pan in a 350° oven for 5-10 minutes or cook in a skillet over low heat until golden brown, stirring occasionally.*

Glazed Cranberry Biscuits

My family likes biscuits for breakfast. One Sunday, I decided to make those golden goodies extra special by adding white chips, dried cranberries and a simple orange glaze.

—LORI DANIELS BEVERLY, WV

PREP: 30 MIN. • **BAKE:** 15 MIN.
MAKES: ABOUT 1 DOZEN

- 2 cups all-purpose flour
- 2 teaspoons baking powder
- ½ teaspoon salt
- ½ teaspoon grated orange peel
- ½ teaspoon ground cinnamon
- ¼ cup shortening
- ¼ cup cold butter
- ¾ cup 2% milk
- ¼ cup orange juice
- 1 cup dried cranberries
- ½ cup white baking chips

DRIZZLE
- 1½ cups confectioners' sugar
- 2 tablespoons orange juice
- ¼ teaspoon orange extract

1. In a large bowl, combine the first five ingredients. Cut in shortening and butter until mixture resembles coarse crumbs. Stir in milk and orange juice just until moistened. Stir in the cranberries and baking chips.

2. Turn onto a lightly floured surface; knead gently 8-10 times. Pat or roll out to ¾-in. thickness; cut with a floured 2½-in. biscuit cutter.

3. Place 2 in. apart on a greased baking sheet. Bake at 400° for 12-16 minutes or until lightly browned. In a small bowl, combine confectioners' sugar, orange juice and extract; drizzle over biscuits. Serve warm.

Contest Winner

Swiss & Caraway Flatbreads

My mom came across this rustic-looking flatbread recipe many years ago and always made it on Christmas Eve. Now I make it for my own family throughout the year. It's easy to double or cut in half depending on how many you're serving.

—DIANE BERGER SEQUIM, WA

PREP: 20 MIN. + RISING • **BAKE:** 10 MIN.
MAKES: 2 LOAVES (16 PIECES EACH)

- 2 loaves (1 pound each) frozen bread dough, thawed
- ¼ cup butter, melted
- ¼ cup canola oil
- 1 tablespoon dried minced onion
- 1 tablespoon Dijon mustard
- 2 teaspoons caraway seeds
- 1 teaspoon Worcestershire sauce
- 1 tablespoon dry sherry, optional
- 2 cups (8 ounces) shredded Swiss cheese

1. On a lightly floured surface, roll each portion of dough into a 15x10-in. rectangle. Transfer to two greased 15x10x1-in. baking pans. Cover with kitchen towels; let rise in a warm place until doubled, about 45 minutes.

2. Preheat oven to 425°. Using fingertips, press several dimples into dough. In a small bowl, whisk melted butter, oil, onion, mustard, caraway seeds, Worcestershire sauce and, if desired, sherry until blended; brush over dough. Sprinkle with cheese. Bake 10-15 minutes or until golden brown. Serve warm.

FREEZE OPTION *Cut the cooled flatbreads into pieces. Freeze in resealable plastic freezer bags. To use, reheat flatbreads on an ungreased baking sheet in a preheated 425° oven until heated through.*

Jumbo Caramel Banana Muffins

Love banana bread? Then you'll be thrilled with my muffin recipe. The sweet caramel icing you drizzle on the top gives them exceptional flavor!

—**KATHERINE MCCLELLAND**
DEEP BROOK, NS

PREP: 20 MIN. • **BAKE:** 25 MIN. + COOLING
MAKES: 6 MUFFINS

- ¼ cup shortening
- 1 cup sugar
- 1 large egg
- 1½ cups mashed ripe bananas (about 3 large)
- 1 teaspoon vanilla extract
- 1½ cups all-purpose flour
- 1 teaspoon baking soda
- ¼ teaspoon salt

CARAMEL ICING
- 2 tablespoons butter
- ¼ cup packed brown sugar
- 1 tablespoon 2% milk
- ½ cup confectioners' sugar

1. In a large bowl, cream shortening and sugar until light and fluffy. Beat in egg. Beat in bananas and vanilla. Combine the flour, baking soda and salt; add to creamed mixture just until moistened.

2. Fill paper-lined jumbo muffin cups three-fourths full. Bake at 350° for 23-28 minutes or until a toothpick inserted near the center comes out clean. Cool for 5 minutes before removing from pan to a wire rack to cool completely.

3. For icing, in a small saucepan, melt butter over medium heat. Stir in brown sugar and milk; bring to a boil. Cool slightly. Beat in the confectioners' sugar until smooth. Transfer to a small resealable plastic bag; cut a small hole in a corner of the bag and drizzle over muffins.

Bacon Walnut Bread with Honey Butter

My savory loaf filled with bacon bits, walnuts and blue cheese dressing is complemented by the sweetness of honey-flavored butter. Cut yourself a thick slice, slather on the butter and enjoy!

—**PAM IVBULS** OMAHA, NE

PREP: 25 MIN. • **BAKE:** 40 MIN. + COOLING
MAKES: 1 LOAF (16 SLICES) AND ¾ CUP HONEY BUTTER

- 2 cups all-purpose flour
- 2 teaspoons baking powder
- ½ teaspoon baking soda
- ¼ teaspoon salt
- ¼ teaspoon coarsely ground pepper
- 1 cup half-and-half cream
- ¾ cup refrigerated blue cheese salad dressing
- 2 large eggs
- 1 tablespoon honey
- ⅔ cup coarsely chopped walnuts
- ½ cup bacon bits

HONEY BUTTER
- ¾ cup butter, softened
- 2 tablespoons honey

1. Preheat oven to 325°. In a large bowl, whisk the first five ingredients. In another bowl, whisk the cream, salad dressing, eggs and honey until blended. Add to flour mixture; stir just until moistened. Fold in walnuts and bacon bits.

2. Transfer to a greased and floured 9x5-in. loaf pan. Bake 40-50 minutes or until a toothpick inserted in center comes out clean. Cool bread in pan 10 minutes before removing to wire rack to cool completely.

3. In a small bowl, beat honey butter ingredients. Serve with bread.

Contest Winner

HERBTASTIC BREADS

Packing an extra flavor punch, herbs can take your baked goods from ordinary to over-the-top tasty. With just a little basil, thyme, oregano or rosemary, these recipes are ready to become your new favorites.

Contest Winner

Herbed Dinner Rolls

After I had a baby, a friend dropped off dinner, including these rolls, which start in a bread machine. They were so delicious that I quickly bought my own machine so I could make them myself.
—**DANA LOWRY** HICKORY, NC

PREP: 20 MIN. + RISING • **BAKE:** 15 MIN. • **MAKES:** 16 ROLLS

- 1 cup water (70° to 80°)
- 2 tablespoons butter, softened
- 1 large egg
- ¼ cup sugar
- 1 teaspoon salt
- ½ teaspoon each dried basil, oregano, thyme and rosemary, crushed
- 3¼ cups bread flour
- 2¼ teaspoons active dry yeast
  Additional butter, melted
  Coarse salt, optional

1. In a bread machine pan, place the water, butter, egg, sugar, salt, seasonings, flour and yeast in order suggested by manufacturer. Select dough setting (check dough after 5 minutes of mixing; add 1 to 2 tablespoons of water or flour if needed).

2. When cycle is complete, turn dough onto a lightly floured surface. Divide dough into 16 portions; shape each into a ball. Place 2 in. apart on greased baking sheets. Cover and let rise in a warm place until doubled, about 30 minutes.

3. Bake at 375° for 12-15 minutes or until golden brown. Brush with butter and sprinkle with coarse salt if desired. Remove from pans to wire racks.

NOTE *We recommend you do not use a bread machine's time-delay feature for this recipe.*

Pesto Pinwheel Buns

A spinach-basil pesto gives a terrific boost to this recipe. We love these savory pinwheels.
—***TASTE OF HOME* TEST KITCHEN**

PREP: 30 MIN. + RISING • **BAKE:** 25 MIN. • **MAKES:** 1 DOZEN

- 1 package (¼ ounce) active dry yeast
- 3 tablespoons warm water (110° to 115°)
- ½ cup warm 2% milk (110° to 115°)
- 2 tablespoons butter, softened
- 1 large egg
- 1 tablespoon sugar
- ¾ teaspoon salt
- 2¼ to 2¾ cups all-purpose flour

PESTO
- 1 cup fresh baby spinach
- 1 cup fresh basil leaves
- 2 garlic cloves
- ¼ cup walnut halves, toasted
- ¼ cup grated Parmesan cheese
- ⅛ teaspoon pepper
- ¼ cup olive oil

1. In a large bowl, dissolve yeast in warm water. Add milk, butter, egg, sugar, salt and 1½ cups flour. Beat until smooth. Stir in enough remaining flour to form a firm dough.

2. Turn onto a lightly floured surface; knead until smooth and elastic, about 6-8 minutes. Place in a greased bowl, turning once to grease the top. Cover and let dough rise in a warm place until doubled, about 1 hour.

3. Meanwhile, place the spinach, basil, garlic, walnuts, cheese and pepper in a food processor; cover and process until blended. While processing, gradually add oil in a steady stream. Set aside.

4. Punch dough down. Turn onto a lightly floured surface. Roll into a 12x10-in. rectangle. Spread pesto to within ½ in. of edges. Roll up jelly-roll style, starting with a long side; pinch seam to seal. Cut into 12 rolls.

5. Place rolls cut side up in a greased 13x9-in. baking pan. Cover and let rise until doubled, about 40 minutes.

6. Bake at 350° for 25-30 minutes or until golden brown. Remove from pan to a wire rack. Serve warm. Refrigerate any leftovers.

Herby Parmesan Bread

I've been making my Parmesan bread for so many years, I can no longer remember where the recipe came from. Thanks to a convenient baking mix, I can get a loaf in the oven in a flash.

—**LESLEY ARCHER** CHAPALA, MEXICO

PREP: 10 MIN. • **BAKE:** 35 MIN. + COOLING
MAKES: 1 LOAF (12 SLICES)

- 3¾ cups biscuit/baking mix
- 1 cup plus 2 tablespoons grated Parmesan cheese, divided
- 1 teaspoon Italian seasoning
- ½ teaspoon salt
- 1 large egg
- 1 can (5 ounces) evaporated milk
- ¾ cup water

1. Preheat oven to 350°. In a large bowl, combine biscuit mix, 1 cup cheese, Italian seasoning and salt. In a small bowl, whisk egg, milk and water. Stir into dry ingredients just until moistened. Transfer to a greased 8x4-in. loaf pan. Sprinkle with remaining cheese.

2. Bake 35-40 minutes or until a toothpick inserted in center comes out clean. Cool 10 minutes before removing from pan to a wire rack.

Rustic Garden Herb Biscuits

The rosemary butter takes warm biscuits to another level. I use fresh herbs from the garden, but dried herbs can work, too.

—**MICHELLE GAUER** SPICER, MN

PREP: 25 MIN. • **BAKE:** 25 MIN.
MAKES: 12 BISCUITS (¼ CUP ROSEMARY BUTTER)

- 3¾ cups all-purpose flour
- 6 tablespoons sugar
- 3 teaspoons baking powder
- 2 teaspoons dried minced onion
- 2 teaspoons minced fresh basil
- 2 teaspoons minced fresh parsley
- 1 teaspoon salt
- 1 teaspoon snipped fresh dill
- 1 garlic clove, minced
- ¾ teaspoon baking soda
- ½ teaspoon minced fresh rosemary
- 1 cup cold butter, cubed
- ¾ cup shredded Monterey Jack cheese
- 1½ cups buttermilk
- ¼ cup chopped roasted sweet red peppers

ROSEMARY BUTTER

- ¼ cup butter, softened
- 1 teaspoon honey
- ½ garlic clove, minced
  Dash minced fresh rosemary

1. Preheat oven to 350°. In a large bowl, whisk the first 11 ingredients. Cut in butter until mixture resembles coarse crumbs. Stir in cheese. Add buttermilk and peppers; stir just until moistened.

2. Drop mixture by ⅓ cupfuls into greased muffin cups. Bake 25-30 minutes or until golden brown. Cool 5 minutes before removing from pan to a wire rack.

3. In a small bowl, mix remaining ingredients until blended. Serve warm biscuits with rosemary butter.

Spicy Salsa Muffins

We used to buy slightly spicy muffins at a farmers market in Coweta, Oklahoma. One day I got the recipe, and now I make them every other week. They're a change of pace from the usual muffins.

—**GINGER SULLIVAN** CUTLER BAY, FL

PREP: 20 MIN. • **BAKE:** 15 MIN. + COOLING
MAKES: 1 DOZEN

- 1 cup all-purpose flour
- 1 cup cornmeal
- 3 tablespoons sugar
- 3 teaspoons baking powder
- ¼ teaspoon salt
- ¾ cup chunky salsa
- ½ cup half-and-half cream
- 6 tablespoons butter, melted
- 1 large egg, lightly beaten

1. In a large bowl, combine the flour, cornmeal, sugar, baking powder and salt. In another bowl, combine the salsa, cream, butter and egg. Stir into dry ingredients just until moistened.
2. Fill greased muffin cups three-fourths full. Bake at 400° for 15-18 minutes or until a toothpick inserted near the center comes out clean. Cool for 5 minutes before removing from pan to a wire rack. Serve warm.

Crusty Homemade Bread

Watch your family come flocking for a fresh slice of this bread. Love it plain, or stir in a few favorites such as cheese, garlic, herbs or dried fruits.

—**MEGUMI GARCIA** MILWAUKEE, WI

PREP: 20 MIN. + RISING
BAKE: 50 MIN. + COOLING
MAKES: 1 LOAF (16 SLICES)

- 1½ teaspoons active dry yeast
- 1¾ cups water (70° to 75°)
- 3½ cups plus 1 tablespoon all-purpose flour, divided
- 2 teaspoons salt
- 1 tablespoon cornmeal or additional flour

1. In a small bowl, dissolve yeast in water. In a large bowl, mix 3½ cups flour and salt. Using a rubber spatula, stir in yeast mixture to form a soft, sticky dough. Do not knead. Cover with plastic wrap; let rise at room temperature 1 hour.

2. Punch down dough. Turn onto a lightly floured surface; pat into a 9-in. square. Fold square into thirds, forming a 9x3-in. rectangle. Fold rectangle into thirds, forming a 3-in. square. Turn dough over; place in a greased bowl. Cover with plastic wrap; let rise at room temperature until almost doubled, about 1 hour.
3. Punch down dough and repeat folding process. Return dough to bowl; refrigerate, covered, overnight.
4. Dust bottom of a disposable foil roasting pan with cornmeal. Turn dough onto a floured surface. Knead gently 6-8 times; shape into a 6-in. round loaf. Place in prepared pan; dust top with remaining 1 tablespoon flour. Cover pan with plastic wrap; let rise at room temperature until dough expands to a 7½-in. loaf, about 1¼ hours.
5. Preheat oven to 500°. Using a sharp knife, make a slash (¼ in. deep) across top of loaf. Cover pan tightly with foil. Bake on lowest oven rack 25 minutes.

6. Reduce oven setting to 450°. Remove foil; bake bread 25-30 minutes longer or until deep golden brown. Remove loaf to a wire rack to cool.
FOR CHEDDAR CHEESE BREAD
Prepare dough as directed. After refrigerating dough overnight, knead in 4 ounces diced sharp cheddar cheese before shaping.

FOR RUSTIC CRANBERRY & ORANGE BREAD *Prepare dough as directed. After refrigerating dough overnight, knead in 1 cup dried cranberries and 4 teaspoons grated orange peel before shaping.*

FOR GARLIC & OREGANO BREAD
Prepare dough as directed. After refrigerating dough overnight, microwave ½ cup peeled and quartered garlic cloves with ¼ cup 2% milk on high for 45 seconds. Drain garlic, discarding milk; knead garlic and 2 tablespoons minced fresh oregano into dough before shaping.

Italian Meatball Buns

One of the greatest gifts I love to share with my six grandkids is making special recipes just for them. The meatballs inside the rolls are an appetizing surprise.

—TRINA LINDER-MOBLEY CLOVER, SC

PREP: 30 MIN. + RISING • **BAKE:** 15 MIN.
MAKES: 2 DOZEN

- 12 **frozen bread dough dinner rolls**
- 1 **package (12 ounces) frozen fully cooked Italian meatballs, thawed**
- 2 **tablespoons olive oil**
- ¼ **cup grated Parmesan cheese**
- ¼ **cup minced fresh basil**
- 1½ **cups marinara sauce, warmed**

1. Let frozen dough stand at room temperature 25-30 minutes or until it is softened.

2. Cut each roll in half. Wrap each portion around a meatball, enclosing meatball completely; pinch dough firmly to seal. Place on greased baking sheets, seam side down. Cover with kitchen towels; let rise in a warm place until almost doubled, about 1½-2 hours.

3. Preheat the oven to 350°. Bake buns 12-15 minutes or until golden brown. Brush tops with oil; sprinkle with cheese and basil. Serve with marinara sauce.

Crisscross Apple Crowns

Wake 'em up on chilly mornings with the tempting aroma of apples and cinnamon filling the house. I love making these for breakfast. They're different and so easy.

—TERESA MORRIS LAUREL, DE

PREP: 30 MIN. • **BAKE:** 20 MIN.
MAKES: 8 SERVINGS

- 1⅓ **cups chopped peeled tart apples**
- ⅓ **cup chopped walnuts**
- ⅓ **cup raisins**
- ½ **cup sugar, divided**
- 2 **tablespoons all-purpose flour**
- 2 **teaspoons ground cinnamon, divided**
  Dash salt
- 1 **package (16.3 ounces) large refrigerated flaky biscuits**
- 2 **teaspoons butter, melted**

1. In a large microwave-safe bowl, combine the apples, walnuts, raisins, 3 tablespoons sugar, flour, ¾ teaspoon cinnamon and salt. Microwave on high for 2-3 minutes or until almost tender.

2. Flatten each biscuit into a 5-in. circle. Combine remaining sugar and cinnamon; sprinkle a rounded teaspoonful of sugar mixture over each. Top each with ¼ cup apple mixture. Bring up edges to enclose mixture; pinch edges to seal.

3. Place seam side down in ungreased muffin cups. Brush tops with butter; sprinkle with remaining sugar mixture. With a sharp knife, cut an "X" in the top of each.

4. Bake at 350° for 18-22 minutes or until golden brown. Cool for 5 minutes before removing crowns from pan to a wire rack.

Contest Winner

> ### BEST BAKING APPLES
>
> For recipes such as Crisscross Apple Crowns, you'll need tart baking apples. There are many to choose from, including Baldwin, Cortland, Golden Russet, Granny Smith, Ida Red, Jonathan, Lady Apple, McIntosh, Macoun, Newtown Pippin, Northern Spy, Rhode Island Greening, Rome Beauty, Winesap, Wolf River or York Imperial.

Sweet Potato Cinnamon Bread

My family loves quick breads. This one is moist and spicy, so naturally it's become one of our favorites. If you don't have mini loaf pans, the recipe works just as well in a regular pan—you just need to bake it a little longer.

—**NANCY FOUST** STONEBORO, PA

PREP: 20 MIN. • **BAKE:** 35 MIN. + COOLING
MAKES: 4 LOAVES (6 SLICES EACH)

- 3½ cups all-purpose flour
- 2⅔ cups sugar
- 2 teaspoons baking soda
- 1 teaspoon salt
- ½ teaspoon baking powder
- 1½ teaspoons ground cinnamon
- 1 teaspoon ground ginger
- ½ teaspoon ground cloves
- 4 large eggs
- 2 cups mashed sweet potatoes
- ⅔ cup canola oil
- ⅔ cup 2% milk
- 1½ cups raisins
- 1 cup chopped walnuts

1. Preheat oven to 350°. In a large bowl, whisk the first eight ingredients. In another bowl, whisk eggs, sweet potatoes, oil and milk until blended. Add to flour mixture; stir just until moistened. Fold in raisins and walnuts.

2. Transfer to four greased 5¾x3x2-in. loaf pans. Bake for 35-40 minutes or until a toothpick inserted in center comes out clean. Cool in pans 10 minutes before removing to wire racks to cool.

FOR LARGER LOAVES *Prepare recipe as directed, using two greased 9x5-in. loaf pans. Bake in preheated 350° oven 55-60 minutes or until a toothpick comes out clean. Makes: 2 loaves (12 slices each).*

Java Muffins

I rely on these muffins to get me going in the morning. They're especially good with a cup of coffee.

—**ZAINAB AHMED** MOUNTLAKE TERRACE, WA

START TO FINISH: 30 MIN. • **MAKES:** 1 DOZEN

- ¼ cup butter, softened
- 1 cup packed brown sugar
- 2 large eggs
- ¼ cup unsweetened applesauce
- ½ cup buttermilk
- ½ cup strong brewed coffee
- 1 tablespoon instant coffee granules
- ½ teaspoon vanilla extract
- 1 cup all-purpose flour
- ¾ cup whole wheat flour
- 1½ teaspoons baking powder
- ½ teaspoon baking soda
- ½ teaspoon ground cinnamon
- ¼ teaspoon salt
- ½ cup finely chopped pecans, divided

1. Preheat oven to 375°. In a large bowl, beat butter and brown sugar until crumbly, about 2 minutes. Add eggs; mix well. Beat in applesauce. In a small bowl, whisk buttermilk, coffee, coffee granules and vanilla until granules are dissolved; gradually add to butter mixture.

2. In another bowl, whisk flours, baking powder, baking soda, cinnamon and salt. Add to butter mixture; stir just until moistened. Fold in ¼ cup pecans.

3. Coat muffin cups with cooking spray or use paper liners; fill three-fourths full. Sprinkle with remaining pecans. Bake 15-20 minutes or until a toothpick inserted in center comes out clean. Cool 5 minutes before removing from pan to a wire rack. Serve warm.

Jumbo Blueberry Muffins

Michigan is the top blueberry producer. I often enjoy trying recipes with them, like a jumbo version of a classic muffin.

—**JACKIE HANNAHS** CEDAR SPRINGS, MI

PREP: 15 MIN. • **BAKE:** 20 MIN. • **MAKES:** 8 JUMBO MUFFINS

- ½ cup butter, softened
- 1 cup sugar
- 2 large eggs
- ½ cup buttermilk
- 1 teaspoon vanilla extract
- 2 cups all-purpose flour
- 2 teaspoons baking powder
- ¼ teaspoon salt
- 2 cups fresh or frozen blueberries

TOPPING

- 3 tablespoons sugar
- ⅛ teaspoon ground cinnamon
- ⅛ teaspoon ground nutmeg

1. Preheat oven to 400°. In a large bowl, cream butter and sugar until light and fluffy. Add eggs, one at a time, beating well after each addition. Beat in buttermilk and vanilla. In another bowl, whisk flour, baking powder and salt. Add to creamed mixture; stir just until moistened. Fold in the blueberries.

2. Fill greased or paper-lined jumbo muffin cups two-thirds full. Mix topping ingredients; sprinkle over tops. Bake for 20-25 minutes or until a toothpick inserted in center comes out clean. Cool 5 minutes before removing from the pan to a wire rack. Serve warm.

FOR STANDARD-SIZE MUFFINS *Make batter as directed; fill greased or paper-lined standard muffin cups two-thirds full. Bake in a preheated 400° oven for 15-20 minutes or until a toothpick comes out clean. Makes: about 16 standard-sized muffins.*

Southwestern Corn Bread

I put a wonderful new twist on my grandma's classic corn bread. Extra flavored butter can be kept in the refrigerator for about a week and used in other recipes or on seeded toast.

—**ELIZABETH CHARPIOT** SANTA ROSA, CA

PREP: 20 MIN. • **BAKE:** 25 MIN.
MAKES: 15 SERVINGS (½ CUP BUTTER)

- 2 cups all-purpose flour
- 2 cups yellow cornmeal
- ½ cup sugar
- 4 teaspoons baking powder
- 1 teaspoon baking soda
- 1 teaspoon salt
- 1 teaspoon dried minced garlic
- 1 teaspoon dried minced onion
- 1 teaspoon paprika
- 1 teaspoon chili powder
- 2 cups buttermilk
- ½ cup canola oil
- 2 large eggs
- 1 jar (7 ounces) roasted sweet red peppers, drained, patted dry and chopped
- 1 cup frozen corn, thawed
- ¼ cup minced chives

CHILI HONEY-LIME BUTTER

- ½ cup butter, softened
- 1 tablespoon lime juice
- 1 tablespoon honey
- 1 teaspoon chili powder
- 1 teaspoon grated lime peel

1. In a large bowl, combine the first 10 ingredients. In a small bowl, whisk the buttermilk, oil and eggs. Stir into dry ingredients just until moistened. Fold in red peppers, corn and chives.

2. Transfer to a greased 13x9-in. baking dish. Bake at 400° for 23-28 minutes or until a toothpick inserted near the center comes out clean. Remove bread to a wire rack.

3. In a small bowl, combine the butter, lime juice, honey, chili powder and lime peel. Serve with warm corn bread.

Praline-Topped Apple Bread

Apples and candied pecans make this bread simply stunning. It'll stand out among the usual coffee cakes you see at brunches.

—SONJA BLOW NIXA, MO

PREP: 30 MIN. • **BAKE:** 50 MIN. + COOLING
MAKES: 1 LOAF (16 SLICES)

- 2 cups all-purpose flour
- 2 teaspoons baking powder
- ½ teaspoon baking soda
- ½ teaspoon salt
- 1 cup sugar
- 1 cup (8 ounces) sour cream
- 2 large eggs
- 3 teaspoons vanilla extract
- 1½ cups chopped peeled Granny Smith apples
- 1¼ cups chopped pecans, toasted, divided
- ½ cup butter, cubed
- ½ cup packed brown sugar

1. Preheat oven to 350°. In a large bowl, mix flour, baking powder, baking soda and salt. In another bowl, beat sugar, sour cream, eggs and vanilla until well blended. Stir into flour mixture just until moistened. Fold in apples and 1 cup pecans.

2. Transfer to a greased 9x5-in. loaf pan. Bake 50-55 minutes or until a toothpick inserted in center comes out clean. Cool in pan 10 minutes. Remove to a wire rack to cool the bread completely.

3. In a small saucepan, combine butter and brown sugar. Bring to a boil, stirring constantly to dissolve sugar; boil 1 minute. Spoon over bread. Sprinkle with remaining pecans; let stand until set.

NOTE *To toast nuts, bake in a shallow pan in a 350° oven for 5-10 minutes or cook in a skillet over low heat until lightly browned, stirring occasionally.*

PICK THE RIGHT PAN

For best results with quick breads, bake in a light aluminum pan rather than a darker nonstick pan. (If you use a glass pan, lower your oven temperature by 25°.)

Contest Winner

Petite Sticky Buns

No kneading is required to bake these muffin-tin sticky buns. Be careful not to overbake them, or they'll be difficult to get out of the pan.

—LISA NAUGLE FAYETTEVILLE, PA

PREP: 30 MIN. + RISING • **BAKE:** 15 MIN.
MAKES: 2 DOZEN

- 3 to 3¾ cups all-purpose flour
- ¼ cup sugar
- 1 package (¼ ounce) active dry yeast
- 1 teaspoon salt
- 1¼ cups milk
- ¼ cup butter, cubed
- 1 large egg

TOPPING

- 1 cup packed brown sugar
- ¾ cup butter, cubed
- ¾ cup chopped pecans, toasted
- 2 tablespoons honey
- 1 teaspoon ground cinnamon
- ½ teaspoon maple flavoring

1. In a large bowl, combine 2 cups flour, sugar, yeast and salt. In a small saucepan, heat the milk and butter to 120°-130°. Add to the dry ingredients; beat just until moistened. Add egg; beat until smooth. Stir in enough remaining flour to form a soft dough (dough will be sticky). Do not knead. Cover and let rise in a warm place until doubled, about an hour.

2. In a small saucepan over low heat, cook and stir topping ingredients until butter is melted. Drop by rounded teaspoonfuls into 24 well-greased muffin cups.

3. Stir dough down. Fill prepared muffin cups half full. Cover and let rise in a warm place until doubled, about 30 minutes.

4. Place muffin cups on foil-lined baking sheets. Bake at 375° for 12-15 minutes or until golden brown. Cool for 2 minutes before inverting onto baking sheets. Transfer to serving platters. Serve warm.

Winter Fruit Coffee Cake

Filled with apples, pears and raisins, this spice cake is dressed up with a streusel topping. The heavenly scent of it baking will have your family gathered in the kitchen, waiting for a piece.

—*TASTE OF HOME* TEST KITCHEN

PREP: 20 MIN. + STANDING
BAKE: 30 MIN. + COOLING
MAKES: 15 SERVINGS

- ½ **cup golden raisins**
- ¼ **cup brandy**

TOPPING
- 1 **cup packed brown sugar**
- 1 **teaspoon ground cinnamon**
- 2 **tablespoons butter, softened**
- ½ **cup chopped pecans**

CAKE
- ½ **cup butter, softened**
- 1 **cup packed brown sugar**
- 2 **large eggs**
- 1 **teaspoon vanilla extract**
- 2 **cups all-purpose flour**
- 3 **teaspoons baking powder**
- 1 **teaspoon baking soda**
- ¾ **teaspoon ground cinnamon**
- ¼ **teaspoon ground nutmeg**
- ⅛ **teaspoon ground cloves**
- ½ **teaspoon salt**
- 1 **cup sour cream**
- ¾ **cup chopped peeled apple**
- ½ **cup chopped peeled ripe pear**

1. In a small bowl, soak the raisins in brandy for 1 hour.

2. In a small bowl, combine brown sugar and cinnamon. With clean hands, work butter into sugar mixture until well combined. Add pecans. Refrigerate for 15 minutes.

3. Meanwhile, in a large bowl, cream butter and sugar until light and fluffy. Beat in eggs and vanilla. Combine the flour, baking powder, baking soda, spices and salt; add to the creamed mixture alternately with sour cream. Fold in the apple, pear and raisins (do not drain raisins). Pour into a greased 13x9-in. baking dish. Sprinkle with the topping.

4. Bake at 350° for 28-32 minutes or until a toothpick inserted near the center comes out clean. Cool cake on a wire rack.

Cheese-Filled Garlic Rolls

To change up plain old dinner rolls, I added mozzarella. Now my family wants them at every gathering. And I don't mind one bit!

—**ROSALIE FITTERY** PHILADELPHIA, PA

PREP: 20 MIN. + RISING • **BAKE:** 15 MIN.
MAKES: 2 DOZEN

- 1 **loaf (1 pound) frozen bread dough, thawed**
- 24 **cubes part-skim mozzarella cheese (¾ inch each), about 10 ounces**
- 3 **tablespoons butter, melted**
- 2 **teaspoons minced fresh parsley**
- 1 **garlic clove, minced**
- ½ **teaspoon Italian seasoning**
- ½ **teaspoon crushed red pepper flakes**
- 2 **tablespoons grated Parmigiano-Reggiano cheese**

1. Divide dough into 24 portions. Shape each portion around a cheese cube to cover completely; pinch to seal. Place each roll in a greased muffin cup, seam side down. Cover with kitchen towels; let rise in a warm place until doubled, about 30 minutes. Preheat oven to 350°.

2. In a small bowl, mix butter, parsley, garlic, Italian seasoning and pepper flakes. Brush over rolls; sprinkle with cheese. Bake 15-18 minutes or until golden brown.

3. Cool 5 minutes before removing from pans. Serve warm.

MAIN DISHES

Comforting, cozy, delicious, savory—no matter what word you choose to describe these main dishes, you're right! Select entrees that will hit the spot for your next lunch, dinner or even special occasion.

Ham and Broccoli Biscuit Bake

Whenever I cook this creamy dish, I'm on alert to make sure my husband doesn't nibble before I bring it to the table. I chide him, but really, who could resist the golden crust bubbling to the top?

—**AMY WHEELER** BALTIMORE, MD

PREP: 20 MIN. • **BAKE:** 25 MIN.
MAKES: 6 SERVINGS

- 2½ cups frozen chopped broccoli
- 1 can (10¾ ounces) condensed cream of potato soup, undiluted
- 1¼ cups 2% milk, divided
- 1 teaspoon garlic pepper blend
- ½ teaspoon crushed red pepper flakes
- ¼ teaspoon pepper
- 2 cups cubed fully cooked ham
- 1 cup (4 ounces) shredded cheddar-Monterey Jack cheese
- 1½ cups biscuit/baking mix
- 1 large egg, beaten

1. Preheat oven to 350°. Combine the broccoli, soup, ¾ cup milk and seasonings in a large saucepan; bring to a boil. Reduce heat; add the ham and cheese. Cook and stir until cheese is melted. Pour into a greased 11x7-in. baking dish.
2. Combine the biscuit mix, egg and remaining milk in a small bowl just until moistened. Drop the batter by tablespoonfuls over ham mixture; spread gently.
3. Bake, uncovered, 25-30 minutes or until golden brown.

Cheeseburger Cups

A terrific recipe for moms with young kids and busy lives, this simple, inexpensive dish is table-ready in a half hour. Best of all, kids will go crazy for these darling dinner bites!

—**JERI MILLHOUSE** ASHLAND, OH

START TO FINISH: 30 MIN.
MAKES: 5 SERVINGS

- 1 pound ground beef
- ½ cup ketchup
- 2 tablespoons brown sugar
- 1 tablespoon prepared mustard
- 1½ teaspoons Worcestershire sauce
- 1 tube (12 ounces) refrigerated buttermilk biscuits
- ½ cup cubed process cheese (Velveeta)

1. In a large skillet, cook beef over medium heat until no longer pink; drain. Stir in the ketchup, brown sugar, mustard and Worcestershire sauce. Remove from heat; set aside.
2. Press each biscuit onto the bottom and up the sides of a greased muffin cup. Spoon beef mixture into cups; top with cheese cubes. Bake at 400° for 14-16 minutes or until golden brown.
FREEZE OPTION *Freeze cooled pastries in a freezer container, separating the layers with waxed paper. To use, thaw pastries in refrigerator for 8 hours. Reheat on a baking sheet in a preheated 375° oven until heated through.*

Company Pot Roast

The aroma of this roast slowly cooking in the oven is heavenly. It gives the home such a cozy feeling, even on the chilliest winter days.

—ANITA OSBORNE THOMASBURG, ON

PREP: 20 MIN. • **BAKE:** 2¾ HOURS
MAKES: 6 SERVINGS

- 1 boneless beef chuck roast (3 to 4 pounds)
- 2 tablespoons olive oil
- 1 cup sherry or beef broth
- ½ cup reduced-sodium soy sauce
- ¼ cup sugar
- 2 teaspoons beef bouillon granules
- 1 cinnamon stick (3 inches)
- 8 medium carrots, cut into 2-inch pieces
- 6 medium potatoes, peeled and cut into 1½-inch pieces
- 1 medium onion, sliced
- 2 tablespoons cornstarch
- 2 tablespoons cold water

1. Brown roast in oil in a Dutch oven on all sides; drain. Combine the sherry, soy sauce, sugar, bouillon and cinnamon stick; pour over roast.
2. Cover and bake at 325° for 2¾-3¼ hours or until meat and vegetables are tender, adding the carrots, potatoes and onion during the last 30 minutes of cooking.
3. Remove roast and vegetables to a serving platter; keep warm. Combine cornstarch and water until smooth. Stir into pan. Bring to a boil; cook and stir for 2 minutes or until thickened. Serve with roast and vegetables.

Chicken Sausages with Polenta

I get a kick out of serving this dish— everyone seems to be on time for dinner when they know it's on the menu.

—ANGELA SPENGLER TAMPA, FL

START TO FINISH: 30 MIN.
MAKES: 6 SERVINGS

- 4 teaspoons olive oil, divided
- 1 tube (1 pound) polenta, cut into ½-inch slices
- 1 each medium green, sweet red and yellow peppers, thinly sliced
- 1 medium onion, thinly sliced
- 1 package (12 ounces) fully cooked Italian chicken sausage links, thinly sliced
- ¼ cup grated Parmesan cheese
- 1 tablespoon minced fresh basil

1. In a large nonstick skillet, heat 2 teaspoons oil over medium heat. Add the polenta; cook 9-11 minutes on each side or until golden brown. Keep warm.
2. Meanwhile, in another large skillet, heat remaining oil over medium-high heat. Add peppers and onion; cook and stir until tender. Remove from pan.
3. Add sausages to same pan; cook and stir 4-5 minutes or until browned. Return pepper mixture to pan; heat through. Serve with polenta; sprinkle with cheese and basil.

Turkey Club Roulades

Weeknights turn elegant when these short-prep roulades with common ingredients are on the menu. Not a fan of turkey? Substitute lightly pounded chicken breasts.

—*TASTE OF HOME* TEST KITCHEN

PREP: 20 MIN. • **COOK:** 15 MIN. • **MAKES:** 8 SERVINGS

- ¾ **pound fresh asparagus, trimmed**
- 8 **turkey breast cutlets (about 1 pound)**
- 1 **tablespoon Dijon-mayonnaise blend**
- 8 **slices deli ham**
- 8 **slices provolone cheese**
- ½ **teaspoon poultry seasoning**
- ½ **teaspoon pepper**
- 8 **bacon strips**

SAUCE
- ⅔ **cup Dijon-mayonnaise blend**
- 4 **teaspoons 2% milk**
- ¼ **teaspoon poultry seasoning**

1. Bring 4 cups water to a boil in a large saucepan. Add the asparagus; cook, uncovered, for 3 minutes or until crisp-tender. Drain and immediately place asparagus in ice water. Drain and pat dry. Set aside.

2. Spread the turkey cutlets with Dijon-mayonnaise. Layer with ham, cheese and asparagus. Sprinkle with the poultry seasoning and pepper. Roll up tightly and wrap with bacon.

3. Cook roulades in a large skillet over medium-high heat for 12-15 minutes, turning occasionally, or until the bacon is crisp and turkey is no longer pink. Combine the sauce ingredients; serve with roulades.

Pineapple-Glazed Pork Roast

Some dishes are just so versatile that you can serve them for both family dinners and when entertaining company. This one gets lots of accolades.

—**NANCY WHITFORD** EDWARDS, NY

PREP: 10 MIN. • **BAKE:** 50 MIN. + STANDING • **MAKES:** 10 SERVINGS

- 1 **boneless pork loin roast (2½ pounds)**
- ¾ **teaspoon salt**
- ¼ **teaspoon pepper**
- ⅓ **cup pineapple preserves**
- 2 **tablespoons stone-ground mustard**
- ¼ **teaspoon dried basil**
- 1 **can (20 ounces) unsweetened pineapple tidbits, drained**

1. Preheat oven to 350°. Place roast on a rack in a shallow roasting pan, fat side up. Sprinkle with salt and pepper. Roast 25 minutes.

2. Meanwhile, for glaze, in a small bowl, whisk preserves, mustard and basil; brush half of mixture over roast. Add pineapple to roasting pan. Roast 25-35 minutes longer or until a thermometer reads 145°.

3. Remove roast from oven and brush with remaining glaze; tent loosely with foil. Let stand 10 minutes before slicing. Using a slotted spoon, serve pineapple with pork.

Italian Meatball Tortes

Full of hearty flavors, these dinner pies stuffed with tomatoes, mozzarella and savory homemade meatballs will be a hit with your family. The preparation takes some time, but the results are well worth it.

—SANDY BLESSING OCEAN SHORES, WA

PREP: 1¼ HOURS + RISING • **BAKE:** 30 MIN.
MAKES: 2 TORTES (6 SERVINGS EACH)

- 1 package (¼ ounce) active dry yeast
- ¼ cup warm water (110° to 115°)
- ¾ cup warm milk (110° to 115°)
- ¼ cup sugar
- ¼ cup shortening
- 1 large egg
- 1 teaspoon salt
- 3½ to 3¾ cups all-purpose flour

MEATBALLS
- 1 can (5 ounces) evaporated milk
- 2 large eggs, lightly beaten
- 1 cup quick-cooking oats
- 1 cup crushed saltines
- ½ cup chopped onion
- ½ cup chopped celery
- 2 teaspoons salt
- 2 teaspoons chili powder
- ½ teaspoon garlic powder
- ½ teaspoon pepper
- 3 pounds ground beef

FILLING
- 1 can (15 ounces) crushed tomatoes
- ½ cup chopped onion
- ⅓ cup grated Parmesan cheese
- 1½ teaspoons dried basil
- 1½ teaspoons dried oregano
- 1 teaspoon minced fresh parsley
- 1 teaspoon salt
- 1½ cups (6 ounces) shredded part-skim mozzarella cheese

1. In a large bowl, dissolve yeast in warm water. Add the milk, sugar, shortening, egg, salt and 2 cups flour. Beat until smooth. Stir in enough remaining flour to form a soft dough.

2. Turn onto a floured surface; knead until smooth and elastic, about 6-8 minutes. Place in a greased bowl, turning once to grease the top. Cover and let rise in a warm place until doubled, 1-1½ hours.

3. In a large bowl, combine milk, eggs, oats, saltines, onion, celery and seasonings. Crumble beef over mixture and mix well. Shape into 1½-in. balls. In a large skillet over medium heat, cook meatballs in batches until no longer pink.

4. Meanwhile, place the tomatoes and onion in a small saucepan. Bring to a boil. Reduce heat; simmer, uncovered, for 10 minutes or until slightly thickened. Stir in Parmesan cheese, herbs and salt.

5. Punch dough down. Divide into three portions. Roll two portions into 11-in. circles; line the bottoms and press partially up the sides of two greased 9-in. springform pans. Roll third portion into a 12x10-in. rectangle; cut into twelve 10x1-in. strips.

6. Place meatballs in prepared crusts; top with the tomato mixture and mozzarella cheese. Make lattice crusts with strips of dough; trim and seal edges. Cover and let rise for 30 minutes.

7. Preheat oven to 350°. Bake 30-35 minutes or until golden brown. Cut into wedges.

Homey Mac & Cheese

I also call this "My Grandson's Mac & Cheese." Zachary has been to Iraq and Afghanistan with both the Marines and Navy, and I've been privileged to make his favorite casserole for him for more than 20 years.

—ALICE BEARDSELL OSPREY, FL

PREP: 20 MIN. • **BAKE:** 25 MIN.
MAKES: 8 SERVINGS

- 2½ cups uncooked elbow macaroni
- ¼ cup butter, cubed
- ¼ cup all-purpose flour
- ½ teaspoon salt
- ¼ teaspoon pepper
- 3 cups 2% milk
- 5 cups (20 ounces) shredded sharp cheddar cheese, divided
- 2 tablespoons Worcestershire sauce
- ½ teaspoon paprika

1. Preheat oven to 350°. Cook the macaroni according to package directions for al dente.
2. Meanwhile, in a large saucepan, heat butter over medium heat. Stir in flour, salt and pepper until smooth; gradually whisk in the milk. Bring to a boil, stirring constantly; cook and stir 2-3 minutes or until thickened.
3. Reduce heat. Stir in 3 cups cheese and Worcestershire sauce until cheese is melted.
4. Drain macaroni; stir into the sauce. Transfer to a greased 10-in. ovenproof skillet. Bake, uncovered, 20 minutes. Top with remaining cheese; sprinkle with paprika. Bake 5-10 minutes longer or until bubbly and the cheese is melted.

Contest Winner

Sage Pork Chops with Cider Pan Gravy

Pork chops topped with sage and a creamy, cider-flavored sauce make for a quick weeknight dinner. You can serve these lightly seasoned chops with rice, couscous or noodles.

—ERICA WILSON BEVERLY, MA

START TO FINISH: 30 MIN.
MAKES: 4 SERVINGS

- 4 bone-in center-cut pork loin chops (6 ounces each)
  Salt and pepper to taste
- 3 tablespoons dried sage leaves
- ¼ cup all-purpose flour
- 2 tablespoons butter
- 2 tablespoons canola oil
- ½ cup apple cider or juice
- ½ cup reduced-sodium chicken broth
- ¼ cup heavy whipping cream
  Minced fresh parsley

1. Sprinkle pork chops with salt and pepper; rub with sage. Place flour in a small shallow bowl; coat the chops with flour.
2. In a large skillet over medium heat, brown chops in butter and oil on both sides. Remove and keep warm.
3. Add the cider, stirring to loosen any browned bits from pan. Cook, uncovered, for 3 minutes. Stir in the broth; cook 3 minutes longer. Add cream; cook for 2-3 minutes or until gravy is slightly thickened. Return chops to the pan; cover and cook for 6-8 minutes or until a thermometer reads 160°. Garnish with parsley.

Pepperoni Lasagna Roll-Ups

Pizza-inspired roll-ups work well for potlucks because you can make them in advance and reheat as needed. They travel well, too.

—**JAMIE MILLER** MAPLE GROVE, MN

PREP: 45 MIN. • **BAKE:** 55 MIN.
MAKES: 16 SERVINGS

- 16 uncooked lasagna noodles
- ½ pound bulk Italian sausage
- ½ pound sliced baby portobello mushrooms
- ¼ cup chopped sweet onion
- 1 jar (24 ounces) tomato basil pasta sauce
- 1½ teaspoons brown sugar
- 1½ teaspoons fennel seed, crushed
- ½ teaspoon dried tarragon
- 1⅛ teaspoons salt, divided
- ⅛ teaspoon crushed red pepper flakes, optional
- 1 package (3½ ounces) sliced pepperoni
- 2½ cups (10 ounces) shredded part-skim mozzarella cheese
- 2½ cups part-skim ricotta cheese
- 2 cups grated Parmesan cheese, divided
- 2 large eggs, lightly beaten
- 6 tablespoons minced fresh parsley, divided
- 3 tablespoons minced fresh basil or 1 tablespoon dried basil
- ½ teaspoon pepper

1. Cook noodles according to package directions.

2. Meanwhile, in a Dutch oven, cook sausage, mushrooms and onion over medium heat until meat is no longer pink; drain and transfer to a large bowl. Stir in pasta sauce, brown sugar, fennel seed, tarragon, ⅛ teaspoon salt and pepper flakes, if desired.

3. In the same pan, cook the sliced pepperoni for 4-5 minutes or until lightly browned; remove to paper towels to drain.

4. In another large bowl, combine the mozzarella, ricotta, 1 cup Parmesan, eggs, 4 tablespoons parsley, basil, pepper and remaining salt.

5. Drain noodles. Spread 1 cup meat sauce in a greased 13x9-in. baking dish. Spread ¼ cup cheese mixture over each noodle; top with 3 or 4 pepperoni slices. Carefully roll up; place seam side down in prepared dish. Top with remaining meat sauce; sprinkle with remaining Parmesan.

6. Cover dish and bake at 350° for 55-60 minutes or until bubbly. Sprinkle with the remaining parsley before serving.

Coconut-Crusted Turkey Strips

My granddaughter shared these baked turkey strips with me. With a plum dipping sauce, they're just right for a light dinner.

—**AGNES WARD** STRATFORD, ON

START TO FINISH: 30 MIN.
MAKES: 6 SERVINGS

- 2 large egg whites
- 2 teaspoons sesame oil
- ½ cup flaked coconut, toasted
- ½ cup dry bread crumbs
- 2 tablespoons sesame seeds, toasted
- ½ teaspoon salt
- 1½ pounds turkey breast tenderloins, cut into ½-inch strips
  Cooking spray

DIPPING SAUCE
- ½ cup plum sauce
- ⅓ cup unsweetened pineapple juice
- 1½ teaspoons prepared mustard
- 1 teaspoon cornstarch

1. Preheat oven to 425°. In a shallow bowl, whisk the egg whites and oil. In another shallow bowl, mix coconut, bread crumbs, sesame seeds and salt. Dip turkey in egg mixture, then in coconut mixture, patting to help the coating adhere.

2. Place on baking sheets coated with cooking spray; spritz the turkey with cooking spray. Bake 10-12 minutes or until the turkey is no longer pink, turning once.

3. Meanwhile, in a small saucepan, mix sauce ingredients. Bring to a boil; cook and stir 1-2 minutes or until thickened. Serve turkey with sauce.

NOTE *To toast coconut, bake in a shallow pan in a 350° oven for 5-10 minutes or cook in a skillet over low heat until golden brown, stirring occasionally.*

> ### HOW TO SEPARATE EGGS
>
> To separate egg whites from the yolk, place an egg separator over a custard cup; crack egg into the separator. It's easier to separate eggs when they are cold.

*Nothing says "Dinner is served!" quite like a casserole. Choose one of these comforting bakes,
then watch your family scramble for kitchen table seats before it's even out of the oven!*

Contest Winner

Sausage Spinach Pasta Bake

I've sometimes swapped in other meats, such as chicken sausage,
veal or ground pork, and added in summer squash, zucchini,
green beans and mushrooms, depending on what's in season.
Also, fresh herbs can really add a lot to the dish.
—**KIM FORNI** LACONIA, NH

PREP: 35 MIN. • **BAKE:** 25 MIN. • **MAKES:** 10 SERVINGS

- 1 **package (16 ounces) whole wheat spiral pasta**
- 1 **pound Italian turkey sausage links, casings removed**
- 1 **medium onion, chopped**
- 5 **garlic cloves, minced**
- 1 **can (28 ounces) crushed tomatoes**
- 1 **can (14½ ounces) diced tomatoes, undrained**
- 1 **teaspoon dried oregano**
- 1 **teaspoon dried basil**
- ¼ **teaspoon pepper**
- 1 **package (10 ounces) frozen chopped spinach, thawed and squeezed dry**
- ½ **cup half-and-half cream**
- 2 **cups (8 ounces) shredded part-skim mozzarella cheese**
- ½ **cup grated Parmesan cheese**

1. Preheat oven to 350°. Cook the pasta according to
package directions.
2. Meanwhile, in a large skillet, cook turkey and onion over
medium heat until meat is no longer pink. Add garlic. Cook
1 minute longer; drain. Stir in tomatoes, oregano, basil and
pepper. Bring to a boil. Reduce heat; simmer, uncovered,
10 minutes.
3. Drain pasta; stir into turkey mixture. Add spinach and
cream; heat through. Transfer to a 13x9-in. baking dish
coated with cooking spray. Sprinkle with cheeses. Bake,
uncovered, 25-30 minutes or until golden brown.

Polish Casserole

When I first made this dish, my 2-year-old liked it so much that he
wanted it for every meal! If you don't have penne, you can use any
pasta that will hold the sauce.
—**CRYSTAL JO BRUNS** ILIFF, CO

PREP: 25 MIN. • **BAKE:** 45 MIN.
MAKES: 2 CASSEROLES (6 SERVINGS EACH)

- 4 **cups uncooked penne pasta**
- 1½ **pounds smoked Polish sausage or kielbasa, cut into ½-inch slices**
- 2 **cans (10¾ ounces each) condensed cream of mushroom soup, undiluted**
- 1 **jar (16 ounces) sauerkraut, rinsed and well drained**
- 3 **cups (12 ounces) shredded Swiss cheese, divided**
- 1⅓ **cups 2% milk**
- 4 **green onions, chopped**
- 2 **tablespoons Dijon mustard**
- 4 **garlic cloves, minced**

1. Preheat oven to 350°. Cook pasta according to package
directions; drain and transfer to a large bowl. Stir in the
sausage, soup, sauerkraut, 2 cups cheese, milk, onions,
mustard and garlic.
2. Spoon into two greased 8-in. square baking dishes;
sprinkle with remaining cheese. Bake, uncovered, for
45-50 minutes or until golden brown and bubbly.
FREEZE OPTION *Cover and freeze unbaked casserole up to
3 months. Thaw in the refrigerator overnight. Remove from
the refrigerator 30 minutes before baking. Preheat oven to
350°. Bake, uncovered, 50-55 minutes or until golden brown
and bubbly.*

Cajun Beef Casserole

Even if your picky eaters usually avoid the veggies, they won't complain when you bring this cheesy casserole with a corn bread crust to the table. For less heat, reduce the amount of seasoning.
—*TASTE OF HOME* TEST KITCHEN

PREP: 15 MIN. • **BAKE:** 25 MIN. • **MAKES:** 6 SERVINGS

- 1 package (8½ ounces) corn bread/muffin mix
- 1 pound ground beef
- 2 cans (14½ ounces each) diced tomatoes, drained
- 2 cups frozen mixed vegetables, thawed
- 1 can (6 ounces) tomato paste
- 1 to 2 teaspoons Cajun seasoning
- 1 cup (4 ounces) shredded cheddar cheese
- 2 green onions, thinly sliced

1. Prepare the corn bread batter according to package directions. Spread into a greased 11x7-in. baking dish.
2. In a large skillet, cook beef over medium heat until meat is no longer pink; drain. Add the tomatoes, vegetables, tomato paste and seasoning. Bring to a boil. Reduce heat; simmer, uncovered, for 5 minutes. Pour over corn bread batter. Sprinkle with cheese.
3. Bake, uncovered, at 350° for 25-30 minutes or until golden brown. Sprinkle with onions.
FREEZE OPTION *Wrap individual portions of cooled casserole in plastic wrap and transfer to a resealable plastic bag. To use, partially thaw in refrigerator overnight. Remove from refrigerator 30 minutes before baking. Preheat oven to 350°. Unwrap casserole and transfer to a baking dish. Bake until a thermometer inserted into center reads 165°.*

Italian Pork and Potato Casserole

When this dish is baking, it always brings back fond memories of home. My mother created the recipe years ago, using the ingredients she had on hand.
—**THERESA KREYCHE** TUSTIN, CA

PREP: 10 MIN. • **BAKE:** 45 MIN. • **MAKES:** 6 SERVINGS

- 6 cups sliced red potatoes
- 3 tablespoons water
- 1 garlic clove, minced
- ½ teaspoon salt
- ⅛ teaspoon pepper
- 6 boneless pork loin chops (6 ounces each)
- 1 jar (24 ounces) marinara sauce
- ¼ cup shredded Parmesan cheese

1. Place the potatoes and water in a microwave-safe dish. Cover and microwave on high for 5 minutes or until almost tender; drain.
2. Place potatoes in a 13x9-in. baking dish coated with cooking spray. Sprinkle with garlic, salt and pepper. Top with pork chops and marinara sauce. Cover and bake at 350° for 40-45 minutes or until a thermometer inserted in pork reads 145° and potatoes are tender.
3. Sprinkle with cheese. Bake, uncovered, 3-5 minutes longer or until the cheese is melted. Let stand 5 minutes before serving.

Italian Sausage-Stuffed Zucchini

I've had to be creative when getting my crew to eat vegetables, so I decided to make stuffed zucchini inspired by pizza. It worked! We like to include sausage for a main dish, but it could be a meatless side dish, too.

—DONNA MARIE RYAN TOPSFIELD, MA

PREP: 35 MIN. • **BAKE:** 20 MIN.
MAKES: 6 SERVINGS

- 6 medium zucchini (about 8 ounces each)
- 1 pound Italian turkey sausage links, casings removed
- 2 medium tomatoes, seeded and chopped
- 1 cup panko (Japanese) bread crumbs
- ⅓ cup grated Parmesan cheese
- ⅓ cup minced fresh parsley
- 2 tablespoons minced fresh oregano or 2 teaspoons dried oregano
- 2 tablespoons minced fresh basil or 2 teaspoons dried basil
- ¼ teaspoon pepper
- ¾ cup shredded part-skim mozzarella cheese

1. Preheat oven to 350°. Cut each zucchini lengthwise in half. Scoop out pulp, leaving a ¼-in. shell; chop pulp. Place the zucchini shells in a large microwave-safe dish. In batches, microwave, covered, on high for 2-3 minutes or until crisp-tender.
2. In a large skillet, cook sausage and zucchini pulp over medium heat 6-8 minutes or until sausage is no longer pink, breaking sausage into crumbles; drain. Stir in tomatoes, bread crumbs, Parmesan cheese, herbs and pepper. Spoon into shells.
3. Place in two ungreased 13x9-in. baking dishes. Bake, covered, for 15-20 minutes or until the zucchini is tender. Sprinkle with mozzarella cheese. Bake, uncovered, 5-8 minutes longer or until cheese is melted.

Contest Winner

Cream Cheese and Swiss Lasagna

I like to fix the chunky meat sauce for this dish the day before so the flavors can blend. It serves 12, making it ideal for a big gathering.

—BETTY PEARSON EDGEWATER, MD

PREP: 40 MIN. + SIMMERING
BAKE: 55 MIN. + STANDING
MAKES: 12 SERVINGS

- 1½ pounds lean ground beef (90% lean)
- 1 pound bulk Italian sausage
- 1 medium onion, finely chopped
- 3 garlic cloves, minced
- 2 cans (15 ounces each) tomato sauce
- 1 can (14½ ounces) Italian diced tomatoes, undrained
- 1 can (6 ounces) tomato paste
- 2 teaspoons dried oregano
- 1 teaspoon dried basil
- 1 teaspoon Italian seasoning
- ½ teaspoon sugar
- ½ teaspoon salt
- ¼ teaspoon pepper
- 9 no-cook lasagna noodles
- 12 ounces cream cheese, softened
- 2 cups shredded part-skim mozzarella cheese, divided
- 2 cups shredded Parmesan cheese
- 2 cups shredded Swiss cheese

1. In a Dutch oven over medium heat, cook the beef, sausage and onion until the meat is no longer pink. Add garlic; cook 1 minute longer. Drain. Stir in the tomato sauce, tomatoes, tomato paste, oregano, basil, Italian seasoning, sugar, salt and pepper. Bring to a boil. Reduce heat; simmer, uncovered, for 30 minutes.
2. Spread 1 cup of sauce in a greased 13x9-in. baking dish. Top with three noodles. Drop a third of the cream cheese by teaspoonfuls over the top. Sprinkle with ½ cup mozzarella and ⅔ cup each of Parmesan cheese and Swiss cheese; spoon a third of the remaining sauce over the top. Repeat with layers of noodles, cheeses and sauce twice (dish will be full). Place dish on a baking sheet.
3. Cover dish and bake at 350° for 45 minutes. Sprinkle with remaining mozzarella cheese. Bake, uncovered, 10-15 minutes longer or until bubbly and cheese is melted. Let stand for 15 minutes before cutting.

Savory Turkey Potpies

This will perk you up on a cold, rainy day. You can use chicken in place of turkey, and I like to serve the potpies with a fresh green salad or cranberry sauce on the side.

—**JUDY WILSON** SUN CITY WEST, AZ

PREP: 25 MIN. • **BAKE:** 20 MIN.
MAKES: 8 SERVINGS

- 1 **small onion, chopped**
- ¼ **cup all-purpose flour**
- 3 **cups chicken stock**
- 3 **cups cubed cooked turkey breast**
- 1 **package (16 ounces) frozen peas and carrots**
- 2 **medium red potatoes, cooked and cubed**
- 3 **tablespoons minced fresh parsley**
- 1 **tablespoon minced fresh thyme**
- ¼ **teaspoon pepper**
- 1 **sheet refrigerated pie pastry**
  Additional fresh parsley or thyme leaves, optional
- 1 **large egg**
- 1 **teaspoon water**
- ½ **teaspoon kosher salt**

1. In a Dutch oven coated with cooking spray, saute the onion until tender. In a small bowl, whisk flour and stock until smooth; gradually stir into Dutch oven. Bring to a boil; cook and stir 2 minutes or until thickened. Remove from heat. Add turkey, peas and carrots, potatoes, parsley, thyme and pepper; stir gently.

2. Preheat oven to 425°. Divide the turkey mixture among eight 10-oz. ramekins. On a lightly floured surface, unroll pastry. Cut out eight 3-in. circles. Gently press parsley into the pastry, if desired. Place over turkey mixture. Beat egg and water; brush over tops. Sprinkle with salt.

3. Place ramekins on a baking sheet. Bake 20-25 minutes or until crusts are golden brown.

FREEZE OPTION *Securely wrap baked and cooled potpies in plastic wrap and foil; freeze. To use, partially thaw in refrigerator overnight. Remove from refrigerator 30 minutes before baking. Preheat oven to 425°. Unwrap potpies; bake in oven until heated through and a thermometer inserted in center reads 165°. Cover top with foil to prevent overbrowning if necessary.*

Parm-Breaded Pork Chops

The king of Italian cheeses brings a sweet, nutty taste to the buttery cracker coating on these tasty chops. I love how this comes together quickly, but tastes like you spent a long time preparing it.

—**MELANIE HOGAN** BIRMINGHAM, AL

PREP: 10 MIN. • **BAKE:** 25 MIN.
MAKES: 6 SERVINGS

- ¼ **cup all-purpose flour**
- 1 **large egg**
- 2 **tablespoons 2% milk**
- 1 **cup crushed Ritz crackers**
- 3 **tablespoons grated Parmesan cheese**
- ½ **teaspoon salt**
- ⅛ **teaspoon pepper**
- 6 **boneless pork loin chops (4 ounces each)**
- ¼ **cup butter, melted**

1. Place flour in a shallow bowl. In a separate shallow bowl, whisk egg and milk. In a third bowl, combine the crackers, cheese, salt and pepper. Dip pork chops in the flour, egg mixture, then cracker mixture.

2. Place butter in a 13x9-in. baking dish; add pork chops. Bake, uncovered, at 350° for 25-30 minutes or until a thermometer reads 145°. Let stand for 5 minutes before serving.

Contest Winner

Saucy Garlic Chicken

Roasted garlic lends a richness to this appetizing entree. The recipe can be assembled in advance and popped into the oven when guests arrive.

—**JOANNA JOHNSON** FLOWER MOUND, TX

PREP: 40 MIN. + COOLING • **BAKE:** 35 MIN. • **MAKES:** 6 SERVINGS

- 4 **whole garlic bulbs**
- 2 **tablespoons olive oil, divided**
- 1 **package (9 ounces) fresh baby spinach**
- ¾ **teaspoon salt, divided**
- ½ **teaspoon coarsely ground pepper, divided**
- 6 **boneless skinless chicken breast halves (6 ounces each)**
- 6 **tablespoons butter, cubed**
- 6 **tablespoons all-purpose flour**
- 3 **cups 2% milk**
- 2½ **cups grated Parmesan cheese, divided**
- ⅛ **teaspoon nutmeg**
  Hot cooked pasta
  Chopped tomato and minced fresh parsley, optional

1. Remove papery outer skin from garlic (do not peel or separate cloves). Cut tops off of garlic bulbs; brush bulbs with 1 tablespoon oil. Wrap each bulb in heavy-duty foil. Bake at 425° for 30-35 minutes or until softened. Cool for 10-15 minutes.

2. Meanwhile, place spinach in a greased 13x9-in. baking dish; sprinkle with ¼ teaspoon each of salt and pepper. In a large skillet, brown chicken in remaining oil on both sides; place over spinach.

3. In a large saucepan, melt the butter. Stir in flour until smooth; gradually add milk. Bring to a boil; cook and stir for 1-2 minutes or until thickened. Stir in 2 cups cheese, nutmeg and remaining salt and pepper.

4. Transfer to a blender; squeeze the softened garlic into blender. Cover and process until smooth. Pour mixture over chicken.

5. Cover and bake at 425° for 30-35 minutes or until a thermometer reads 170° and sauce is bubbly. Uncover; sprinkle with remaining cheese. Bake 5 minutes longer. Serve with pasta. Sprinkle with tomato and parsley if desired.

FREEZE OPTION *Substitute 5 ounces frozen chopped spinach that has been thawed and squeezed dry for fresh spinach. Cool unbaked casserole and sprinkle with remaining cheese; cover and freeze. To use, partially thaw in refrigerator overnight. Remove from refrigerator 30 minutes before baking. Preheat oven to 425°. Bake casserole as directed, increasing time as necessary to heat through and for a thermometer inserted into chicken to read 170°.*

Pesto Grilled Salmon

Using just a few ingredients, this fresh and easy summertime dish is sure to become a family favorite.

—**SONYA LABBE** WEST HOLLYWOOD, CA

START TO FINISH: 30 MIN. • **MAKES:** 12 SERVINGS

- 1 **salmon fillet (3 pounds)**
- ½ **cup prepared pesto**
- 2 **green onions, finely chopped**
- ¼ **cup lemon juice**
- 2 **garlic cloves, minced**

1. Moisten a paper towel with cooking oil; using long-handled tongs, rub on the grill rack to coat lightly. Place salmon skin side down on rack. Grill, covered, over medium heat or broil 4 in. from the heat for 5 minutes.

2. In a small bowl, combine pesto, onions, lemon juice and garlic. Carefully spoon some of pesto mixture over salmon. Grill 15-20 minutes longer or until fish flakes easily with a fork, basting occasionally with remaining pesto mixture.

Chicken Cordon Bleu Pasta

Facebook fans of my blog, *Chef in Training,* inspired me to create this pasta casserole out of ingredients I had on hand. Success! I took the dish for another tasty spin and added a bit of smoky bacon and toasted bread crumbs.
—**NIKKI BARTON** PROVIDENCE, UT

PREP: 25 MIN. • **BAKE:** 20 MIN. • **MAKES:** 6 SERVINGS

- 3 **cups uncooked penne pasta**
- 2 **cups heavy whipping cream**
- 1 **package (8 ounces) cream cheese, softened and cubed**
- 1½ **cups (6 ounces) shredded Swiss cheese, divided**
- ½ **teaspoon onion powder**
- ½ **teaspoon garlic salt**
- ¼ **teaspoon pepper**
- 3 **cups sliced cooked chicken breasts**
- ¾ **cup crumbled cooked bacon**
- ¾ **cup cubed fully cooked ham**
- 3 **tablespoons dry bread crumbs**

1. Preheat oven to 350°. Cook pasta according to package directions for al dente.

2. Meanwhile, in a large saucepan, heat the cream and cream cheese over medium heat until smooth, stirring occasionally. Stir in 1 cup Swiss cheese, onion powder, garlic salt and pepper until blended.

3. Drain pasta; stir in chicken, bacon and ham. Add sauce; toss to coat. Transfer to a greased 13x9-in. baking dish. Sprinkle with remaining Swiss cheese and bread crumbs. Bake, uncovered, 18-22 minutes or until heated through.

Muffin-Pan Meat Loaves

I used to have a catering business, and my specialty was comfort food. My clients went nuts over these mini loaves. I often use an 8x8 pan or a loaf pan, but a muffin tin really cuts the cooking time.
—**VANGIE PANAGOTOPULOS** MOORESTOWN, NJ

START TO FINISH: 30 MIN. • **MAKES:** 6 SERVINGS

- 2 **large eggs, lightly beaten**
- ¾ **cup shredded Mexican cheese blend**
- 1 **tablespoon chili powder**
- 1 **tablespoon Worcestershire sauce**
- 2 **garlic cloves, minced**
- 1½ **teaspoons hot pepper sauce**
- 1 **teaspoon dried parsley flakes**
- ½ **teaspoon salt**
- ¼ **teaspoon pepper**
- ¾ **pound lean ground beef (90% lean)**
- ¾ **pound ground turkey**

TOPPING
- ½ **cup ketchup**
- 3 **tablespoons brown sugar**
- 1 **teaspoon prepared mustard**

1. Preheat oven to 375°. In a large bowl, combine the first nine ingredients. Add beef and turkey; mix lightly but thoroughly. Place ⅓ cup mixture into each of 12 ungreased muffin cups, pressing lightly.

2. In a small bowl, mix topping ingredients; spoon over meat loaves. Bake, uncovered, 15-20 minutes or until a thermometer reads 165°.

FREEZE OPTION *Bake the meat loaves without topping. Cool meat loaves and freeze, covered, on a waxed paper-lined baking sheet until firm. Transfer the meat loaves to resealable plastic freezer bags; return to freezer. To use, partially thaw in refrigerator overnight. Place meat loaves on a greased shallow baking pan. Prepare topping as directed; spread over tops. Bake in a preheated 350° oven until heated through.*

Zippy Sirloin Steak

The spicy coating on this steak brings the heat, and it's such an easy rub to put together. Steak leftovers can make an impressive main-dish salad.

—**LISA FINNEGAN** FORKED RIVER, NJ

PREP: 15 MIN. + MARINATING
GRILL: 20 MIN. • **MAKES:** 6 SERVINGS

- 1 tablespoon paprika
- 2 teaspoons pepper
- 1½ teaspoons kosher salt
- 1½ teaspoons brown sugar
- 1½ teaspoons ground cumin
- 1½ teaspoons chili powder
- 1 teaspoon sugar
- ¼ teaspoon cayenne pepper
- 1 beef sirloin tip steak (1½ pounds)

1. In a small bowl, combine the first eight ingredients. Rub over both sides of beef. Cover and refrigerate for 2 hours.

2. Moisten a paper towel with cooking oil; using long-handled tongs, rub on the grill rack to coat lightly. Grill beef, covered, over medium heat or broil 4 in. from the heat for 8-10 minutes on each side or until meat reaches desired doneness (for medium-rare, a thermometer should read 145°; medium, 160°; well-done, 170°). Let stand for 5 minutes before slicing.

Contest Winner

Catfish Parmesan

Mississippi is the nation's largest producer of farm-raised catfish. My family loves this dish, and asks for it often. I love that it's so simple to prepare.

—**MRS. W. D. BAKER** STARKVILLE, MS

PREP: 15 MIN. • **BAKE:** 20 MIN.
MAKES: 6 SERVINGS

- ¾ cup dry bread crumbs
- 3 tablespoons grated Parmesan cheese
- 2 tablespoons chopped fresh parsley
- ½ teaspoon salt
- ¼ teaspoon paprika
- ⅛ teaspoon each pepper, dried oregano and basil
- 6 fresh or frozen catfish fillets (3 to 5 ounces each)
- ½ cup butter, melted

1. In a shallow bowl, combine bread crumbs, Parmesan cheese, parsley and seasonings. Dip catfish in butter, then in the crumb mixture. Arrange in a greased 13x9-in. baking dish.

2. Bake, uncovered, at 375° for 20-25 minutes or until the fish flakes easily with a fork.

Dad's Lemony Grilled Chicken

Lemon juice, onions and garlic add tangy flavor to my grilled chicken.

—**MIKE SCHULZ** TAWAS CITY, MI

PREP: 20 MIN. + MARINATING
GRILL: 30 MIN. • **MAKES:** 8 SERVINGS

- 1 cup olive oil
- ⅔ cup lemon juice
- 6 garlic cloves, minced
- 1 teaspoon salt
- ½ teaspoon pepper
- 2 medium onions, chopped
- 8 chicken drumsticks (2 pounds)
- 8 bone-in chicken thighs (2 pounds)

1. In a small bowl, whisk the first five ingredients until blended; stir in the onions. Pour 1½ cups marinade into a large resealable plastic bag. Add the chicken; seal bag and turn it to coat. Refrigerate overnight. Cover and refrigerate remaining marinade.

2. Prepare grill for indirect heat. Drain chicken, discarding marinade in bag. Place chicken on grill rack, skin side up. Grill, covered, over indirect medium heat 15 minutes. Turn; grill for 15-20 minutes longer or until a thermometer reads 170°-175°, basting occasionally with reserved marinade.

Sausage & Mushroom Stuffed Squash

This dish just says "comfort" to me, especially because so many of the flavors are familiar.

—**ELIANE ONEYEAR** RIVER FOREST, IL

PREP: 45 MIN. • **BAKE:** 20 MIN.
MAKES: 6 SERVINGS

- 3 medium acorn squash
- 1½ cups water
- 1 pound bulk pork sausage
- ½ pound sliced baby portobello mushrooms
- 1 large onion, chopped
- 1 celery rib, chopped
- 1 garlic clove, minced
- ½ cup white wine or beef broth
- 1 can (10¾ ounces) condensed cream of mushroom soup, undiluted
- 1 cup salad croutons
- ½ cup 2% milk
- ⅓ cup shredded Parmesan cheese
- 1 cup (4 ounces) sharp shredded cheddar cheese, divided

1. Cut squash in half; discard seeds. Place cut side down in an ungreased 15x10x1-in. baking pan. Add water. Cover squash and bake at 350° for 40-50 minutes or until tender.

2. Meanwhile, in a large skillet, cook the sausage, mushrooms, onion, celery and garlic over medium heat until meat is no longer pink; drain. Add the wine. Bring to a boil; cook until liquid is reduced by half. Stir in the soup, croutons, milk, Parmesan and ¾ cup cheddar cheese.

3. Drain water from squash. Turn the squash over; stuff with the sausage mixture. Sprinkle with remaining cheddar cheese. Bake, uncovered, for 20-25 minutes or until heated through.

> **ANOTHER NAME FOR PORTOBELLOS**
> Did you know? Baby portobello mushrooms are also known as cremini mushrooms.

Burrito Pie

Layers of cheese, meat sauce and tortillas create a satisfying Mexican lasagna that kids of all ages will love. The recipe makes two casseroles, so you'll have an easy meal to freeze for later, too.

—**RENEE STARRET** BENTON, LA

PREP: 40 MIN. • **BAKE:** 30 MIN.
MAKES: 2 CASSEROLES (6 SERVINGS EACH)

- 2 **pounds ground beef**
- 1 **medium onion, chopped**
- 2 **garlic cloves, minced**
- 2 **cans (15 ounces each) Ranch Style beans (pinto beans in seasoned tomato sauce)**
- 1 **bottle (16 ounces) taco sauce**
- 1 **can (10 ounces) diced tomatoes and green chilies, undrained**
- 1 **can (4 ounces) chopped green chilies**
- 1 **can (3.8 ounces) sliced ripe olives, drained**
- 12 **flour tortillas (8 inches), halved**
- 4 **cups (16 ounces) shredded Colby-Monterey Jack cheese**

1. In a large skillet, cook beef and onion over medium heat until meat is no longer pink. Add garlic; cook 1 minute longer. Drain. Stir in the beans, taco sauce, tomatoes, chilies and olives. Bring to a boil. Reduce heat; simmer, uncovered, for 20-25 minutes or until slightly thickened.

2. Spread 1 cup meat mixture in each of two greased 11x7-in. baking dishes. Layer with 4 tortilla halves, 1 cup meat mixture and ⅔ cup cheese. Repeat twice.

3. Cover and freeze one casserole for up to 3 months. Cover and bake the remaining casserole at 350° for 20 minutes. Uncover; bake 10-15 minutes longer or until bubbly and cheese is melted. Let stand for 5 minutes before serving.

TO USE FROZEN CASSEROLE *Thaw in the refrigerator overnight. Remove from the refrigerator 30 minutes before baking. Cover and bake at 350° for 25 minutes. Uncover; bake 10-15 minutes longer or until bubbly and cheese is melted. Let stand for 5 minutes before serving.*

Contest Winner

Maple-Glazed Corned Beef

Corned beef gets a touch of sweetness with a maple syrup glaze. Even people who say they don't care for corned beef will ask for seconds when served this one. This recipe was passed down from my great-grandmother.

—**GAYLE MACKLIN** VAIL, AZ

PREP: 25 MIN. • **COOK:** 2½ HOURS • **MAKES:** 12 SERVINGS

- 2 **corned beef briskets with spice packets (3 pounds each)**
- 1 **large sweet onion, sliced**
- 12 **garlic cloves, peeled and halved**
- ¼ **cup kosher salt**
- ¼ **cup whole peppercorns**
- 8 **bay leaves**
- 2 **tablespoons dried basil**
- 2 **tablespoons dried oregano**
- 4 **quarts water**
- 3 **cups beef broth**
- ¼ **cup maple syrup**
- ⅓ **cup packed brown sugar**

1. Place briskets and contents of the spice packets in a stockpot. Add onion, garlic, salt, peppercorns, bay leaves, basil and oregano. Pour in water and beef broth. Bring to a boil. Reduce heat; cover and simmer for 2½-3 hours or until meat is tender.

2. Transfer meat to a broiler pan. Brush with maple syrup; sprinkle with brown sugar. Broil 4-6 in. from the heat for 2-3 minutes or until glazed. Thinly slice across the grain.

Shrimp-Stuffed Poblano Peppers

Since my mom enjoys shrimp and food with some spice, I decided to create shrimp-stuffed poblanos to surprise her. She was delighted with it!

—**TINA GARCIA-ORTIZ** TAMPA, FL

PREP: 35 MIN. • **BAKE:** 10 MIN. • **MAKES:** 8 SERVINGS

- 4 large poblano peppers
- 2 tablespoons butter, melted, divided
- 1 teaspoon coarsely ground pepper
- ½ teaspoon kosher salt
- 1 small onion, finely chopped
- 2 celery ribs, chopped
- 4 ounces cream cheese, softened
- 1 pound chopped cooked peeled shrimp
- 1¾ cups shredded Mexican cheese blend
- 1½ cups cooked rice
- 2 tablespoons lemon juice
- 2 teaspoons dried cilantro flakes
- ½ teaspoon onion powder
- ½ teaspoon garlic powder

TOPPING
- 1 cup panko (Japanese) bread crumbs
- ¼ cup grated Parmesan cheese
- 2 tablespoons butter, melted

1. Cut the peppers in half lengthwise and discard seeds. Place peppers, cut side down, in an ungreased 15x10x1-in. baking pan. Brush with 1 tablespoon butter; sprinkle with pepper and salt. Bake, uncovered, at 350° for 10-15 minutes or until tender.

2. Meanwhile, in a large skillet, saute onion and celery in remaining butter until tender. Stir in cream cheese until melted. Add the shrimp, cheese blend, rice, lemon juice and seasonings; heat through. Spoon into pepper halves.

3. Place in an ungreased 15x10x1-in. baking pan. Combine the topping ingredients; sprinkle over peppers. Bake, uncovered, at 350° for 10-15 minutes or until topping is golden brown.

NOTE *Wear disposable gloves when cutting hot peppers; the oils can burn skin. Avoid touching your face.*

Kansas City-Style Ribs

Our family recipe for ribs has evolved over the years to near perfection. These country-style beauties are legendary in our close circle.

—**LINDA SCHEND** KENOSHA, WI

PREP: 1 HOUR + CHILLING • **GRILL:** 1 HOUR 25 MIN.
MAKES: 12 SERVINGS

- 1⅓ cups packed brown sugar
- 2 teaspoons each garlic powder, onion powder and smoked paprika
- 1¼ teaspoons each ground cumin, coarsely ground pepper and cayenne pepper
- 12 bone-in country-style pork ribs (about 7 pounds)

SAUCE
- 2 tablespoons canola oil
- 1 medium onion, finely chopped
- 1 cup tomato sauce
- ⅓ cup dark brown sugar
- ¼ cup ketchup
- ¼ cup molasses
- 1 tablespoon apple cider vinegar
- 2 teaspoons Worcestershire sauce
- 1 teaspoon salt
- 1 teaspoon ground mustard
- ¼ teaspoon smoked paprika
- ¼ teaspoon cayenne pepper

1. In a small bowl, mix the brown sugar and seasonings; sprinkle over ribs. Refrigerate, covered, at least 1 hour.

2. For sauce, in a large saucepan, heat oil over medium heat. Add onion; cook and stir 5-6 minutes or until tender. Stir in remaining ingredients; bring to a boil, stirring occasionally. Remove from heat.

3. Wrap ribs in a large piece of heavy-duty foil; seal edges of foil. Grill, covered, over indirect medium heat 1¼-1¾ hours or until ribs are tender.

4. Carefully remove ribs from foil. Place ribs over direct medium heat; baste with some of the sauce. Grill, covered, for 8-10 minutes or until browned, turning and basting ribs occasionally with remaining sauce.

Bacon & Tomato-Topped Meat Loaf

I started with a meat loaf recipe I had that includes horseradish and added a few other complementary elements. The results? A tender, savory meat loaf.

—**CHERYL MORING** NEW EDINBURG, AR

PREP: 30 MIN. • **BAKE:** 1 HOUR
MAKES: 6 SERVINGS

- 1 small onion, finely chopped
- 1 celery rib, finely chopped
- 1 small green pepper, finely chopped
- 1 tablespoon canola oil
- 1 garlic clove, minced
- 1 large egg, lightly beaten
- 1 tablespoon prepared horseradish
- 1 tablespoon dry red wine or beef broth
- 1 teaspoon prepared mustard
- 1 teaspoon Worcestershire sauce
- 1 cup soft bread crumbs
- 1 tablespoon all-purpose flour
- 1 tablespoon brown sugar
- 1 teaspoon salt
- 1 teaspoon Cajun seasoning
- 1 teaspoon pepper
- ½ teaspoon chili powder
- 1 pound lean ground beef (90% lean)
- ½ pound bulk pork sausage
- ½ pound bacon strips

TOPPING
- 1 can (14½ ounces) diced tomatoes, drained
- 1 can (8 ounces) tomato sauce

1. In a large skillet, saute the onion, celery and green pepper in oil until tender. Add the garlic; cook 1 minute longer. Transfer to a large bowl; cool slightly.

2. Add the egg, horseradish, wine, mustard, Worcestershire sauce, bread crumbs, flour, brown sugar and the seasonings. Crumble beef and sausage over mixture and mix well. Pat into an ungreased 9x5-in. loaf pan. Place the bacon strips over meat loaf; tuck in the ends.

3. Bake, uncovered, at 350° for 55 minutes. Combine the tomatoes and tomato sauce; spoon over the loaf. Bake 5-10 minutes longer or until no pink remains and a thermometer reads 160°.

Crumb-Crusted Pork Roast with Root Vegetables

Perfect for fall, this hearty meal combines sweet roasted veggies with a wonderful crumb coating.

—*TASTE OF HOME* TEST KITCHEN

PREP: 25 MIN. • **BAKE:** 1 HOUR + STANDING
MAKES: 8 SERVINGS

- 1 boneless pork loin roast (2 to 3 pounds)
- 4 teaspoons honey
- 1 tablespoon molasses
- 1½ teaspoons spicy brown mustard
- 2 teaspoons rubbed sage
- 1 teaspoon dried thyme
- 1 teaspoon dried rosemary, crushed
- ½ cup soft whole wheat bread crumbs
- 2 tablespoons grated Parmesan cheese
- 1 large rutabaga, peeled and cubed
- 1 large sweet potato, peeled and cubed
- 1 large celery root, peeled and cubed
- 1 large onion, cut into wedges
- 2 tablespoons canola oil
- ½ teaspoon salt
- ¼ teaspoon pepper

1. Preheat oven to 350°. Place roast on a rack in a shallow roasting pan coated with cooking spray. In a small bowl, mix the honey, molasses and mustard; brush over roast.

2. In a large bowl, mix sage, thyme and rosemary. In a small bowl, toss bread crumbs with Parmesan cheese and 2 teaspoons of the herb mixture; press onto roast.

3. Add vegetables, oil, salt and pepper to remaining herb mixture; toss to coat. Arrange vegetables around roast.

4. Roast for 1-1½ hours or until a thermometer reads 145°. Remove from pan; let stand 10 minutes before slicing. Serve with vegetables.

Pecan Chicken with Blue Cheese Sauce

Special in every way, this chicken is coated with pecans and drizzled with a rich blue cheese sauce. It's an important recipe in my collection.

—**MAGGIE RUDDY** ALTOONA, IA

PREP: 15 MIN. • **BAKE:** 20 MIN.
MAKES: 4 SERVINGS

- 4 **boneless skinless chicken breast halves (5 ounces each)**
- ¼ **teaspoon salt**
- ⅛ **teaspoon pepper**
- ¼ **cup all-purpose flour**
- 1 **tablespoon minced fresh rosemary or 1 teaspoon dried rosemary, crushed**
- ¼ **cup butter, melted**
- 1 **tablespoon brown sugar**
- ¾ **cup finely chopped pecans**

SAUCE
- 1 **cup heavy whipping cream**
- ⅓ **cup crumbled blue cheese**
- 1 **tablespoon finely chopped green onion**
- ¼ **teaspoon salt**
- ¼ **teaspoon pepper**

1. Sprinkle chicken with salt and pepper. In a shallow bowl, combine the flour and rosemary; in a separate shallow bowl, combine butter and brown sugar. Place pecans in another shallow bowl. Coat chicken with flour mixture, then dip in butter mixture and coat with pecans.

2. Transfer to a greased baking sheet. Bake at 375° for 20-25 minutes or until a thermometer reads 170°.

3. Meanwhile, place cream in a small saucepan. Bring to a boil; cook and stir for 8-10 minutes or until thickened. Stir in the cheese, onion, salt and pepper. Serve with chicken.

Crusted Red Snapper

This dish is elegant but still weeknight-ready. The veggies steam and flavor the fish from below, while the crunchy topping adds instant appeal.

—**KELLY REMINGTON** ARCATA, CA

PREP: 25 MIN. • **BAKE:** 20 MIN.
MAKES: 6 SERVINGS

- 2 **medium tomatoes, chopped**
- 1 **each medium green, sweet yellow and red peppers, chopped**
- 1 **cup chopped leeks (white portion only)**
- ½ **cup chopped celery leaves**
- 2 **garlic cloves, minced**
- 6 **red snapper fillets (4 ounces each)**

TOPPING
- ½ **cup panko (Japanese) bread crumbs**
- ½ **cup coarsely crushed baked Parmesan and Tuscan herb potato chips**
- ¼ **cup grated Parmesan cheese**
- ½ **teaspoon salt**
- ½ **teaspoon paprika**
- ¼ **teaspoon cayenne pepper**
- ¼ **teaspoon pepper**
- 2 **tablespoons butter, melted**

1. In a 15x10x1-in. baking pan coated with cooking spray, combine the tomatoes, peppers, leeks, celery leaves and garlic; arrange the fillets over vegetable mixture.

2. In a small bowl, combine the bread crumbs, chips, cheese, salt, paprika, cayenne and pepper; stir in butter. Sprinkle over fillets. Bake, uncovered, at 425° for 18-22 minutes or until fish flakes easily with a fork.

Contest Winner

Bayou Sausage Stew

My husband and I worked on this recipe together. We make a big pot of stew and freeze it to enjoy throughout the winter. We sometimes stir in sauteed shrimp for a delicious addition.

—**LISA NELSON** BLUFFTON, SC

PREP: 20 MIN. • **COOK:** 20 MIN. • **MAKES:** 9 SERVINGS

- 1 pound smoked sausage, halved lengthwise and cut into ¼-inch slices
- 2 large onions, chopped
- 1 large green pepper, chopped
- 8 green onions, sliced
- 1 cup minced fresh parsley
- ¼ cup olive oil
- 6 garlic cloves, minced
- 1 cup white wine
- 1 can (28 ounces) diced tomatoes, undrained
- 1 package (16 ounces) frozen sliced okra
- 1 can (8 ounces) tomato sauce
- 2 tablespoons soy sauce
- 1 tablespoon Louisiana-style hot sauce
  Hot cooked rice

1. In a Dutch oven, saute the first five ingredients in oil until the vegetables are tender. Add garlic; cook 1 minute longer. Add wine, stirring to loosen browned bits from pan.

2. Stir in the tomatoes, okra, tomato sauce, soy sauce and hot sauce; bring to a boil. Reduce heat; simmer, uncovered, for 4-5 minutes or until okra is tender. Serve with rice.

FREEZE OPTION *Freeze cooled stew in freezer containers. To use, partially thaw in refrigerator overnight. Microwave, covered, on high in a microwave-safe dish until heated through, gently stirring and adding a little broth or water if necessary. Serve with rice.*

Citrus-Spiced Roast Chicken

I am the designated Thanksgiving host in my family because of my chipotle citrus roast turkey. I use the same recipe for chicken so we can enjoy it year-round.

—**ROBIN HAAS** CRANSTON, RI

PREP: 20 MIN. • **BAKE:** 1 HOUR + STANDING • **MAKES:** 6 SERVINGS

- 3 tablespoons orange marmalade
- 4½ teaspoons chopped chipotle peppers in adobo sauce
- 3 garlic cloves, minced
- ¾ teaspoon salt, divided
- ½ teaspoon ground cumin
- 1 broiler/fryer chicken (4 pounds)

1. Preheat oven to 350°. Mix marmalade, chipotle peppers, garlic, ½ teaspoon salt and cumin. With fingers, carefully loosen skin from chicken; rub mixture under the skin.

2. Place chicken on a rack in a shallow roasting pan, breast side up. Tuck wings under chicken; tie drumsticks together. Rub skin with remaining salt. Roast 1-1¼ hours or until a thermometer inserted into thickest part of thigh reads 170°-175°, covering with foil halfway through cooking to prevent overbrowning.

3. Remove chicken from oven; let stand, loosely covered, 15 minutes before carving. Remove and discard the skin before serving.

FREEZE OPTION *Bake meat loaf without sauce. Securely wrap and freeze cooled meat loaf in plastic wrap and foil. To use, partially thaw meat loaf in refrigerator overnight. Unwrap meat loaf and place on a greased shallow baking pan. Prepare sauce as directed; spread half of the sauce over the meat loaf. Reheat meat loaf in a preheated 350° oven until heated through and a thermometer inserted into center reads 165°. Serve with remaining sauce.*

Glazed Spiral-Sliced Ham

In my mind, few foods in a special occasion spread are as tempting as a big baked ham. I always hope for leftovers so we can have ham sandwiches in the following days.

—**EDIE DESPAIN** LOGAN, UT

PREP: 10 MIN. • **BAKE:** 1 HOUR 35 MIN. • **MAKES:** 12 SERVINGS

- 1 **spiral-sliced fully cooked bone-in ham (7 to 9 pounds)**
- ½ **cup pineapple preserves**
- ½ **cup seedless raspberry jam**
- ¼ **cup packed brown sugar**
- ¼ **teaspoon ground cloves**

1. Preheat oven to 300°. Place ham directly on roasting pan, cut side down. Bake, covered, 1¼-1¾ hours.

2. In a bowl, mix the remaining ingredients. Spread over ham. Bake, uncovered, for 20-30 minutes longer or until a thermometer reads 140° (do not overcook).

Moist & Savory Meat Loaf

You can stop searching for the perfect meat loaf recipe because we think this is it. There's so much to love in this mixture of beef, pork and sauteed onion bound by cheese cracker crumbs.

—**TASTE OF HOME** TEST KITCHEN

PREP: 20 MIN. • **BAKE:** 1¼ HOURS + STANDING
MAKES: 8 SERVINGS

- 1 **medium onion, chopped**
- 2 **teaspoons canola oil**
- 2 **large eggs, lightly beaten**
- ⅓ **cup 2% milk**
- 2 **teaspoons Worcestershire sauce**
- 2 **teaspoons Dijon mustard**
- ⅔ **cup finely crushed cheese crackers**
- 1 **teaspoon salt**
- ½ **teaspoon pepper**
- ½ **teaspoon dried thyme**
- 1½ **pounds ground beef**
- ½ **pound ground pork**
- ¾ **cup ketchup**
- ¼ **cup packed brown sugar**

1. Saute onion in oil in a small skillet until tender. Cool to room temperature.

2. Combine the eggs, milk, Worcestershire sauce, mustard, crackers, salt, pepper, thyme and onion in a large bowl. Crumble beef and pork over mixture and mix well. Shape into a loaf; place in a greased 11x7-in. baking dish.

3. Bake, uncovered, at 350° for 1 hour. Combine ketchup and brown sugar; spread half of sauce over meat loaf. Bake for 15-20 minutes longer or until no pink remains and a thermometer reads 160°. Let stand for 10 minutes before slicing. Serve with remaining sauce.

Beef & Blue Cheese Tart

Mushrooms and blue cheese elevate regular ground beef. This rustic tart is ideal for company.

—**JUDY BATSON** TAMPA, FL

PREP: 20 MIN. • **BAKE:** 15 MIN.
MAKES: 6 SERVINGS

- ½ **pound lean ground beef (90% lean)**
- 1¾ **cups sliced fresh mushrooms**
- ½ **medium red onion, thinly sliced**
- ¼ **teaspoon salt**
- ¼ **teaspoon pepper**
- 1 **tube (13.8 ounces) refrigerated pizza crust**
- ½ **cup reduced-fat sour cream**
- 2 **teaspoons Italian seasoning**
- ½ **teaspoon garlic powder**
- ¾ **cup crumbled blue cheese**

1. In a large skillet, cook the beef, mushrooms and onion over medium heat until meat is no longer pink; drain. Stir in salt and pepper; set aside.

2. On a lightly floured surface, roll crust into a 15x12-in. rectangle. Transfer to a parchment paper-lined baking sheet.

3. In a small bowl, combine the sour cream, Italian seasoning and garlic powder; spread over crust to within 2 in. of edges. Spoon beef mixture over top. Fold up edges of crust over filling, leaving center uncovered.

4. Bake at 425° for 15-18 minutes or until crust is golden. Using the parchment paper, slide tart onto a wire rack. Sprinkle with blue cheese; let stand for 5 minutes before slicing.

Hearty Beef & Cabbage Pockets

I found this recipe many years ago and experimented until I had it just right. If you can't find the frozen rolls, you can use a homemade dough.

—**ELAINE CLARK** WELLINGTON, KS

PREP: 1 HOUR + RISING • **BAKE:** 15 MIN.
MAKES: 2 DOZEN

- 24 **frozen dough Texas-size whole wheat dinner rolls (3 pounds total), thawed**
- 1½ **pounds lean ground beef (90% lean)**
- ½ **pound reduced-fat bulk pork sausage**
- 1 **large onion, chopped**
- 1 **pound carrots, grated**
- 2 **cans (4 ounces each) chopped green chilies**
- 2 **tablespoons prepared mustard**
- ½ **teaspoon salt**
- ½ **teaspoon pepper**
- 1 **small head cabbage, shredded**
- 2 **large egg whites**
- 2 **teaspoons water**
   Caraway seeds

1. Let the dough stand at room temperature 30-40 minutes or until softened. In a Dutch oven, cook beef, sausage and onion over medium heat for 12-15 minutes or until meat is no longer pink, breaking it into crumbles; drain. Stir in carrots, chilies, mustard, salt and pepper. Add the cabbage in batches; cook and stir until tender.

2. On a lightly floured surface, press or roll each dinner roll into a 5-in. circle. Top with a heaping ⅓ cup of filling; bring edges of dough up over filling and pinch to seal.

3. Place on baking sheets coated with cooking spray, seam side down. Cover with kitchen towels; let rise in a warm place until almost doubled, about 45 minutes. Preheat oven to 350°.

4. Whisk egg whites and water; brush over tops. Sprinkle with caraway seeds. Bake 15-20 minutes or until golden brown.

FREEZE OPTION *Freeze baked and cooled pockets in resealable plastic freezer bags. To use, reheat pockets on a baking sheet coated with cooking spray in a preheated 350° oven for 30-35 minutes or until heated through; cover loosely with foil if needed to prevent overbrowning.*

Pork with Strawberry-Port Sauce

I never thought to add fruit to barbecue sauce, but after I saw a contest-winning recipe with the two, I decided to try something similar with pork. I'm glad I did!

—LILY JULOW LAWRENCEVILLE, GA

PREP: 25 MIN. • **GRILL:** 10 MIN.
MAKES: 8 SERVINGS (2 CUPS SAUCE)

- 2 tablespoons butter
- 2 medium onions, finely chopped
- 1¼ teaspoons salt, divided
- ½ teaspoon pepper, divided
- 1 cup strawberry spreadable fruit
- ¼ cup port wine or chicken broth
- 2 tablespoons balsamic vinegar
- ½ teaspoon ground mustard
- 1 cup grape tomatoes, halved
- 2 tablespoons minced fresh basil
- 2 teaspoons lime juice
- 8 pork rib chops (1-inch thick and 8 ounces each)

1. In a large skillet, heat butter over medium-high heat. Add the onions, ¾ teaspoon salt and ¼ teaspoon pepper; cook and stir until tender. Stir in the spreadable fruit, wine, vinegar and mustard. Bring to a boil; cook and stir for 3-4 minutes or until slightly thickened. Add the tomatoes; cook 2-3 minutes or until softened. Stir in basil and lime juice.

2. Moisten a paper towel with cooking oil; using long-handled tongs, rub it on the grill rack to coat lightly. Sprinkle chops with remaining salt and pepper. Grill, covered, over medium heat or broil 4 in. from heat 4-6 minutes on each side or until a thermometer reads 145°. Let stand 5 minutes before serving. Serve with sauce.

BBQ & Ranch Chicken Pizza

I wanted something different for dinner and came up with this pizza. The kids loved it, and so did my friends. Best of all, it takes advantage of leftover chicken and convenience items.

—SUE SITLER BLOOMSBURG, PA

START TO FINISH: 30 MIN.
MAKES: 8 SERVINGS

- 2 tubes (8 ounces each) refrigerated crescent rolls
- ½ cup hickory smoke-flavored barbecue sauce, divided
- ¼ cup prepared ranch salad dressing
- 3 cups cubed cooked chicken breasts
- 2 cups (8 ounces) shredded pizza cheese blend

1. Preheat oven to 375°. Unroll both tubes of crescent dough and press onto the bottom and up the sides of an ungreased 15x10x1-in. baking pan, pressing perforations to seal. Bake 8-10 minutes or until lightly browned.

2. In a small bowl, mix ¼ cup of barbecue sauce and salad dressing; spread over crust. In another bowl, toss chicken with remaining barbecue sauce. Arrange over top. Sprinkle with cheese. Bake 15-20 minutes longer or until crust is golden brown and cheese is melted.

MEALS IN MINUTES

It's happened to us all—sometimes that dinner hour just sneaks up on you! When you need a fast meal, turn to these quick-fix recipes: they're table-ready in 30 minutes... or less! Your family will love the new dishes.

Easy Meatball Stroganoff

This recipe has fed not only my own family, but many neighborhood kids! They come running when I make this supper. It's one of those things you throw together after work on a busy day because you know it always works.

—JULIE MAY HATTIESBURG, MS

START TO FINISH: 30 MIN.
MAKES: 4 SERVINGS

- 3 cups uncooked egg noodles
- 1 tablespoon olive oil
- 1 package (12 ounces) frozen fully cooked Italian meatballs, thawed
- 1½ cups beef broth
- 1 teaspoon dried parsley flakes
- ¾ teaspoon dried basil
- ½ teaspoon salt
- ½ teaspoon dried oregano
- ¼ teaspoon pepper
- 1 cup heavy whipping cream
- ¾ cup sour cream

1. Cook egg noodles according to package directions for al dente; drain.
2. Meanwhile, in a large skillet, heat oil over medium-high heat. Brown meatballs; remove from pan. Add broth, stirring to loosen browned bits from pan. Add seasonings. Bring to a boil; cook 5-7 minutes or until liquid is reduced to ½ cup.
3. Add meatballs, noodles and cream. Bring to a boil. Reduce heat; simmer, covered, 3-5 minutes or until slightly thickened. Stir in sour cream; heat mixture through.

Barbecue Pork and Penne Skillet

I'm the proud mother of wonderful and active children. Delicious, quick meals like this one are perfect for everyone to enjoy together after the errands, school activities and soccer practice are over.

—JUDY ARMSTRONG PRAIRIEVILLE, LA

START TO FINISH: 25 MIN.
MAKES: 8 SERVINGS

- 1 package (16 ounces) penne pasta
- 1 cup chopped sweet red pepper
- ¾ cup chopped onion
- 1 tablespoon butter
- 1 tablespoon olive oil
- 3 garlic cloves, minced
- 1 carton (16 ounces) refrigerated fully cooked barbecued shredded pork
- 1 can (14½ ounces) diced tomatoes with mild green chilies, undrained
- ½ cup beef broth
- 1 teaspoon ground cumin
- 1 teaspoon pepper
- ¼ teaspoon salt
- 1¼ cups shredded cheddar cheese
- ¼ cup chopped green onions

1. Cook pasta according to package directions. Meanwhile, in a large skillet, saute red pepper and onion in butter and oil until tender. Add garlic; saute 1 minute longer. Stir in the pork, tomatoes, broth, cumin, pepper and salt; heat through.
2. Drain pasta. Add pasta and cheese to pork mixture; stir until blended. Sprinkle with green onions.

Hash Brown-Topped Steak

My husband and I enjoy cooking together. One night, we were craving grilled steak and cheese-stuffed baked potatoes, but didn't want to wait for the baking. Here's what we invented instead.

—**JUDY ARMSTRONG** PRAIRIEVILLE, LA

START TO FINISH: 30 MIN.
MAKES: 4 SERVINGS

- 2 **tablespoons butter**
- 1 **small onion, chopped**
- 3 **garlic cloves, minced**
- 2 **cups frozen shredded hash brown potatoes, thawed**
- ¾ **teaspoon salt, divided**
- 1 **cup (4 ounces) shredded Jarlsberg cheese**
- 1 **beef top sirloin steak (1 inch thick and 1½ pounds), cut into 4 portions**
- ½ **teaspoon pepper**
- 2 **tablespoons minced fresh chives**

1. In a large skillet, heat butter over medium-high heat. Add onion; cook and stir 2-3 minutes or until tender. Add garlic; cook 2 minutes longer.

2. Stir in the hash browns and ¼ teaspoon salt; spread in an even layer. Reduce heat to medium; cook 5 minutes. Turn hash browns over; cook, covered, 5-6 minutes longer or until heated through and the bottom is lightly browned. Sprinkle with cheese; cover and remove from heat. Keep warm.

3. Sprinkle beef with pepper and remaining salt. Grill, covered, over medium heat 5-7 minutes on each side or until meat reaches desired doneness (for medium-rare, a thermometer should read 145°; medium, 160°; well-done, 170°).

4. Remove steaks from heat; top each with one-fourth of the potato mixture. Sprinkle with chives.

Hearty Italian White Bean Soup

A bowlful of this soup is so satisfying. With lots of filling beans, veggies and potato nuggets, the meatless recipe even hits the spot with meat lovers.

—**KRISTINA KRUMMEL** ELKINS, AR

START TO FINISH: 30 MIN.
MAKES: 6 SERVINGS

- 1 **tablespoon olive oil**
- 1 **medium potato, peeled and cut into ½-inch cubes**
- 2 **medium carrots, chopped**
- 1 **medium onion, chopped**
- 2 **celery ribs, chopped**
- 1 **medium zucchini, chopped**
- 1 **teaspoon finely chopped seeded jalapeno pepper**
- 1 **can (15½ ounces) navy beans, rinsed and drained**
- 2 **to 2½ cups vegetable or chicken broth**
- 1 **can (8 ounces) tomato sauce**
- 2 **tablespoons minced fresh parsley or 2 teaspoons dried parsley flakes**
- 1½ **teaspoons minced fresh thyme or ½ teaspoon dried thyme**

1. In a Dutch oven, heat oil over medium-high heat. Add potato and carrots; cook and stir 3 minutes. Add onion, celery, zucchini and jalapeno; cook and stir 3-4 minutes or until vegetables are crisp-tender.

2. Stir in remaining ingredients; bring to a boil. Reduce heat; simmer, covered, 12-15 minutes or until the vegetables are tender.

FREEZE OPTION *Freeze cooled soup in freezer containers. To use, partially thaw in refrigerator overnight. Heat through in a saucepan, stirring occasionally and adding a little broth or water if necessary.*

NOTE *Wear disposable gloves when cutting hot peppers; the oils can burn skin. Avoid touching your face.*

QUICK PARSLEY SNIP

Instead of dirtying a cutting board for mincing parsley, place parsley in a small glass container and snip sprigs with kitchen shears until minced. It's so fast and efficient!

Chicken Salad Pizzas

Sometimes it just takes a creative spin to get the kids excited about an otherwise grown-up dish. Add the word "pizza" to this gorgeous piled-high salad, and you won't have to worry about convincing any picky eaters.
—*TASTE OF HOME* TEST KITCHEN

START TO FINISH: 30 MIN. • **MAKES:** 5 SERVINGS

- 5 ounces cream cheese, softened
- ⅓ cup mayonnaise
- ½ teaspoon plus ⅛ teaspoon garlic powder, divided
- 1 pound boneless skinless chicken breasts, cubed
- 1 medium sweet yellow pepper, chopped
- 1 medium green pepper, chopped
- 1 medium red onion, halved and sliced
- ¼ teaspoon salt
- 2 teaspoons olive oil
- 5 whole pita breads, warmed
- 1⅔ cups fresh arugula or baby spinach
- 1 can (11 ounces) mandarin oranges, drained
- 4 bacon strips, cooked and crumbled
- ⅔ cup shredded cheddar cheese

1. Combine the cream cheese, mayonnaise and ½ teaspoon garlic powder in a small bowl; set aside.
2. Cook the chicken, peppers, onion, salt and remaining garlic powder in oil in a large skillet over medium heat until chicken is no longer pink. Spread cream cheese mixture over pita breads; top with arugula, chicken mixture and oranges. Sprinkle with bacon and cheddar cheese.

Shrimp Salad with Cilantro Vinaigrette

This pretty dish has such a sunny tropical flavor, you'll think that you are sitting at a beachside cantina in Acapulco.
—**HEIDI HALL** NORTH SAINT PAUL, MN

START TO FINISH: 25 MIN. • **MAKES:** 4 SERVINGS

- 3 tablespoons olive oil
- 2 tablespoons lime juice
- 1 to 2 teaspoons dried cilantro flakes
- 1 small garlic clove, minced
- ¾ teaspoon sugar
- ¼ teaspoon salt
- ⅛ teaspoon pepper

SALAD
- 1 teaspoon olive oil
- ½ pound uncooked large shrimp, peeled and deveined
- ¼ teaspoon chili powder
- ⅛ teaspoon salt
- ⅛ teaspoon ground cumin
- 1 small garlic clove, minced
- 5 cups chopped hearts of romaine
- 1 cup fresh or frozen corn, thawed
- 1 cup frozen peas, thawed
- ½ cup chopped sweet red pepper
- 1 medium ripe avocado, peeled and thinly sliced

1. In a bowl, whisk the first seven ingredients until blended. In a skillet, heat oil over medium-high heat. Add shrimp, chili powder, salt and cumin; cook and stir 2-3 minutes or until shrimp turn pink. Add garlic; cook 1 minute longer. Remove from heat.
2. In a bowl, combine the romaine, corn, peas and red pepper; drizzle with dressing and toss to coat. Top with avocado and shrimp.

Contest Winner

Turkey Mushroom Sandwich Bowls

My grandmother was an amazing cook. I've tried to re-create some of her magic here in these creamy, mushroom-packed, French roll bowl sandwiches.

—**ANGELA LEINENBACH** MECHANICSVLLE, VA

START TO FINISH: 30 MIN. • **MAKES:** 4 SERVINGS

- 4 **French rolls**
- ¼ **cup butter, melted**
- 1½ **cups sliced fresh mushrooms**
- 1 **medium onion, thinly sliced**
- 2 **tablespoons canola oil**
- ½ **cup dry vermouth or chicken broth**
- 2 **tablespoons all-purpose flour**
- ½ **teaspoon salt**
- ¼ **teaspoon pepper**
- 1¼ **cups heavy whipping cream**
- 4 **cups cubed cooked turkey**
  Minced fresh chives

1. Cut a ½-in. slice off the top of each roll; set aside tops. Hollow out centers, leaving ¼-in. shells (discard removed bread or save for another use). Brush tops and inside of rolls with butter; place on a baking sheet. Bake at 325° for 10-15 minutes or until lightly browned.

2. Meanwhile, in a large skillet, saute mushrooms and onion in oil until tender. Add vermouth, stirring to loosen browned bits from pan. Bring to a boil; cook until liquid is almost evaporated. Combine the flour, salt, pepper and cream; stir until smooth. Stir into skillet; bring to a boil. Reduce heat; cook and stir for 1-2 minutes or until sauce is thickened. Stir in turkey; heat through. Spoon into the hollowed rolls; garnish with chives. Replace tops.

Pepperoni Pizza Skillet

On hectic school nights, no household should be without a 30-minute supper the whole family loves. This cheesy skillet is one you'll turn to frequently, with no objections.

—**ANNA MILLER** QUAKER CITY, OH

START TO FINISH: 30 MIN. • **MAKES:** 8 SERVINGS

- 5 **cups uncooked wide egg noodles**
- 1½ **pounds ground beef**
- ½ **cup chopped onion**
- ½ **cup chopped green pepper**
- 1½ **cups chopped pepperoni**
- 1 **jar (14 ounces) pizza sauce**
- 1 **can (10¾ ounces) condensed cream of mushroom soup, undiluted**
- 1 **can (4½ ounces) sliced mushrooms, drained**
- ½ **cup grated Parmesan cheese**
- ¼ **teaspoon garlic powder**
- ¼ **teaspoon dried oregano**
- ½ **cup shredded part-skim mozzarella cheese**

1. Cook noodles according to package directions.

2. Meanwhile, in a large skillet, cook the beef, onion and pepper over medium heat until meat is no longer pink; drain. Stir in the pepperoni, pizza sauce, soup, mushrooms, Parmesan cheese, garlic powder and oregano.

3. Drain noodles; stir into skillet and heat through. Sprinkle with mozzarella cheese.

Baked Cod Piccata with Asparagus

It takes longer for the oven to preheat than it does to prepare this stunning dish. While it's baking, I throw together a quick side salad.
—**BARBARA LENTO** HOUSTON, PA

START TO FINISH: 30 MIN.
MAKES: 4 SERVINGS

- 1 pound fresh asparagus, trimmed
- ¼ cup water
- 1 pound cod fillet, cut into four pieces
- 2 tablespoons lemon juice
- 1 teaspoon salt-free lemon-pepper seasoning
- ½ teaspoon garlic powder
- 2 tablespoons butter, cubed
- 2 teaspoons capers
  Minced fresh parsley, optional

1. Place asparagus in an ungreased 11x7-in. baking dish; add water. Arrange cod over asparagus. Sprinkle with lemon juice, lemon pepper and garlic powder. Dot with the butter; sprinkle with capers.
2. Bake, uncovered, at 400° for 12-15 minutes or until fish flakes easily with a fork and asparagus is tender. If desired, sprinkle with parsley.

Angel Hair Primavera

I love to make pasta primavera when summer is in full swing and the vegetables are at their best. You can toss in almost any vegetable that's in season. I seem to change up this dish often.
—**TRE BALCHOWSKY** SAUSALITO, CA

START TO FINISH: 30 MIN.
MAKES: 4 SERVINGS

- 1 tablespoon olive oil
- 2 medium zucchini, coarsely chopped
- 1 cup fresh baby carrots, halved lengthwise
- 1 cup fresh or frozen corn
- 1 small red onion, cut into thin wedges
- 1 cup cherry tomatoes, halved
- 2 garlic cloves, minced
- 1 package (4.8 ounces) Pasta Roni angel hair pasta with herbs
- ½ cup chopped walnuts, toasted
- ¼ cup shredded Parmesan cheese
  Coarsely ground pepper

1. In a large skillet, heat oil over medium-high heat. Add zucchini, carrots, corn and onion; cook and stir 10-12 minutes or until carrots are tender. Stir in the tomatoes and garlic; cook 1 minute longer.
2. Meanwhile, prepare pasta mix according to package directions. Add to vegetable mixture; toss to combine. Sprinkle with the walnuts, cheese and pepper.
NOTE *To toast nuts, bake in a shallow pan in a 350° oven for 5-10 minutes or cook in a skillet over low heat until lightly browned, stirring occasionally.*

Grilled Steak Salad with Tomatoes & Avocado

My family loves a good steak dinner, but with full schedules, I'm often thinking about ways to put new and simple twists on the classic meal. This salad quickly became one of my husband's most-requested weeknight dishes.

—LYNDSAY WELLS LADYSMITH, BC

START TO FINISH: 30 MIN.
MAKES: 6 SERVINGS

- 1 **beef top sirloin steak (1¼ inches thick and 1½ pounds)**
- 1 **tablespoon olive oil**
- 3 **teaspoons Creole seasoning**
- 2 **large tomatoes, chopped**
- 1 **can (15 ounces) white kidney or cannellini beans, rinsed and drained**
- 1 **can (15 ounces) black beans, rinsed and drained**
- 3 **green onions, chopped**
- ¼ **cup minced fresh cilantro**
- 2 **teaspoons grated lemon peel**
- 2 **tablespoons lemon juice**
- ¼ **teaspoon salt**
- 1 **medium ripe avocado, peeled and cubed (½ inch)**

1. Rub both sides of steak with oil; sprinkle with Creole seasoning. Grill, covered, over medium heat or broil 4 in. from heat 5-8 minutes on each side or until meat reaches desired doneness (for medium-rare, a thermometer should read 145°; medium, 160°; well-done, 170°). Let stand 5 minutes.

2. In a large bowl, combine tomatoes, beans, green onions, cilantro, lemon peel, lemon juice and salt; gently stir in avocado. Cut steak into slices; serve with bean mixture.

NOTE *The following spices may be substituted for 3 teaspoons Creole seasoning: ¾ teaspoon each salt, garlic powder and paprika; and ⅛ teaspoon each dried thyme, ground cumin and cayenne pepper.*

Pear, Ham & Cheese Pastry Pockets

I came up with this recipe on the fly one night. Add a cup of soup and supper's ready. The sweet-savory flavor combo makes it a good brunch choice, too.

—TERRI CRANDALL GARDNERVILLE, NV

START TO FINISH: 30 MIN.
MAKES: 8 SERVINGS

- 1 **package (17.3 ounces) frozen puff pastry, thawed**
- ¼ **cup honey Dijon mustard**
- 1 **large egg, lightly beaten**
- 8 **slices deli ham**
- 4 **slices Muenster cheese, halved diagonally**
- 1 **medium red pear, very thinly sliced**
- 1 **small red onion, thinly sliced**

1. Preheat oven to 400°. Unfold each sheet of puff pastry. Cut each into four squares. Spread 1½ teaspoons of the mustard over each square to within ½ in. of edges. Brush egg over the edges of pastry.

2. On one corner of each square, layer ham, cheese, pear and onion. Fold opposite corner over filling, forming a triangle; press edges with a fork to seal. Transfer to ungreased baking sheets. Brush tops with remaining egg.

3. Bake 10-14 minutes or until golden brown. Serve warm.

FREEZE OPTION *Freeze cooled pockets in a freezer container, separating with waxed paper. To use, reheat pockets on a baking sheet in a preheated 400° oven until crisp and heated through.*

FIESTA-READY EATS

Turn any weeknight into a fiesta with the no-fuss dinner ideas shared here. They each come together in 30 minutes and promise to spice up your dinner routine!

Turkey Taco Salad

I discovered this taco salad while I was on a health kick. My husband and I can't get enough of it now. When I served it at a family birthday party, everyone eagerly asked for the recipe.

—**ANGELA MATSON** AMBOY, WA

START TO FINISH: 30 MIN. • **MAKES:** 4 SERVINGS

- 12 ounces ground turkey
- 1 medium sweet red pepper, chopped
- 1 small sweet yellow pepper, chopped
- ⅓ cup chopped onion
- 3 garlic cloves, minced
- 1½ cups salsa
- ½ cup canned kidney beans, rinsed and drained
- 2 teaspoons chili powder
- 1 teaspoon ground cumin
- 8 cups torn romaine
- 2 tablespoons fresh cilantro leaves
-   Optional toppings: chopped tomatoes, shredded cheddar cheese and crushed tortilla chips

1. In a large skillet, cook turkey, peppers, onion and garlic over medium heat 6-8 minutes or until turkey is no longer pink and vegetables are tender, breaking up turkey into crumbles; drain.

2. Stir in salsa, beans, chili powder and cumin; heat through. Divide romaine among four plates. Top with the turkey mixture; sprinkle with cilantro and toppings of your choice. Serve immediately.

Smothered Burritos

My brother-in-law teased that I knew how to make only five things using ground beef. To prove him wrong, I came back with these comforting burritos.

—**KIM KENYON** GREENWOOD, MO

START TO FINISH: 25 MIN. • **MAKES:** 4 SERVINGS

- 1 can (10 ounces) green enchilada sauce
- ¾ cup salsa verde
- 1 pound ground beef
- 4 flour tortillas (10 inches)
- 1½ cups (6 ounces) shredded cheddar cheese, divided

1. Preheat oven to 375°. In a small bowl, mix enchilada sauce and salsa verde.

2. In a large skillet, cook beef over medium heat 8-10 minutes or until no longer pink, breaking into crumbles; drain. Stir in ½ cup sauce mixture.

3. Spoon ⅔ cup beef mixture across center of each tortilla; top each with 3 tablespoons cheese. Fold bottom and sides of tortilla over filling and roll up.

4. Place in a greased 11x7-in. baking dish. Pour remaining sauce mixture over top; sprinkle with remaining ¾ cup cheese. Bake, uncovered, 10-15 minutes or until cheese is melted.

Pork Quesadillas with Fresh Salsa

I threw this together one night when I was in the mood for quesadillas but didn't feel like going out. The homemade salsa is so tasty and versatile, you might want to double the recipe.
—**ADAM GAYLORD** NATICK, MA

START TO FINISH: 30 MIN. • **MAKES:** 4 SERVINGS (¾ CUP SALSA)

- 1 **tablespoon olive oil**
- 1 **each small green, sweet red and orange peppers, sliced**
- 1 **medium red onion, sliced**
- ¾ **pound thinly sliced cooked pork (about 3 cups)**
- ¼ **teaspoon salt**
- ⅛ **teaspoon pepper**

SALSA
- 2 **medium tomatoes, seeded and chopped**
- 1 **tablespoon chopped red onion**
- 1 **tablespoon minced fresh cilantro**
- 2 **teaspoons olive oil**
- 1 **to 2 teaspoons chopped seeded jalapeno pepper**
- 1 **teaspoon cider vinegar**
- ⅛ **teaspoon salt**
   Dash pepper

QUESADILLAS
- 4 **flour tortillas (10 inches)**
- 1½ **cups (6 ounces) shredded part-skim mozzarella cheese**

1. In a large skillet, heat oil over medium-high heat. Add peppers and onion; cook 4-5 minutes or until tender, stirring occasionally. Stir in pork, salt and pepper; heat through. Meanwhile, in a small bowl, combine salsa ingredients.
2. Place tortillas on a griddle. Layer one-half of each tortilla with ¼ cup cheese, 1 cup pork mixture and 2 tablespoons cheese; fold other half over filling.
3. Cook over medium heat 1-2 minutes on each side or until golden brown and cheese is melted. Cut into wedges. Serve with salsa.
NOTE *Wear disposable gloves when cutting hot peppers; the oils can burn skin. Avoid touching your face.*

Weeknight Taco Soup

This soup turned out delicious on the first try. You could also add cooked ground beef or cubed stew meat dredged in seasoned flour and browned for a meaty meal.
—**AMANDA SWARTZ** GODERICH, ON

START TO FINISH: 30 MIN. • **MAKES:** 6 SERVINGS (2½ QUARTS)

- 1 **tablespoon canola oil**
- 1 **large onion, chopped**
- 1 **medium sweet red pepper, chopped**
- 1 **medium green pepper, chopped**
- 1 **can (28 ounces) diced tomatoes, undrained**
- 3 **cups vegetable broth**
- 1 **can (15 ounces) pinto beans, rinsed and drained**
- 1½ **cups frozen corn**
- 1 **envelope taco seasoning**
- ¼ **teaspoon salt**
- ¼ **teaspoon pepper**
- 1 **package (8.8 ounces) ready-to-serve long grain rice**
- 1 **cup (8 ounces) sour cream**
   Optional toppings: shredded cheddar cheese, crushed tortilla chips and additional sour cream

1. In a Dutch oven, heat oil over medium heat. Add onion and peppers; cook and stir 3-5 minutes or until crisp-tender.
2. Add tomatoes, broth, beans, corn, taco seasoning, salt and pepper; bring to a boil. Reduce heat; simmer, uncovered, 10-15 minutes or until vegetables are tender. Reduce heat. Stir in rice and sour cream; heat through. Serve with toppings as desired.
FREEZE OPTION *Freeze cooled soup in freezer containers. To use, partially thaw in refrigerator overnight. Heat through in a saucepan, stirring occasionally and adding a little broth if necessary.*

Sweet-Chili Salmon with Blackberries

My garden is often my best cooking inspiration. Because I have a large berry patch, I especially enjoy using just-picked berries to add natural sweetness and pop to savory dishes.
—**ROXANNE CHAN** ALBANY, CA

START TO FINISH: 25 MIN.
MAKES: 4 SERVINGS

- 1 cup fresh or frozen blackberries, thawed
- 1 cup finely chopped English cucumber
- 1 green onion, finely chopped
- 2 tablespoons sweet chili sauce, divided
- 4 salmon fillets (6 ounces each)
- ½ teaspoon salt
- ½ teaspoon pepper

1. In a small bowl, combine the blackberries, cucumber, green onion and 1 tablespoon chili sauce; toss to coat. Moisten a paper towel with cooking oil; using long-handled tongs, rub on grill rack to coat lightly. Sprinkle salmon with salt and pepper.
2. Place fillets on grill rack, skin side down. Grill, covered, over medium-high heat or broil 4 in. from heat 10-12 minutes or until fish flakes easily with a fork, brushing with remaining chili sauce during the last 2-3 minutes of cooking. Serve with blackberry mixture.

Pasta & Broccoli Sausage Simmer

I created this meal when I had a lot of broccoli on hand. My family requests it at least once a week, which is handy because we always have the ingredients.
—**LISA MONTGOMERY** ELMIRA, ON

START TO FINISH: 30 MIN.
MAKES: 8 SERVINGS

- 3 cups uncooked spiral pasta
- 2 pounds smoked kielbasa or Polish sausage, cut into ¼-inch slices
- 2 medium bunches broccoli, cut into florets
- 1 cup sliced red onion
- 2 cans (14½ ounces each) diced tomatoes, undrained
- 2 tablespoons minced fresh basil or 2 teaspoons dried basil
- 2 tablespoons minced fresh parsley or 2 teaspoons dried parsley flakes
- 2 teaspoons sugar

1. Cook pasta according to directions.
2. Meanwhile, in a Dutch oven, saute the sausage, broccoli and onion for 5-6 minutes or until the broccoli is crisp-tender.
3. Add the tomatoes, basil, parsley and sugar. Cover and simmer for 10 minutes. Drain pasta; stir into the sausage mixture.

Asparagus, Bacon & Herbed Cheese Pizza

Here's a zesty, fresh pizza that's especially nice with spring asparagus but lovely all year round when you add mozzarella and bacon.

—DAHLIA ABRAMS DETROIT, MI

START TO FINISH: 30 MIN.
MAKES: 6 SERVINGS

- 1 prebaked 12-inch pizza crust
- 6 teaspoons olive oil, divided
- 1 cup (4 ounces) shredded part-skim mozzarella cheese
- 2¼ cups cut fresh asparagus (1-inch pieces)
- 8 bacon strips, cooked and crumbled
- ½ cup garlic-herb spreadable cheese (about 3 ounces)
- ¼ teaspoon crushed red pepper flakes

1. Preheat oven to 450°. Place crust on an ungreased 12-in. pizza pan or baking sheet; brush top with 4 teaspoons oil. Top with mozzarella cheese, asparagus and bacon. Drop spreadable cheese by teaspoonfuls over pizza. Sprinkle with pepper flakes; drizzle with remaining oil.
2. Bake 12-15 minutes or until cheese is lightly browned.

Simple Chicken Stir-Fry

With three kids at home and a full-time job, I always needed dinners that were quick and simple. This peanutty stir-fry is still a favorite after 15 years.

—CHERYL MURPHY DELTA, BC

START TO FINISH: 25 MIN.
MAKES: 4 SERVINGS

- 2 tablespoons canola oil, divided
- 1 pound boneless skinless chicken breasts, cut into 1-inch cubes
- 1 medium green pepper, chopped
- 3 garlic cloves, minced
- 2 teaspoons minced fresh gingerroot
- 1½ cups salsa
- ½ cup creamy peanut butter
- 2 tablespoons reduced-sodium soy sauce
  Hot cooked rice

1. In a large skillet, heat 1 tablespoon oil over medium-high heat. Add chicken; stir-fry 4-6 minutes or until no longer pink. Remove from pan.
2. In same skillet, heat remaining oil. Add pepper; cook and stir 2-3 minutes or until crisp-tender. Add garlic and ginger; cook 1 minute longer. Add salsa, peanut butter and soy sauce; stir until peanut butter is blended. Stir in chicken; heat through. Serve with rice.

Bean & Cheese Quesadillas

My son doesn't eat meat, so I created this recipe as a way for me to cook one meal for the family instead of two: everyone loves it. It's so easy, my toddler grandson helps me make it!
—**TINA MCMULLEN** SALINA, KS

START TO FINISH: 30 MIN. • **MAKES:** 6 SERVINGS

- 1 can (16 ounces) refried beans
- ½ cup canned petite diced tomatoes
- 2 green onions, chopped
- 12 flour tortillas (8 inches)
- 2 cups (8 ounces) shredded cheddar cheese
  Sour cream and salsa, optional

1. In a small bowl, mix beans, tomatoes and green onions. Spread half of the tortillas with bean mixture. Sprinkle with cheese; top with remaining tortillas.

2. Heat a griddle over medium heat. Place tortillas on griddle in batches. Cook 2-3 minutes on each side or until golden brown and cheese is melted. If desired, serve with sour cream and salsa.

Glazed Shrimp & Asparagus

With its spicy Asian flavor, this shrimp and asparagus combo is excellent for both a special occasion and a weeknight dinner.
—**JOAN DUCKWORTH** LEE'S SUMMIT, MO

START TO FINISH: 30 MIN. • **MAKES:** 4 SERVINGS

- 8 ounces uncooked whole wheat angel hair pasta
- 1 tablespoon cornstarch
- ¾ cup cold water
- 1 tablespoon soy sauce
- 1 tablespoon honey
- 1 pound uncooked large shrimp, peeled and deveined
- 3 teaspoons peanut or canola oil, divided
- 1 teaspoon sesame oil
- 1 pound fresh asparagus, trimmed and cut into 2- to 3-in. lengths
- 1 tablespoon minced fresh gingerroot
- 2 garlic cloves, minced
- ¼ teaspoon crushed red pepper flakes
- 1 tablespoon sesame seeds

1. Cook pasta according to package directions. In a small bowl, combine the cornstarch, water, soy sauce and honey until smooth; set aside.

2. In a large skillet or wok, stir-fry shrimp in 1 teaspoon peanut oil and the sesame oil until shrimp turn pink. Remove and keep warm.

3. Stir-fry asparagus in remaining peanut oil for 2 minutes. Add the ginger, garlic, pepper flakes and sesame seeds; stir-fry 2 minutes longer or until asparagus is crisp-tender.

4. Stir cornstarch mixture and add to the pan. Bring to a boil; cook and stir for 2 minutes or until thickened. Add shrimp; heat through. Drain pasta; serve with the shrimp mixture.

Mom's Spanish Rice

My mom is famous for her Spanish rice, the ultimate comfort food. When I want a taste of home, I pull out this recipe.
—**JOAN HALLFORD** FORT WORTH, TX

START TO FINISH: 20 MIN. • **MAKES:** 4 SERVINGS

- 1 **pound lean ground beef (90% lean)**
- 1 **large onion, chopped**
- 1 **medium green pepper, chopped**
- 1 **can (15 ounces) tomato sauce**
- 1 **can (14½ ounces) no-salt-added diced tomatoes, drained**
- 1 **teaspoon ground cumin**
- 1 **teaspoon chili powder**
- ½ **teaspoon garlic powder**
- ¼ **teaspoon salt**
- 2⅔ **cups cooked brown rice**

1. In a large skillet, cook beef, onion and pepper over medium heat 6-8 minutes or until beef is no longer pink and onion is tender, breaking up beef into crumbles; drain.
2. Stir in tomato sauce, tomatoes and seasonings; bring to a boil. Add rice; heat through, stirring occasionally.

Broiled Chicken & Artichokes

My wife and I first made this chicken entree as newlyweds and have been hooked ever since. You can't beat a cozy, affordable dinner at home.
—**CHRIS KOON** MIDLOTHIAN, VA

START TO FINISH: 15 MIN. • **MAKES:** 8 SERVINGS

- 8 **boneless skinless chicken thighs (about 2 pounds)**
- 2 **jars (7½ ounces each) marinated quartered artichoke hearts, drained**
- 2 **tablespoons olive oil**
- 1 **teaspoon salt**
- ½ **teaspoon pepper**
- ¼ **cup shredded Parmesan cheese**
- 2 **tablespoons minced fresh parsley**

1. Preheat the boiler. In a large bowl, toss the chicken and artichokes with oil, salt and pepper. Transfer to a broiler pan.
2. Broil 3 in. from heat 8-10 minutes or until a thermometer inserted in chicken reads 170°, turning chicken and artichokes halfway through cooking. Sprinkle with cheese. Broil 1-2 minutes longer or until cheese is melted. Sprinkle with parsley.

Summer Fish Skillet

On crazy nights when you have other proverbial fish to fry, this fresh Mediterranean medley will offer the help you need.
—*TASTE OF HOME* **TEST KITCHEN**

START TO FINISH: 30 MIN.
MAKES: 4 SERVINGS

- 2 packages (7.6 ounces each) frozen lemon butter grilled fish fillets
- 1 tablespoon olive oil
- 2 medium yellow summer squash, halved and sliced
- 2 medium sweet orange peppers, chopped
- ½ cup chopped red onion
- 2 cups fresh salsa, drained
- 4 ounces feta cheese, cubed
- 2 packages (8.8 ounces each) ready-to-serve rice pilaf with orzo pasta

1. In a large skillet, cook the fish fillets in oil over medium heat for 15-20 minutes, turning once or until fish flakes easily with a fork; remove and keep warm.
2. In the same skillet, saute the squash, peppers and onion until tender. Add salsa; cook 2 minutes longer. Return fish to skillet. Add cheese and heat through.
3. Prepares rice pilaf according to package directions. Serve with fish and vegetables.

Bacon & Rosemary Chicken

Your family will devour this entree. The sauce is a blend of wonderful ingredients without too much effort on your end!
—**YVONNE STARLIN** WESTMORELAND, TN

START TO FINISH: 30 MIN.
MAKES: 4 SERVINGS

- 4 boneless skinless chicken breast halves (5 ounces each)
- ½ teaspoon salt
- ¼ teaspoon pepper
- ¼ cup all-purpose flour
- 5 bacon strips, chopped
- 1 tablespoon butter
- 4 garlic cloves, thinly sliced
- 1 tablespoon minced fresh rosemary or 1 teaspoon dried rosemary, crushed
- ⅛ teaspoon crushed red pepper flakes
- 1 cup reduced-sodium chicken broth
- 2 tablespoons lemon juice

1. Pound chicken breasts slightly with a meat mallet to uniform thickness; sprinkle with salt and pepper. Place flour in a shallow bowl. Dip chicken in flour to coat both sides; shake off excess.
2. In a large skillet, cook bacon over medium heat until crisp, stirring occasionally. Remove with a slotted spoon; drain on paper towels. Discard drippings, reserving 2 tablespoons in pan. Cook chicken in butter and reserved drippings 4-6 minutes on each side or until a thermometer reads 165°. Remove and keep warm.
3. Add garlic, rosemary and pepper flakes to skillet; cook and stir 1 minute. Add broth and lemon juice; bring to a boil. Cook until liquid is reduced by half. Return chicken and bacon to the skillet; heat through.

Creamy Ham Penne

Mixing spreadable cheese with whole wheat pasta, broccoli and milk creates a main dish that's too good to resist.
—**BARBARA PLETZKE** HERNDON, VA

START TO FINISH: 30 MIN.
MAKES: 4 SERVINGS

- 2 cups uncooked whole wheat penne pasta
- 2 cups fresh broccoli florets
- 1 cup fat-free milk
- 1 package (6½ ounces) reduced-fat garlic-herb spreadable cheese
- 1 cup cubed fully cooked ham
- ¼ teaspoon pepper

In a large saucepan, cook penne according to package directions, adding broccoli during the last 5 minutes of cooking; drain. Remove and set aside. In the same pan, combine milk and spreadable cheese. Cook and stir over medium heat for 3-5 minutes or until cheese is melted. Add ham, pepper and penne mixture; heat through.

Quick Ravioli & Spinach Soup

I love my Italian-American traditions, but I didn't have time to make a classic Italian wedding soup. So I decided to improvise this shortcut version with ravioli.
—**CYNTHIA BENT** NEWARK, DE

START TO FINISH: 25 MIN.
MAKES: 6 SERVINGS

- 2 cartons (32 ounces each) chicken broth
- ¼ teaspoon onion powder
  Dash pepper
- 1 package (9 ounces) refrigerated small cheese ravioli
- 4 cups coarsely chopped fresh spinach (about 4 ounces)
- 3 cups shredded cooked chicken
  Grated Parmesan cheese, optional

In a large saucepan, combine the broth, onion powder and pepper; bring to a boil. Add ravioli; cook, uncovered, for 7-10 minutes or until tender. Add spinach and chicken during the last 3 minutes of cooking. If desired, serve with cheese.

Stovetop Goulash

I came up with this recipe after trying goulash at a local restaurant. The blend of spices gives it great taste.
—**KAREN SCHELERT** PORTAND, OR

START TO FINISH: 25 MIN.
MAKES: 4 SERVINGS

- 1 pound ground beef
- 1 package (16 ounces) frozen mixed vegetables, thawed
- 2 cans (10¾ ounces each) condensed tomato soup, undiluted
- 1 cup water
- 1 small onion, chopped
- 2 teaspoons Worcestershire sauce
- 1 teaspoon garlic salt
- 1 teaspoon chili powder
- ½ teaspoon dried oregano
- ½ teaspoon paprika
- ⅛ teaspoon ground cinnamon
- ⅛ teaspoon pepper
- 1 package (24 ounces) refrigerated mashed potatoes

1. Cook beef in a large skillet over medium heat until no longer pink; drain. Add mixed vegetables, soup, water, onion, Worcestershire sauce and seasonings; bring to a boil. Reduce heat; simmer, uncovered, for 10 minutes or until slightly thickened. **2.** Meanwhile, heat the potatoes according to package directions. Serve with goulash.

Southern Skillet Chops

The Creole seasoning adds the right amount of heat to these pork chops. Black-eyed peas make the perfect accompaniment.

—**IRENE SULLIVAN** LAKE MILLS, WI

START TO FINISH: 25 MIN. • **MAKES:** 4 SERVINGS

- 4 **bone-in pork loin chops (8 ounces each)**
- 2 **teaspoons plus ⅛ teaspoon Creole seasoning, divided**
- 2 **tablespoons canola oil**
- 2 **cans (14½ ounces each) diced tomatoes with mild green chilies, undrained**
- 1 **can (15½ ounces) black-eyed peas, rinsed and drained**
  Shredded cheddar cheese, optional

1. Sprinkle pork chops with 2 teaspoons Creole seasoning. In a large skillet, brown the pork chops in oil. Remove and keep warm.

2. Drain one can tomatoes; discard liquid. Add tomatoes to skillet with the remaining can of undrained tomatoes, black-eyed peas and remaining Creole seasoning, stirring to loosen browned bits from pan.

3. Bring to a boil and return chops to pan. Reduce heat; simmer, uncovered, for 2-4 minutes or until a thermometer inserted in the pork reads 145°. Sprinkle with cheese if desired. Let stand for 5 minutes.

NOTE *The following spices may be substituted for 1 teaspoon Creole seasoning: ¼ teaspoon each salt, garlic powder and paprika; and a pinch each of dried thyme, ground cumin and cayenne pepper.*

Mushroom Beef Stew

Forget beef stew that takes all day to prepare. This version is just as tasty, and it's ready to eat in a fraction of the time! You'll love the quick-cooking beef tips and loads of fresh veggies.

—*TASTE OF HOME* TEST KITCHEN

START TO FINISH: 30 MIN. • **MAKES:** 8 SERVINGS

- 1 **pound sliced baby portobello mushrooms**
- 1 **pound fresh baby carrots, sliced**
- 1 **large onion, chopped**
- 3 **tablespoons butter**
- 3 **garlic cloves, minced**
- 1 **teaspoon dried rosemary, crushed**
- 3 **tablespoons all-purpose flour**
- 1 **teaspoon pepper**
- 4 **cups water**
- 4 **teaspoons beef base**
- 2 **packages (17 ounces each) refrigerated beef tips with gravy**
  Hot cooked egg noodles and crumbled blue cheese

1. Saute the mushrooms, carrots and onion in butter in a Dutch oven until tender. Add garlic and rosemary; cook 1 minute longer. Stir in flour and pepper until blended; gradually add water. Stir in beef base.

2. Bring to a boil; cook and stir for 2 minutes or until thickened. Add beef tips with gravy; heat through. Serve with noodles and cheese.

NOTE *Look for beef base near the broth and bouillon.*

Penne Gorgonzola with Chicken

Having a recipe like this in your back pocket will come in handy if you're hosting a dinner party. The mix of wine, broth, cream and cheese creates a robust, silky sauce that nicely coats the pasta.
—**IMELDA SCHROEDER** PORT MURRAY, NJ

START TO FINISH: 30 MIN. • **MAKES:** 8 SERVINGS

- 1 package (16 ounces) penne pasta
- 1 pound boneless skinless chicken breasts, cut into ½-inch pieces
- 1 tablespoon olive oil
- 1 large garlic clove, minced
- ¼ cup white wine
- 1 cup heavy whipping cream
- ¼ cup chicken broth
- 2 cups (8 ounces) crumbled Gorgonzola cheese
- 6 to 8 fresh sage leaves, thinly sliced
  Salt and pepper to taste
  Grated Parmigiano-Reggiano cheese and minced fresh parsley

1. Cook pasta according to package directions. Meanwhile, in a large skillet over medium heat, brown chicken in oil on all sides. Add garlic; cook 1 minute longer. Add wine, stirring to loosen browned bits from pan.
2. Add the cream and broth; cook until sauce is slightly thickened and chicken is no longer pink. Stir in Gorgonzola cheese, sage, salt and pepper; cook just until the cheese is melted.
3. Drain pasta; toss with sauce. Sprinkle with Parmigiano-Reggiano cheese and parsley.

Turkey & Noodle Tomato Soup

Turn V8 juice, ramen and frozen veggies into a wonderful soup that really satisfies. I like to serve it with biscuits.
—**JENNIFER BRIDGES** LOS ANGELES, CA

START TO FINISH: 25 MIN. • **MAKES:** 6 SERVINGS (2 QUARTS)

- 1 pound ground turkey
- 1 envelope reduced-sodium onion soup mix
- 1 package (3 ounces) beef ramen noodles
- 1½ teaspoons sugar
- ¾ teaspoon pepper
- ¼ teaspoon salt
- 1 bottle (46 ounces) reduced-sodium V8 juice
- 1 package (16 ounces) frozen mixed vegetables

1. In a Dutch oven, cook the turkey over medium heat 6-8 minutes or until no longer pink, breaking into crumbles; drain. Stir in soup mix, 1½ teaspoons seasoning from the noodles, sugar, pepper and salt. Add V8 juice and vegetables; bring to a boil. Reduce heat; simmer, uncovered, 5 minutes.
2. Break noodles into small pieces; add to soup (discard remaining seasoning or save for another use). Cook 3-5 minutes longer or until noodles are tender, stirring occasionally.
FREEZE OPTION *Freeze cooled soup in freezer containers. To use, partially thaw in refrigerator overnight. Heat through in a saucepan, stirring occasionally and adding a little reduced-sodium broth or water if necessary.*

COOKING FOR TWO

Enjoy a relaxing evening at home—no need to make a reservation when these recipes are waiting for you. They're already perfectly portioned, delectable and just right for tonight!

Peanut Butter & Banana Smoothie

What kid wouldn't love a cold, creamy smoothie when he or she comes in the door after school or sports practice? The recipe is flavored with banana, peanut butter and honey. For a fun variation, substitute chocolate syrup for the honey.

—TRACI WYNNE DENVER, PA

START TO FINISH: 10 MIN. • **MAKES:** 1 SERVING

- ½ cup plain yogurt
- 1 medium ripe banana
- 2 tablespoons nonfat dry milk powder
- 1 tablespoon honey
- 1 tablespoon creamy peanut butter
- 2 ice cubes

In a blender, combine all ingredients; cover and process for 30-40 seconds or until smooth. Stir if necessary. Pour into a chilled glass; serve immediately.

Pureed Butternut Squash Soup

For several years, we've been enjoying this velvety, yet healthy, soup at Thanksgiving. Butternut squash isn't the easiest thing to cut into, so I go ahead and buy mine pre-chopped.

—**CHRISTEN CHALMERS** HOUSTON, TX

START TO FINISH: 30 MIN. • **MAKES:** 2 SERVINGS

- 1 teaspoon butter
- 1 teaspoon olive oil
- ¼ cup chopped onion
- ¼ cup chopped carrot
- 1 garlic clove, minced
- 1½ cups cubed peeled butternut squash
- 1½ cups chicken stock
- ¼ teaspoon dried sage leaves
- ¼ teaspoon salt
- ⅛ teaspoon pepper
    Pinch crushed red pepper flakes

1. In a small saucepan, heat butter and oil over medium heat. Add onion and carrot; cook and stir until tender. Add garlic; cook 1 minute longer.

2. Stir in squash, stock, sage, salt and pepper; bring to a boil. Reduce heat; simmer, covered, 10-15 minutes or until squash is tender. Remove from heat; cool slightly. Process in a blender until smooth. Sprinkle servings with the red pepper flakes.

Sweet Potato Fries with Blue Cheese

I used to hate sweet potatoes as a child, mostly because they came out of a can. When I heard of the many health benefits, I began trying fresh sweet potatoes with my husband. We like to make fries with different toppings like cinnamon, sugar and cayenne pepper. Then we discovered how awesome they are with blue cheese.

—**KATRINA KRUMM** APPLE VALLEY, MN

START TO FINISH: 25 MIN. • **MAKES:** 2 SERVINGS

- 1 tablespoon olive oil
- 2 medium sweet potatoes (about 1¼ pounds), peeled and cut into ½-inch-thick strips
- 1 tablespoon apricot preserves
- ¼ teaspoon salt
- 3 tablespoons crumbled blue cheese

In a large skillet, heat oil over medium heat. Add sweet potatoes; cook 12-15 minutes or until tender and lightly browned, turning occasionally. Add preserves, stirring to coat; sprinkle with salt. Top with cheese.

Orange-Pecan Salmon

Give a classic seafood meal a flavorful twist with the addition of orange and pecan. This saucy salmon is the perfect meal for a romantic dinner for two.

—**PAT NEAVES** LEE'S SUMMIT, MO

PREP: 10 MIN. + MARINATING • **BAKE:** 20 MIN. • **MAKES:** 2 SERVINGS

- ½ cup chopped pecans, toasted
- ½ cup orange marmalade
- ¼ cup reduced-sodium soy sauce
- ⅛ teaspoon salt
- ⅛ teaspoon pepper
- 2 salmon fillets (6 ounces each and 1 inch thick)

1. In a small bowl, combine the first five ingredients. Pour ½ cup marinade into a large resealable plastic bag. Add the salmon; seal bag and turn to coat. Refrigerate for up to 30 minutes. Set aside remaining marinade.

2. Drain and discard marinade from salmon. Place salmon in a greased 11x7-in. baking dish. Bake, uncovered, at 350° for 20-25 minutes or until fish flakes easily with a fork.

3. In a small saucepan, bring reserved marinade to a boil; cook until liquid is reduced to ⅓ cup. Serve with salmon.

Fennel Wild Rice Salad

This is a salad I invented years ago when my sister's family had to go gluten-free. It has since become a family favorite, and Thanksgiving just isn't the same without our wild rice salad!

—**AIMEE DAY** FERNDALE, WA

PREP: 15 MIN. • **COOK:** 55 MIN.
MAKES: 2 SERVINGS

- ⅓ cup uncooked wild rice
- 1 cup water
- 1½ teaspoons lemon juice
- 1½ teaspoons olive oil
- ¼ cup thinly sliced fennel bulb
- 2 tablespoons salted pumpkin seeds or pepitas
- 2 tablespoons dried cherries
- 1 green onion, sliced
- 1 tablespoon minced fresh parsley
- ⅛ teaspoon salt
  Dash pepper

1. Rinse wild rice thoroughly; drain. In a small saucepan, combine water and rice; bring to a boil. Reduce heat; simmer, covered, 50-55 minutes or until rice is fluffy and tender. Drain if necessary.

2. Transfer the rice to a small bowl. Drizzle with lemon juice and oil; toss to coat. Stir in remaining ingredients.

Contest Winner

Crumb-Coated Chicken & Blackberry Salsa

Maple lends a sweet touch to blackberry salsa. Besides chicken, it's also great with fried fish.

—**TAMMY THOMAS** MORRISVILLE, VT

START TO FINISH: 25 MIN.
MAKES: 2 SERVINGS

- ½ cup fresh blackberries
- 1 jalapeno pepper, seeded and minced
- 2 tablespoons minced fresh cilantro
- 2 tablespoons chopped red onion
- 2 tablespoons maple syrup
- 2 tablespoons balsamic vinegar
- 2 boneless skinless chicken breast halves (5 ounces each)
- ⅛ teaspoon salt
- ⅛ teaspoon pepper
- ¼ cup all-purpose flour
- 1 egg, beaten
- ½ cup panko (Japanese) bread crumbs
- 1 tablespoon olive oil

1. In a small bowl, combine the first six ingredients. Cover and refrigerate until serving.

2. Flatten chicken to ¼-in. thickness; sprinkle with salt and pepper. Place the flour, egg and bread crumbs in separate shallow bowls. Coat chicken with flour, dip in egg, then coat with the crumbs.

3. In a large skillet, cook chicken in oil over medium heat for 4-6 minutes on each side or until no longer pink. Serve with salsa.

NOTE *Wear disposable gloves when cutting hot peppers; the oils can burn skin. Avoid touching your face.*

Curry Chicken Soup for Two

Don't be overwhelmed by the long ingredient list—this soup is quick and easy to make. Plus, it's a fantastic way to get your veggies.

—**JANE HACKER** MILWAUKEE, WI

PREP: 20 MIN. • **COOK:** 15 MIN.
MAKES: 2 SERVINGS

- ¼ **pound boneless skinless chicken breasts, cut into ½-inch cubes**
- 1½ **teaspoons canola oil, divided**
- ⅓ **cup chopped onion**
- ¼ **cup chopped carrot**
- ¼ **cup chopped celery**
- ¼ **cup chopped green pepper**
- ½ **cup chopped peeled apple**
- 1 **tablespoon all-purpose flour**
- ⅛ **teaspoon salt**
- 1 **can (14½ ounces) reduced-sodium chicken broth**
- 2 **tablespoons tomato paste**
- 1 **to 1½ teaspoons curry powder**
- ½ **teaspoon ground ginger**
- ⅛ **to ¼ teaspoon crushed red pepper flakes**
- 1 **tablespoon minced fresh parsley**

1. In a large saucepan coated with cooking spray, cook the chicken in ½ teaspoon oil for 4-5 minutes or until juices run clear. Remove chicken and set aside.

2. In the same saucepan, saute the onion, carrot, celery and green pepper in remaining oil for 4 minutes. Add the apple; cook 2 minutes longer. Combine flour and salt. Sprinkle over vegetable mixture; cook and stir for 1 minute. Gradually stir in broth and tomato paste. Bring to a boil; cook and stir 1-2 minutes longer or until slightly thickened.

3. Stir in the curry, ginger and pepper flakes. Return chicken to saucepan and bring to a boil. Reduce the heat; simmer, uncovered, for 8-10 minutes or until the vegetables are tender. Sprinkle with parsley.

Ham & Sweet Potato Packets

I can my own peaches and use them in this recipe. Add a simple salad and you've got a delicious meal.

—**JANET ERNSBARGER** SALINA, KS

PREP: 5 MIN. • **BAKE:** 30 MIN.
MAKES: 2 SERVINGS

- 2 **individual boneless fully cooked ham steaks (5 ounces each)**
- 1 **large sweet potato, peeled and thinly sliced**
- 2 **canned peach halves**
- 1 **tablespoon brown sugar**
- 1 **tablespoon butter**

1. Preheat oven to 350°. Place each ham steak on a double thickness of heavy-duty foil (about 12 in. square). Layer with potato and peach halves. Sprinkle with brown sugar; dot with butter. Fold foil around mixture and seal tightly. Place on a baking sheet.

2. Bake 30-35 minutes or until heated through and potato is tender. Open foil carefully to allow steam to escape.

Raspberry Ice Cream in a Bag

Making homemade ice cream is fun for the whole family, and the fresh raspberry taste of this treat makes it a perfect summer activity. Kids can shake the bags until the liquid changes to ice cream and then enjoy the reward!
—**ERIN HOFFMAN** CANBY, MN

START TO FINISH: 15 MIN. • **MAKES:** 1 CUP

- 1 cup half-and-half cream
- ½ cup fresh raspberries
- ¼ cup sugar
- 2 tablespoons evaporated milk
- 1 teaspoon vanilla extract
- 4 cups coarsely crushed ice
- ¾ cup salt

1. Using two quart-size resealable plastic bags, place one bag inside the other. Place the first five ingredients inside the inner bag. Seal both bags, pressing out as much air as possible.
2. Place the two bags in a gallon-size resealable plastic freezer bag. Add ice and salt. Seal bag, again pressing out as much air as possible.

3. Shake and knead cream mixture until thickened, about 5 minutes. (If desired, wear mittens or wrap bags in a kitchen towel while shaking to protect hands from the cold ice.)

Tomato & Avocado Sandwiches

I'm a vegetarian, and this is my go-to sandwich. It's a combination I never tire of and others enjoy, too. I call it HATS for hummus, avocado, tomato and shallots.
—**SARAH JARAHA** MOORESTOWN, NJ

START TO FINISH: 10 MIN.
MAKES: 2 SERVINGS

- ½ medium ripe avocado, peeled and mashed
- 4 slices whole wheat bread, toasted
- 1 medium tomato, sliced
- 2 tablespoons finely chopped shallot
- ¼ cup hummus

Spread avocado over two slices of toast. Top with tomato and shallot. Spread hummus over remaining toast slices; place over tops.

Fried Rice Omelet

Here's a fun way to use leftover chicken and cooked rice. This delightful omelet is also wonderful for dinner.
—**TASTE OF HOME** TEST KITCHEN

START TO FINISH: 25 MIN.
MAKES: 1 SERVING

- ¼ cup cooked rice
- ¼ cup cubed cooked chicken
- ¼ cup frozen stir-fry vegetable blend, thawed
- 1 tablespoon reduced-sodium teriyaki sauce
- 1 tablespoon butter
- 3 large eggs
- 3 tablespoons water
- ⅛ teaspoon salt
- ⅛ teaspoon pepper

1. In a small nonstick skillet coated with cooking spray, saute the rice, chicken, vegetable blend and teriyaki sauce until heated through. Remove from skillet and set aside.
2. In the same skillet, melt butter over medium-high heat. Whisk the eggs, water, salt and pepper. Add egg mixture to skillet (mixture should set immediately at edges).

3. As eggs set, push cooked edges toward the center, letting uncooked portion flow underneath. When the eggs are set, spoon rice mixture on one side; fold other side over filling. Slide omelet onto a plate.

Waffle Sandwich

Keep 'em going right through to lunchtime with this innovative breakfast idea. I like to serve it with apple slices on the side.
—**MICHELE MCHENRY** BELLINGHAM, WA

START TO FINISH: 20 MIN.
MAKES: 1 SERVING

- 1 slice Canadian bacon
- 1 large egg
- 1 green onion, chopped
- 2 frozen waffles
- 1 tablespoon shredded cheddar cheese
  Sliced tomato, optional

1. In a nonstick skillet coated with cooking spray, cook Canadian bacon over medium-high heat 1-2 minutes on each side or until lightly browned. Remove and keep warm.
2. In a small bowl, whisk egg and green onion; add to the same pan. Cook and stir until egg is thickened and no liquid egg remains.
3. Meanwhile, prepare the waffles according to package directions. Place one waffle on a plate. Top with Canadian bacon, scrambled egg, cheese and, if desired, tomato. Top with remaining waffle.

Bacon, Cremini & Brie Potatoes

This is my version of an ultimate baked potato. Rich Brie, crispy bacon and cremini mushrooms transform the humble baked potato into something really special.
—**JAN VALDEZ** CHICAGO, IL

PREP: 10 MIN. • **BAKE:** 50 MIN.
MAKES: 2 SERVINGS

- 2 **medium potatoes**
- 2 **teaspoons olive oil**
- ¼ **teaspoon salt**
- 3 **bacon strips, chopped**
- ¼ **pound sliced baby portobello (cremini) mushrooms**
- 2 **ounces Brie cheese, sliced**
- 1 **tablespoon minced fresh chives**

1. Scrub and pierce potatoes. Rub potato skins with oil; sprinkle with salt. Bake at 400° for 50-60 minutes or until tender.
2. In a skillet, cook bacon over medium heat until crisp. Remove to paper towels with a slotted spoon; drain, reserving 1 tablespoon of drippings. Saute mushrooms in the drippings.
3. Cut a 2-in. "X" in tops of the potatoes; insert cheese slices. Top with mushrooms, bacon and chives.

Caramel Pumpkin Tiramisu for Two

I'm not fond of traditional tiramisu, so I used pumpkin and bourbon in place of coffee in my recipe. Now I love it! I always make extra sauce and eat it over vanilla ice cream. It's so good, I can't leave it alone!
—**MARY FILIPIAK** FORT WAYNE, IN

PREP: 35 MIN. + CHILLING
MAKES: 2 SERVINGS

- 6 **crisp ladyfinger cookies**
- 4 **teaspoons maple syrup**
- 2 **teaspoons bourbon**
- ⅓ **cup heavy whipping cream, divided**
- 4 **teaspoons sugar**
- ¼ **cup solid-pack pumpkin**
- ¼ **teaspoon ground cinnamon**
  Dash ground ginger
  Dash salt
- 1½ **ounces cream cheese, softened**
- 1 **tablespoon confectioners' sugar**
- **SAUCE**
- ¼ **cup hot caramel ice cream topping**
- 1 **teaspoon bourbon**

1. Using a serrated knife, cut two ladyfingers in half. In a shallow bowl, combine syrup and bourbon. Dip two whole ladyfingers and two halves into mixture; arrange in a single layer in a 9x5-in. loaf pan.
2. In a small bowl, beat ¼ cup cream until it begins to thicken. Gradually add sugar; beat until soft peaks form. In a large bowl, combine the pumpkin, cinnamon, ginger, and salt; fold in whipped cream. In another bowl, beat the cream cheese, confectioners' sugar and remaining cream until thickened.
3. Spread half of pumpkin mixture over ladyfingers in pan. Dip remaining ladyfingers; arrange over the top. Top with remaining pumpkin mixture and the cream cheese mixture. Cover and refrigerate for 8 hours or overnight.
4. In a microwave, heat the caramel sauce; stir in bourbon. Serve warm with tiramisu.
NOTE *This recipe was prepared with Alessi brand ladyfinger cookies.*

DINING FOR ONE

Whether you need a lunch at work, don't want to store lots of leftovers or are craving a quick bite, these single-serving recipes are here for you. Dig in!

Lunch Box Chicken Wrap

Sure, this wrap is kid-friendly, but it's just as exciting to pack for your own lunch box. Using colorful, thin strips of vegetables adds visual interest when the wrap is cut into slices.

—**PEGGY WOODWARD** GREENDALE, WI

START TO FINISH: 10 MIN. • **MAKES:** 1 SERVING

- ¼ cup hummus
- 1 whole wheat tortilla (8 inches), room temperature
- ½ cup fresh baby spinach
- ⅓ cup shredded cooked chicken breast
- 2 carrot sticks
- 2 sweet red pepper strips

Spread hummus over tortilla; top with spinach. Place the chicken, carrot and red pepper in a row near center of tortilla; roll up tightly. If desired, cut crosswise into slices. Wrap securely or pack in an airtight container; refrigerate until serving.

Blueberry Cheesecake Parfait

Fresh blueberries may not seem decadent, but this impressive cheesecake-flavored parfait will make your mouth water.

—**BLAIR LONERGAN** ROCHELLE, VA

START TO FINISH: 10 MIN. • **MAKES:** 1 SERVING

- ½ cup reduced-fat ricotta cheese
- 1 teaspoon sugar
- ¼ teaspoon vanilla extract
- 3 tablespoons blueberry preserves
- ½ cup fresh or frozen blueberries, thawed
- ¼ cup graham cracker crumbs
- 1 tablespoon slivered almonds

In a small bowl, combine the cheese, sugar and vanilla. Spoon 1 tablespoon preserves, 2 tablespoons blueberries, half of the cheese mixture and 2 tablespoons cracker crumbs into a parfait glass. Repeat layers. Top with remaining preserves, blueberries and almonds.

Strawberry Patch Frost

Strawberries get a deliciously chilled treatment in this creamy, pretty pink drink.
—*TASTE OF HOME* **TEST KITCHEN**

START TO FINISH: 5 MIN. • **MAKES:** 1 SERVING

- 2 **tablespoons strawberry jam**
- 1 **teaspoon water**
- 3 **scoops strawberry ice cream**
- ½ **cup sliced fresh strawberries**
- ¼ **cup heavy whipping cream or half-and-half cream**
- 1 **cup chilled strawberry or raspberry sparkling water**
  Whipped cream
  Colored sprinkles

In a tall glass, combine strawberry jam and water. Add ice cream, strawberries and cream. Top with sparkling water. Garnish with whipped cream and sprinkles. Serve immediately.

Portobello Burger with Muffuletta Topping

A tasty tomato-olive mixture, melted cheese and smoky grilled mushroom add so much to this tasty concoction that a guest once called it "one of the best grilled mushroom burgers I've had."
—**TAMRA DUNCAN** LINCOLN, AR

START TO FINISH: 25 MIN. • **MAKES:** 1 SERVING

- 1 **large portobello mushroom, stem removed**
- 1 **teaspoon olive oil**
- ⅛ **teaspoon dried oregano**
  Salt and pepper, to taste
- 1 **plum tomato, chopped**
- 2 **pitted green olives, chopped**
- 1 **tablespoon mayonnaise**
- 1 **multigrain hamburger bun, split and toasted**
- 1 **lettuce leaf**
- 1 **slice provolone cheese**

1. Brush mushroom with oil and sprinkle with oregano. Season with salt and pepper. Using long-handled tongs, moisten a paper towel with cooking oil and lightly coat the grill rack. Grill the mushroom, covered, over medium heat or broil 4 in. from the heat for 6-8 minutes on each side or until tender.
2. Combine tomato and olives; season with salt and pepper. Spread mayonnaise over bun bottom. Top with lettuce, mushroom, cheese and tomato mixture; replace bun top.

Tender Biscuits

Yes, you can make biscuits in 30 minutes! They'll dress up any weeknight meal.
—**ANE BURKE** BELLA VISTA, AR

START TO FINISH: 30 MIN.
MAKES: 2 BISCUITS

- ⅓ cup self-rising flour
- 1 tablespoon grated Parmesan cheese
- ⅛ teaspoon garlic salt
- 3 tablespoons reduced-fat cream cheese
- 3 tablespoons fat-free milk
- 1 tablespoon fat-free plain yogurt

1. In a small bowl, combine the flour, Parmesan cheese and garlic salt. Cut in cream cheese until the mixture resembles coarse crumbs. Stir in milk and yogurt just until moistened.

2. Drop by scant ⅓ cupfuls 2 in. apart onto a baking sheet coated with cooking spray. Bake at 400° for 12-15 minutes or until golden brown. Serve warm.

Beef Barley Soup

Enjoy this hearty soup that's full of the most satisfying ingredients. It'll give you true comfort, especially on a cool day.
—**SUE JURACK** MEQUON, WI

START TO FINISH: 30 MIN.
MAKES: 2 SERVINGS

- 2 tablespoons each chopped carrot, celery and onion
- 1 teaspoon butter
- 1 cup water
- 1 cup reduced-sodium beef broth
- ½ cup cubed cooked roast beef
- ½ cup canned diced tomatoes
- ¼ cup quick-cooking barley
- 2 tablespoons frozen peas
- ¼ teaspoon salt
- ¼ teaspoon dried basil
- ¼ teaspoon dried oregano
- ¼ teaspoon pepper

In a small saucepan, saute the carrot, celery and onion in butter until tender. Add remaining ingredients; bring to a boil. Reduce heat; cover and simmer for 15-20 minutes or until the barley is tender, stirring soup occasionally.

Crispy Buffalo Chicken Roll-Ups

These winning chicken rolls with a crispy crust are both impressive and easy to make. My family and friends absolutely love them!

—**WILLIAM KEYS** KENNETT SQUARE, PA

PREP: 15 MIN. • **BAKE:** 30 MIN.
MAKES: 2 SERVINGS

- 2 **boneless skinless chicken breast halves (6 ounces each)**
- ¼ **teaspoon salt**
- ¼ **teaspoon pepper**
- 2 **tablespoons crumbled blue cheese**
- 2 **tablespoons hot pepper sauce**
- 1 **tablespoon mayonnaise**
- ½ **cup crushed cornflakes**

1. Preheat oven to 400°. Flatten chicken breasts to ¼-in. thickness. Season with salt and pepper; sprinkle with blue cheese. Roll up each from a short side and secure with toothpicks.
2. In a shallow bowl, combine the pepper sauce and mayonnaise. Place cornflakes in a separate shallow bowl. Dip the chicken in pepper sauce mixture, then coat with cornflakes. Place seam side down in a greased 11x7-in. baking dish.
3. Bake, uncovered, 30-35 minutes or until chicken is no longer pink. Discard toothpicks.

Apple, Blue Cheese & Bibb Salad for Two

Red or Golden Delicious apples add a sweet crunch to this simple salad, while a homemade honey-mustard dressing gives it an extra special touch.

—**REBEKAH BEYER** SABETHA, KS

START TO FINISH: 20 MIN.
MAKES: 2 SERVINGS

- 2 **tablespoons olive oil**
- ¾ **teaspoon white balsamic or white wine vinegar**
- ¾ **teaspoon honey**
- ¾ **teaspoon mayonnaise**
- ⅛ **teaspoon mustard seed, toasted**
- ⅛ **teaspoon stone-ground mustard (whole grain)**
  Dash salt
  Dash coarsely ground pepper

SALAD
- 1 **cup torn Bibb or Boston lettuce**
- ¾ **cup chopped Red and/or Golden Delicious apple**
- ¼ **cup crumbled blue cheese**
- 3 **tablespoons walnut halves, toasted**
- 2 **tablespoons golden raisins**

In a small bowl, whisk the first eight ingredients until blended. In a bowl, combine lettuce, apple and cheese. Drizzle with dressing and toss to coat. Sprinkle with walnuts and raisins. Serve immediately.
NOTE *To toast nuts, bake in a shallow pan in a 350° oven for 5-10 minutes or cook in a skillet over low heat until lightly browned, stirring occasionally.*

Contest Winner

Jeweled Plum Tartlets

I developed this dessert as a way to enjoy the seasonal plums in Michigan. The red fruit shines just like jewels in the creamy custard when they emerge from the oven.

—**NICOLE FILIZETTI** STEVENS POINT, WI

PREP: 30 MIN. • **BAKE:** 20 MIN. + COOLING • **MAKES:** 2 SERVINGS

- ½ cup plus 2 teaspoons all-purpose flour, divided
- 4 teaspoons sugar
- ⅛ teaspoon salt
- ¼ cup cold butter, cubed
- 2 medium plums, sliced
- 1 large egg yolk
- 1 tablespoon 2% milk
- 4 teaspoons brown sugar, divided
  Vanilla ice cream

1. In a small bowl, combine ½ cup flour, sugar and salt; cut in butter until mixture resembles coarse crumbs. Press onto the bottom and up the sides of two 4-in. fluted tart pans with removable bottoms. Bake at 325° for 10 minutes or until set.

2. Arrange the plum slices in crusts. In another bowl, combine the egg yolk, milk, 2 teaspoons brown sugar and remaining flour. Spoon over plums; sprinkle with remaining brown sugar.

3. Bake for 20-25 minutes or until a knife inserted near the center comes out clean. Cool on a wire rack. Serve with the ice cream.

Herb-Crusted Perch Fillets with Pea Puree

Become a culinary Picasso when you decorate plates with a creamy pea puree. Flecked with a crisp herb coating, perch is the perfect subject for your canvas.

—**GREGORY ROYSTER** NORTH LAUDERDALE, FL

PREP: 35 MIN. • **COOK:** 10 MIN./BATCH • **MAKES:** 2 SERVINGS

- 1 cup frozen peas
- ½ cup chicken broth
- 1 garlic clove, halved
- 1 tablespoon heavy whipping cream
- 2 tablespoons plus ⅓ cup olive oil, divided
- ¼ cup all-purpose flour
- 1 egg, beaten
- ½ cup panko (Japanese) bread crumbs
- 1 tablespoon dried basil
- 1 tablespoon snipped fresh dill
- 1 tablespoon minced fresh thyme
- 8 perch fillets (about ¾ pound)
- ¼ teaspoon salt
- ⅛ teaspoon white pepper
  Lemon wedges

1. In a small saucepan, combine the peas, broth and garlic. Bring to a boil. Reduce heat; simmer, uncovered, for 4-5 minutes or until peas are tender; cool slightly. Drain peas and garlic; transfer to a food processor. Add cream and 2 tablespoons oil. Cover and process until pureed; set aside.

2. Place flour and egg in separate shallow bowls. In another shallow bowl, combine the bread crumbs, basil, dill and thyme. Sprinkle fillets with salt and pepper. Dip perch, skin side up, in the flour, egg, then bread crumb mixture.

3. In a large skillet, cook the fillets in remaining oil in batches over medium heat for 3-4 minutes on each side or until fish flakes easily with a fork. Serve with pea puree and lemon wedges.

Easy Spiced Morning Mocha

This recipe is a guaranteed morning pick-me-up. It still tastes great when made with low-fat milk, if you want to change it up.
—**VICKIE WRIGHT** OMAHA, NE

START TO FINISH: 10 MIN. • **MAKES:** 1 SERVING

- 1 tablespoon French vanilla powdered nondairy creamer
- 1½ teaspoons sugar
- 1 teaspoon instant coffee granules
- 1 teaspoon baking cocoa
- ¼ teaspoon ground ginger
- ¼ teaspoon ground cinnamon
- 1 cup hot 2% milk or water
  Sweetened whipped cream and additional ground cinnamon

Place the first six ingredients in a mug. Stir in hot milk until blended. Top with whipped cream; sprinkle topping with additional cinnamon.

Full Garden Frittata

I was cooking for a health-conscious friend, and wanted to serve a frittata. To brighten it up, I added classic bruschetta toppings. This has become a staple in my recipe book.
—**MELISSA ROSENTHAL** VISTA, CA

PREP: 25 MIN. • **BAKE:** 10 MIN. • **MAKES:** 2 SERVINGS

- 4 large eggs
- ⅓ cup 2% milk
- ¼ teaspoon salt, divided
- ⅛ teaspoon coarsely ground pepper
- 2 teaspoons olive oil
- ½ medium zucchini, chopped
- ½ cup chopped baby portobello mushrooms
- ¼ cup chopped onion
- 1 garlic clove, minced
- 2 tablespoons minced fresh basil
- 1 teaspoon minced fresh oregano
- 1 teaspoon minced fresh parsley
  Optional toppings: halved grape tomatoes, small fresh mozzarella cheese balls and thinly sliced fresh basil

1. Preheat oven to 375°. In a bowl, whisk the eggs, milk, ⅛ teaspoon salt and pepper. In an 8-in. ovenproof skillet, heat oil over medium-high heat. Add zucchini, mushrooms and onion; cook and stir until tender. Add garlic, herbs and remaining salt; cook 1 minute longer. Pour in egg mixture.
2. Bake, uncovered, 10-15 minutes or until eggs are set. Cut into four wedges. If desired, serve with toppings.

Summer Squash Medley

You can enjoy this dish while the squash is still warm, but it's also great cold. You'll love how it captures the fresh flavors and bright colors of summer.

—**RANI LONG** COLD SPRING, NY

START TO FINISH: 20 MIN.
MAKES: 2 SERVINGS

- 1 medium yellow summer squash, thinly sliced
- 1 tablespoon lemon juice
- 1 tablespoon olive oil
- 2 teaspoons snipped fresh dill or ½ teaspoon dill weed
- 1 small garlic clove, minced
- ½ teaspoon Dijon mustard
- ¼ teaspoon sugar
- ¼ teaspoon salt
- ⅛ teaspoon pepper
- ¼ cup crumbled feta cheese
- 1 medium tomato, diced
- ¼ cup finely chopped sweet onion

1. In a small saucepan, bring ½ in. of water to a boil. Add the squash; cover and boil for 3-4 minutes or until tender. Drain.

2. In a large bowl, combine the lemon juice, oil, dill, garlic, mustard, sugar, salt and pepper. Gently stir in squash and cheese. Transfer to a serving platter. Combine tomato and onion; spoon over squash mixture. Serve dish immediately.

Chicken Creole for Two

I ladle this vegetable-packed chicken dish over jasmine rice, which is a long-grain rice that's not as sticky as most. If you prefer another variety of rice, feel free to substitute the one you like best.

—**VIRGINIA CROWELL** LYONS, OR

PREP: 20 MIN. • **COOK:** 30 MIN.
MAKES: 2 SERVINGS

- ½ cup chopped green pepper
- ¼ cup thinly sliced onion
- ¼ cup chopped celery
- 1 garlic clove, minced
- 1 teaspoon canola oil, divided
- ¾ cup sliced fresh mushrooms
- ¾ cup undrained diced tomatoes
- 2 tablespoons chicken broth
- 1½ teaspoons minced fresh oregano or ½ teaspoon dried oregano
- 1½ teaspoons lemon juice
- ¾ teaspoon minced fresh basil or ¼ teaspoon dried basil
- ⅛ teaspoon salt
- ⅛ teaspoon pepper
- ⅛ teaspoon crushed red pepper flakes
- ½ pound boneless skinless chicken breasts, cubed
  Hot cooked rice
  Minced fresh parsley, optional

1. In a large saucepan, saute the green peppers, onion, celery and garlic in ½ teaspoon oil until tender. Add mushrooms; cook until liquid has evaporated. Stir in the tomatoes, broth, oregano, lemon juice, basil and spices. Bring to a boil. Reduce heat; cover and simmer 5-10 minutes or until slightly thickened and flavors are blended.

2. Meanwhile, in a Dutch oven, saute chicken in remaining oil until no longer pink. Return chicken to pan; stir in sauce. Heat through, stirring to loosen browned bits from pan. Serve over rice; garnish with parsley if desired.

Merlot Filet Mignon

Although this filet is such a simple recipe, you can feel confident serving it to your guests. The rich sauce adds a touch of elegance. Just add a salad and rolls.

—JAUNEEN HOSKING WATERFORD, WI

START TO FINISH: 20 MIN.
MAKES: 2 SERVINGS

- 2 beef tenderloin steaks (8 ounces each)
- 3 tablespoons butter, divided
- 1 tablespoon olive oil
- 1 cup merlot
- 2 tablespoons heavy whipping cream
- ⅛ teaspoon salt

1. In a small skillet, cook steaks in 1 tablespoon butter and oil over medium heat for 4-6 minutes on each side or until meat reaches desired doneness (for medium-rare, a thermometer should read 145°; medium, 160°; well-done, 170°). Remove and keep warm.

2. In the same skillet, add wine, stirring to loosen browned bits from pan. Bring to a boil; cook until liquid is reduced to ¼ cup. Add the cream, salt and remaining butter; bring to a boil. Cook and stir for 1-2 minutes or until slightly thickened and butter is melted. Serve with steaks.

Contest Winner

Veggie Tossed Salad

Getting your veggies in has never been so easy and satisfying. Drizzle your favorite dressing on top.

—EVELYN SLADE FRUITA, CO

START TO FINISH: 10 MIN.
MAKES: 2 SERVINGS

- ¾ cup torn romaine
- ¾ cup fresh baby spinach
- ⅓ cup sliced fresh mushrooms
- ⅓ cup grape tomatoes
- ¼ cup sliced cucumber
- 3 tablespoons sliced ripe olives
- 1½ teaspoons grated Parmesan cheese
- 2 tablespoons reduced-fat Italian salad dressing

In a large bowl, combine the first seven ingredients. Add salad dressing; toss to coat.

Lime-Buttered Broccoli

I grew tired of serving broccoli the same way every time, so I prepared this recipe. The butter sauce turns the tender florets into something undeniably good.

—DENISE ALBERS FREEBURG, IL

START TO FINISH: 20 MIN.
MAKES: 2 SERVINGS

- 2 cups fresh broccoli florets
- 1 tablespoon butter, melted
- 1 teaspoon lime juice
- ⅛ teaspoon salt
- ⅛ teaspoon pepper

1. Place broccoli in a steamer basket; place in a large saucepan over 1 in. of water. Bring to a boil; cover and steam for 3-4 minutes or until crisp-tender.

2. Meanwhile, in a small bowl, combine the remaining ingredients.

3. Drizzle the butter mixture over broccoli; toss to coat.

STEAMING VEGGIES

When steaming vegetables, be sure to follow the recipe's directions for how long to boil for best results. The cooking time begins when the water starts to boil.

SLOW COOKER

Trade time in the kitchen for more memories with loved ones. These slow-cooked dishes make it possible with just a little prep work. Hours later, come back and enjoy the warm and satisfying results.

Pear Cider

This sweetly spiced, pear-flavored beverage will warm you from head to toe. It's a pleasant change of pace from a traditional hot cider.

—TASTE OF HOME TEST KITCHEN

PREP: 5 MIN. • **COOK:** 3 HOURS
MAKES: 20 SERVINGS (¾ CUP EACH)

- 12 **cups unsweetened apple juice**
- 4 **cups pear nectar**
- 8 **cinnamon sticks (3 inches)**
- 1 **tablespoon whole allspice**
- 1 **tablespoon whole cloves**

1. In a 6-qt. slow cooker, combine juice and nectar. Place the cinnamon sticks, allspice and cloves on a double thickness of cheesecloth; bring up corners of cloth and tie with string to form a bag. Place in slow cooker.
2. Cover and cook on low for 3-4 hours or until heated through. Discard spice bag. Serve warm cider in mugs.

Contest Winner

Black Bean 'n' Pumpkin Chili

Believe it or not, I discovered the secret ingredient to make chili really stand out: pumpkin. Be sure to cook up a big batch of this and freeze for later; it tastes just as good reheated.

—DEBORAH VLIET HOLLAND, MI

PREP: 20 MIN. • **COOK:** 4 HOURS
MAKES: 10 SERVINGS (2½ QUARTS)

- 2 **tablespoons olive oil**
- 1 **medium onion, chopped**
- 1 **medium sweet yellow pepper, chopped**
- 3 **garlic cloves, minced**
- 2 **cans (15 ounces each) black beans, rinsed and drained**
- 1 **can (15 ounces) solid-pack pumpkin**
- 1 **can (14½ ounces) diced tomatoes, undrained**
- 3 **cups chicken broth**
- 2½ **cups cubed cooked turkey**
- 2 **teaspoons dried parsley flakes**
- 2 **teaspoons chili powder**
- 1½ **teaspoons ground cumin**
- 1½ **teaspoons dried oregano**
- ½ **teaspoon salt**
  Cubed avocado and thinly sliced green onions, optional

1. In a large skillet, heat oil over medium-high heat. Add onion and pepper; cook and stir until tender. Add garlic; cook 1 minute longer.
2. Transfer to a 5-qt. slow cooker; stir in the remaining ingredients. Cook, covered, on low 4-5 hours. If desired, top with avocado and green onions.

Beef Stroganoff

No more standing and stirring at the stove—this creamy Stroganoff quickly preps in a skillet, then slow-cooks all day while you're away.

—SARAH VASQUES MILFORD, NH

PREP: 20 MIN. • **COOK:** 6 HOURS
MAKES: 7 SERVINGS

- 2 **pounds beef top sirloin steak, cut into thin strips**
- 3 **tablespoons olive oil**
- 1 **cup water**
- 1 **envelope (1½ ounces) beef Stroganoff seasoning for the slow cooker**
- 1 **pound sliced baby portobello mushrooms**
- 1 **small onion, chopped**
- 3 **tablespoons butter**
- ¼ **cup port wine or beef broth**
- 2 **teaspoons ground mustard**
- 1 **teaspoon sugar**
- 1½ **cups (12 ounces) sour cream**
  Hot cooked egg noodles
  Minced fresh parsley, optional

1. In a large skillet, brown the meat in oil. Add water and seasoning mix, stirring to loosen browned bits from pan. Transfer meat and drippings to a 3-qt. slow cooker.
2. In the same skillet, saute the mushrooms and onion in butter until tender. Combine the wine, mustard and sugar; stir into the mushroom mixture. Add to slow cooker; stir to combine.
3. Cover and cook on low for 6-8 hours or until meat is tender. Stir in sour cream. Serve with noodles. Sprinkle with parsley if desired.

Contest Winner

Garlic Green Beans with Gorgonzola

I updated this green bean side dish by adding a touch of white wine, fresh thyme and green onions. You can't go wrong making it for a special occasion.

—NANCY HEISHMAN LAS VEGAS, NV

PREP: 20 MIN. • **COOK:** 3 HOURS
MAKES: 10 SERVINGS

- 2 **pounds fresh green beans, trimmed and halved**
- 1 **can (8 ounces) sliced water chestnuts, drained**
- 4 **green onions, chopped**
- 5 **bacon strips, cooked and crumbled, divided**
- ⅓ **cup white wine or chicken broth**
- 2 **tablespoons minced fresh thyme or 2 teaspoons dried thyme**
- 4 **garlic cloves, minced**
- 1½ **teaspoons seasoned salt**
- 1 **cup (8 ounces) sour cream**
- ¾ **cup crumbled Gorgonzola cheese**

1. Place green beans, water chestnuts, green onions and ¼ cup cooked bacon in a 4-qt. slow cooker. In a small bowl, mix wine, thyme, garlic and seasoned salt; pour over top. Cook, covered, on low 3-4 hours or until green beans are crisp-tender. Drain liquid from beans.
2. Just before serving, stir in sour cream; sprinkle with the cheese and remaining bacon.

Chicken Corn Bread Casserole

Here's a hearty, savory meal for the fall or winter season. I love this recipe because it tastes like Thanksgiving dinner without all the holiday hassle.

—**NANCY BARKER** PEORIA, AZ

PREP: 40 MIN. • **COOK:** 3 HOURS • **MAKES:** 6 SERVINGS

- 5 cups cubed corn bread
- ¼ cup butter, cubed
- 1 large onion, chopped (about 2 cups)
- 4 celery ribs, chopped (about 2 cups)
- 3 cups shredded cooked chicken
- 1 can (10¾ ounces) condensed cream of chicken soup, undiluted
- 1 can (10¾ ounces) condensed cream of mushroom soup, undiluted
- ½ cup reduced-sodium chicken broth
- 1 teaspoon poultry seasoning
- ½ teaspoon salt
- ½ teaspoon rubbed sage
- ¼ teaspoon pepper

1. Preheat oven to 350°. Place bread cubes on an ungreased 15x10x1-in. baking pan. Bake 20-25 minutes or until toasted. Cool on baking pan.

2. In a large skillet, heat butter over medium-high heat. Add onion and celery; cook and stir 6-8 minutes or until tender. Transfer to a greased 4-qt. slow cooker. Stir in corn bread, chicken, soups, broth and seasonings.

3. Cook, covered, on low 3-4 hours or until heated through.

Slow-Cooked Tex-Mex Flank Steak

This flavorful, tender beef dish has been a go-to recipe for many years; it's a meal lifesaver on days when I'm going to be getting home late for dinner.

—**ANNE MERRILL** CROGHAN, NY

PREP: 20 MIN. • **COOK:** 6 HOURS • **MAKES:** 4 SERVINGS

- 1 tablespoon canola oil
- 1 beef flank steak (1½ pounds)
- 1 large onion, sliced
- ⅓ cup water
- 1 can (4 ounces) chopped green chilies
- 2 tablespoons cider vinegar
- 2 to 3 teaspoons chili powder
- 1 teaspoon garlic powder
- 1 teaspoon sugar
- ½ teaspoon salt
- ⅛ teaspoon pepper

1. In a large skillet, heat oil over medium-high heat; brown the steak on both sides. Transfer to a 3-qt. slow cooker.

2. Add onion to same skillet; cook and stir 1-2 minutes or until crisp-tender. Add water to pan; cook 30 seconds, stirring to loosen browned bits from pan. Stir in remaining ingredients; return to a boil. Pour over steak.

3. Cook, covered, on low 6-8 hours or until meat is tender. Slice steak across the grain; serve with onion mixture.

Potato and Leek Soup

Sour cream adds just a hint of tang to this creamy chowder that's packed with vegetables and bacon.

—**MELANIE WOODEN** RENO, NV

PREP: 20 MIN. • **COOK:** 8 HOURS • **MAKES:** 8 SERVINGS (2 QUARTS)

- 4 cups chicken broth
- 3 medium potatoes, peeled and cubed
- 1½ cups chopped cabbage
- 2 medium carrots, chopped
- 1 medium leek (white portion only), chopped
- 1 medium onion, chopped
- ¼ cup minced fresh parsley
- ½ teaspoon salt
- ½ teaspoon caraway seeds
- ½ teaspoon pepper
- 1 bay leaf
- ½ cup sour cream
- 1 pound bacon strips, cooked and crumbled

1. Combine the first 11 ingredients in a 4- or 5-qt. slow cooker. Cover and cook on low for 8-10 hours or until vegetables are tender.

2. Before serving, combine sour cream with 1 cup soup; return all to the slow cooker. Stir in bacon and discard the bay leaf.

German Potato Salad with Sausage

This potato salad is an old family recipe that was updated using cream of potato soup to ease preparation. The sausage and sauerkraut make it a meal.

—**TERESA MCGILL** TROTWOOD, OH

PREP: 30 MIN. • **COOK:** 6 HOURS • **MAKES:** 5 SERVINGS

- 8 bacon strips, finely chopped
- 1 large onion, chopped
- 1 pound smoked kielbasa or Polish sausage, halved and cut into ½-inch slices
- 2 pounds medium red potatoes, cut into chunks
- 1 can (10¾ ounces) condensed cream of potato soup, undiluted
- 1 cup sauerkraut, rinsed and well drained
- ½ cup water
- ¼ cup cider vinegar
- 1 tablespoon sugar
- ½ teaspoon salt
- ½ teaspoon coarsely ground pepper

1. In a large skillet, cook bacon over medium heat until crisp. Remove to paper towels with a slotted spoon to drain. Saute onion in drippings for 1 minute. Add sausage; cook until lightly browned. Add the potatoes; cook 2 minutes longer. Drain.

2. Transfer sausage mixture to a 3-qt. slow cooker. In a small bowl, combine the soup, sauerkraut, water, vinegar, sugar, salt and pepper. Pour over sausage mixture. Sprinkle with bacon. Cover and cook on low for 6-7 hours or until potatoes are tender.

Apple Pie Oatmeal Dessert

Making this comforting dessert brings back memories of time spent with my family around the kitchen table. I serve it warm with sweetened whipped cream or vanilla ice cream as a topper.

—CAROL GREER EARLVILLE, IL

PREP: 15 MIN. • **COOK:** 4 HOURS
MAKES: 6 SERVINGS

- 1 cup quick-cooking oats
- ½ cup all-purpose flour
- ⅓ cup packed brown sugar
- 2 teaspoons baking powder
- 1½ teaspoons apple pie spice
- ¼ teaspoon salt
- 3 large eggs
- 1⅔ cups 2% milk, divided
- 1½ teaspoons vanilla extract
- 3 medium apples, peeled and finely chopped
  Vanilla ice cream, optional

1. In a large bowl, whisk oats, flour, brown sugar, baking powder, pie spice and salt. In a small bowl, whisk eggs, 1 cup milk and vanilla until blended. Add to oat mixture, stirring just until moistened. Fold in apples.

2. Transfer to a greased 3-qt. slow cooker. Cook mixture, covered, on low 4-5 hours or until apples are tender and top is set.

3. Stir in remaining milk. Serve warm or cold, with ice cream if desired.

Contest Winner

Bavarian Pork Loin

I got the recipe for this tender pork roast from an aunt, who made it all the time. What a delicious taste sensation with sauerkraut, carrots, onions and apples.

—EDIE DESPAIN LOGAN, UT

PREP: 25 MIN.
COOK: 6 HOURS + STANDING
MAKES: 10 SERVINGS

- 1 boneless pork loin roast (3 to 4 pounds)
- 1 can (14 ounces) Bavarian sauerkraut, rinsed and drained
- 1¾ cups chopped carrots
- 1 large onion, finely chopped
- ½ cup unsweetened apple juice
- 2 teaspoons dried parsley flakes
- 3 large tart apples, peeled and quartered

1. Cut roast in half; place in a 5-qt. slow cooker. In a small bowl, combine the sauerkraut, carrots, onion, apple juice and parsley; spoon over roast. Cover and cook on low for 4 hours.

2. Add apples to slow cooker. Cover and cook 2-3 hours longer or until meat is tender. Remove roast; let stand for 10 minutes before slicing. Serve with sauerkraut mixture.

ONION-FREE HANDS

To remove the onion smell after you've finished chopping, sprinkle your hands with table salt, rub them together a few times, then rinse. Presto!

—CONNIE S. AMHERST, OH

Butternut Squash with Whole Grains

Fresh thyme really shines in this hearty slow-cooked side featuring nutritious whole grains, vitamin-packed spinach and colorful winter squash.

—*TASTE OF HOME* TEST KITCHEN

PREP: 15 MIN. • **COOK:** 4 HOURS
MAKES: 12 SERVINGS (¾ CUP EACH)

- 1 medium butternut squash (about 3 pounds), cut into ½-inch cubes
- 1 cup uncooked whole grain brown and red rice blend
- 1 medium onion, chopped
- ½ cup water
- 3 garlic cloves, minced
- 2 teaspoons minced fresh thyme or ½ teaspoon dried thyme
- ½ teaspoon salt
- ¼ teaspoon pepper
- 1 can (14½ ounces) vegetable broth
- 1 package (6 ounces) fresh baby spinach

1. In a 4-qt. slow cooker, combine the first eight ingredients. Stir in broth.
2. Cook, covered, on low 4-5 hours or until grains are tender. Stir in spinach before serving.
NOTE *This recipe was tested with RiceSelect Royal Blend Whole Grain Texmati Brown & Red Rice with Barley and Rye. Look for it in the rice aisle.*

Spiced Split Pea Soup

A hint of curry adds the perfect amount of kick to this family-pleasing soup. Just assemble the ingredients in the slow cooker early in the day and come back at night for a filling meal.

—**SUE MOHRE** MOUNT GILEAD, OH

PREP: 25 MIN. • **COOK:** 7 HOURS
MAKES: 10 SERVINGS (2½ QUARTS)

- 4 cups reduced-sodium chicken broth
- 1 cup dried green split peas
- 2 medium potatoes, chopped
- 2 medium carrots, halved and thinly sliced
- 1 medium onion, chopped
- 1 celery rib, thinly sliced
- 3 garlic cloves, minced
- 3 bay leaves
- 4 teaspoons curry powder
- 1 teaspoon ground cumin
- ½ teaspoon coarsely ground pepper
- ½ teaspoon ground coriander
- 1 can (28 ounces) diced tomatoes, undrained

In a 4-qt. slow cooker, combine the first 12 ingredients. Cover and cook on low for 7-9 hours or until peas are tender. Add tomatoes; heat through. Discard bay leaves.

RISE & SHINE

We all know breakfast is the most important meal, so start your day right with some slow-cooked comfort. Kick back and relax while these brunch favorites cook away.

Chili & Cheese Crustless Quiche

This Tex-Mex egg casserole is great for brunch or any meal of the day. If you want to serve it for dinner, just add a green salad.

—**GAIL WATKINS** NORWALK, CA

PREP: 15 MIN. • **COOK:** 3 HOURS + STANDING • **MAKES:** 6 SERVINGS

- 3 **corn tortillas (6 inches)**
- 2 **cans (4 ounces each) whole green chilies**
- 1 **can (15 ounces) chili con carne**
- 1½ **cups (6 ounces) shredded cheddar cheese, divided**
- 4 **large eggs**
- 1½ **cups 2% milk**
- 1 **cup biscuit/baking mix**
- ¼ **teaspoon salt**
- ¼ **teaspoon pepper**
- 1 **teaspoon hot pepper sauce, optional**
- 1 **can (4 ounces) chopped green chilies**
- 2 **medium tomatoes, sliced**
  Sour cream, optional

1. In a greased 4- or 5-qt. slow cooker, layer tortillas, whole green chilies, chili con carne and 1 cup cheese.
2. In a small bowl, whisk eggs, milk, biscuit mix, salt, pepper and, if desired, pepper sauce until blended; pour into slow cooker. Top with chopped green chilies and tomatoes.

3. Cook, covered, on low 3-4 hours or until a thermometer reads 160°, sprinkling with remaining cheese during the last 30 minutes of cooking. Turn off slow cooker; remove insert. Let stand 15 minutes before serving. If desired, top with sour cream.

Carrot Cake Oatmeal

This warm breakfast cereal made in the slow cooker is a great way to get your veggies in the morning. For the extra crunch, I garnish individual servings with ground walnuts or pecans.

—**DEBBIE KAIN** COLORADO SPRINGS, CO

PREP: 10 MIN. • **COOK:** 6 HOURS • **MAKES:** 8 SERVINGS

- 4½ **cups water**
- 1 **can (20 ounces) crushed pineapple, undrained**
- 2 **cups shredded carrots**
- 1 **cup steel-cut oats**
- 1 **cup raisins**
- 2 **teaspoons ground cinnamon**
- 1 **teaspoon pumpkin pie spice**
  Brown sugar, optional

In a 4-qt. slow cooker coated with cooking spray, combine the first seven ingredients. Cover and cook on low for 6-8 hours or until oats are tender and liquid is absorbed. Sprinkle with brown sugar if desired.

Slow Cooker Breakfast Casserole

Here's a breakfast casserole that is very easy on the cook. I can make it the night before and it's waiting in the morning. It's the perfect recipe when I have weekend guests.

—**ELLIE STUTHEIT** LAS VEGAS, NV

PREP: 25 MIN. • **COOK:** 7 HOURS • **MAKES:** 12 SERVINGS

- 1 package (30 ounces) frozen shredded hash brown potatoes
- 1 pound bulk pork sausage, cooked and drained
- 1 medium onion, chopped
- 1 can (4 ounces) chopped green chilies
- 1½ cups (6 ounces) shredded cheddar cheese
- 12 large eggs
- 1 cup 2% milk
- ½ teaspoon salt
- ½ teaspoon pepper

In a greased 5- or 6-qt. slow cooker, layer half the potatoes, sausage, onion, chilies and cheese. Repeat layers. In a large bowl, whisk the eggs, milk, salt and pepper; pour over top. Cover and cook on low for 7-9 hours or until eggs are set.

Raisin Nut Oatmeal

There's no better feeling than waking up to a hot, ready-to-eat breakfast. The oats, fruit and spices in this homey meal cook together while you sleep!

—**VALERIE SAUBER** ADELANTO, CA

PREP: 10 MIN. • **COOK:** 7 HOURS • **MAKES:** 6 SERVINGS

- 3½ cups fat-free milk
- 1 large apple, peeled and chopped
- ¾ cup steel-cut oats
- ¾ cup raisins
- 3 tablespoons brown sugar
- 4½ teaspoons butter, melted
- ¾ teaspoon ground cinnamon
- ½ teaspoon salt
- ¼ cup chopped pecans

In a 3-qt. slow cooker coated with cooking spray, combine the first eight ingredients. Cover and cook mixture on low for 7-8 hours or until liquid is absorbed. Spoon oatmeal into bowls; sprinkle with pecans.

NOTE *You may substitute 1½ cups quick-cooking oats for the steel-cut oats and increase the fat-free milk to 4½ cups.*

Slow Cooker Spiced Poached Pears

I love this dessert because the pretty pears are mostly prepared in advance, making it the ultimate easy treat to serve at dinner parties.

—**JILL MANT** DENVER, CO

PREP: 25 MIN. • **COOK:** 4 HOURS
MAKES: 8 SERVINGS

- 1½ cups dry red wine or cranberry juice
- ⅓ cup packed brown sugar
- 2 tablespoons dried cherries
- 1 tablespoon ground cinnamon
- 1 whole star anise
- 1 dried Sichuan peppercorn, optional
- 4 ripe Bosc pears

GANACHE

- 6 ounces bittersweet chocolate, chopped
- ¼ cup heavy whipping cream

TOPPINGS

- 2 tablespoons pine nuts
- Fresh blackberries
- Sweetened whipped cream, optional

1. In a 3-qt. slow cooker, mix wine, brown sugar, cherries, cinnamon, star anise and, if desired, peppercorn until blended. Peel and cut pears lengthwise in half. Remove cores, leaving a small well in the center of each. Arrange pears in wine mixture.

2. Cook, covered, on low 4-5 hours or until pears are almost tender. Discard star anise and peppercorn.

3. Place chocolate in a small bowl. In a small saucepan, bring cream just to a boil. Pour over chocolate; stir with a whisk until smooth.

4. To serve, remove the pears to dessert dishes; drizzle with some of the poaching liquid. Spoon ganache into wells of pears. Top with pine nuts and blackberries. If desired, serve with whipped cream.

Contest Winner

Cheesy Cauliflower Soup

If you prefer a chunky soup, skip the blender step and stir the cheese and cream into the slow cooker, then heat on high until cheese is melted.

—**SHERYL PUNTER** WOODSTOCK, ON

PREP: 25 MIN. • **COOK:** 5½ HOURS
MAKES: 9 SERVINGS (2¼ QUARTS)

- 1 large head cauliflower, broken into florets
- 2 celery ribs
- 2 large carrots
- 1 large green pepper
- 1 small sweet red pepper
- 1 medium red onion
- 4 cups chicken broth
- ½ teaspoon Worcestershire sauce
- ¼ teaspoon salt
- ⅛ teaspoon pepper
- 2 cups (8 ounces) shredded cheddar cheese
- 2 cups half-and-half cream

1. Place cauliflower in a 4-qt. slow cooker. Chop the celery, carrots, peppers and onion; add to slow cooker. Stir in the broth, Worcestershire sauce, salt and pepper. Cover and cook on low for 5-6 hours or until vegetables are tender.

2. In a blender, process the soup in batches until smooth. Return all to slow cooker; stir in cheese and cream. Cover and cook on high for 30 minutes or until cheese is melted.

Spiced Cran-Apple Brisket

Kids and adults alike seem to become instant fans of this dish after trying it. The apple and cranberry flavors are especially soothing during the winter.

—AYSHA SCHURMAN AMMON, ID

PREP: 20 MIN. • **COOK:** 8 HOURS
MAKES: 9 SERVINGS

- 1 fresh beef brisket (4 pounds)
- ½ cup apple butter
- ¼ cup ruby port wine
- 2 tablespoons cider vinegar
- 1 teaspoon coarsely ground pepper
- ½ teaspoon salt
- 1 medium tart apple, peeled and cubed
- 1 celery rib, chopped
- 1 small red onion, chopped
- ⅓ cup dried apples, diced
- ⅓ cup dried cranberries
- 2 garlic cloves, minced
- 1 tablespoon cornstarch
- 3 tablespoons cold water

1. Cut brisket in half; place in a 5-qt. slow cooker.

2. In a large bowl, combine the apple butter, wine, vinegar, pepper and salt. Stir in tart apple, celery, onion, dried apples, cranberries and garlic. Pour over brisket. Cover and cook on low for 8-10 hours or until meat is tender.

3. Remove meat to a serving platter; keep warm. Skim fat from cooking juices; transfer to a small saucepan. Bring liquid to a boil.

4. Combine cornstarch and water until smooth. Gradually stir into the pan. Bring to a boil; cook and stir for 2 minutes or until thickened. Serve with meat.

NOTES *This is a fresh beef brisket, not corned beef. This recipe was tested with commercially prepared apple butter.*

Shoepeg Corn Side Dish

I took this dish to a potluck and everyone asked for the recipe. If the shoepeg corn isn't available in your grocery store, then regular canned corn works well, too.

—GLORIA SCHUTZ TRENTON, IL

PREP: 20 MIN. • **COOK:** 3 HOURS
MAKES: 8 SERVINGS

- 1 can (14½ ounces) french-style green beans, drained
- 2 cans (7 ounces each) white or shoepeg corn
- 1 can (10¾ ounces) condensed cream of mushroom soup, undiluted
- 1 jar (4½ ounces) sliced mushrooms, drained
- ½ cup slivered almonds
- ½ cup shredded cheddar cheese
- ½ cup sour cream
- ¾ cup french-fried onions

In a 3-qt. slow cooker, combine the first seven ingredients. Cover and cook on low for 3-4 hours or until vegetables are tender, stirring occasionally. Sprinkle with onions during the last 15 minutes of cooking.

Contest Winner

Barbecued Party Starters

These sweet and tangy bites are sure to tide everyone over until dinner. At the buffet, set out some fun toothpicks to make for easy nibbling.

—ANASTASIA WEISS PUNXSUTAWNEY, PA

PREP: 30 MIN. • **COOK:** 2¼ HOURS
MAKES: 16 SERVINGS (⅓ CUP EACH)

- 1 **pound ground beef**
- ¼ **cup finely chopped onion**
- 1 **package (16 ounces) miniature hot dogs, drained**
- 1 **jar (12 ounces) apricot preserves**
- 1 **cup barbecue sauce**
- 1 **can (20 ounces) pineapple chunks, drained**

1. In a large bowl, combine beef and onion, mixing lightly but thoroughly. Shape into 1-in. balls. In a large skillet over medium heat, cook meatballs in two batches until cooked through, turning occasionally.
2. Using a slotted spoon, transfer meatballs to a 3-qt. slow cooker. Add hot dogs; stir in preserves and barbecue sauce. Cook, covered, on high 2-3 hours or until heated through.
3. Stir in pineapple; cook, covered, 15-20 minutes longer or until heated through.

Contest Winner

Caramel Apple Cider

Spiced with cinnamon sticks, allspice and caramel, this warm-you-up sipper is sure to chase away winter's chill. Serve brimming mugs of the hot beverage alongside a platter of cookies at your next special gathering.

—TASTE OF HOME TEST KITCHEN

PREP: 5 MIN. • **COOK:** 2 HOURS
MAKES: 12 SERVINGS (¾ CUP EACH)

- 8 **cups apple cider or juice**
- 1 **cup caramel flavoring syrup**
- ¼ **cup lemon juice**
- 1 **vanilla bean**
- 2 **cinnamon sticks (3 inches)**
- 1 **tablespoon whole allspice**
  Whipped cream, hot caramel ice cream topping and cinnamon sticks (3 inches), optional

1. In a 3-qt. slow cooker, combine the apple cider, caramel syrup and lemon juice. Split vanilla bean and scrape seeds; add seeds to cider mixture. Place the bean, cinnamon sticks and allspice on a double thickness of cheesecloth; bring up corners of cloth and tie with string to form a bag. Add to cider mixture.
2. Cover and cook on low for 2-3 hours or until heated through. Discard spice bag. Pour cider into mugs; garnish with whipped cream, caramel topping and additional cinnamon sticks if desired.
NOTE *This recipe was tested with Torani brand flavoring syrup. Look for it in the coffee section.*

Potluck Macaroni and Cheese

Mac and cheese is one of the most beloved comfort foods. My slow cooker version is soothing, satisfying and creamy, along with giving you lots of time to work on other things!

—JENNIFER BABCOCK CHICOPEE, MA

PREP: 25 MIN. • **COOK:** 2 HOURS
MAKES: 16 SERVINGS (¾ CUP EACH)

- 3 **cups uncooked elbow macaroni**
- 1 **package (16 ounces) process cheese (Velveeta), cubed**
- 2 **cups (8 ounces) shredded Mexican cheese blend**
- 2 **cups (8 ounces) shredded white cheddar cheese**
- 1¾ **cups whole milk**
- 1 **can (12 ounces) evaporated milk**
- ¾ **cup butter, melted**
- 3 **large eggs, lightly beaten**

1. Cook macaroni according to package directions for al dente; drain. Transfer to a greased 5-qt. slow cooker. Stir in remaining ingredients.
2. Cook, covered, on low 2-2½ hours or until a thermometer reads at least 160°, stirring once.

Chicken Thighs with Ginger-Peach Sauce

This slightly sweet Asian chicken is a breeze to make, and the peaches bring a little summer to the table any time of year.

—LISA RENSHAW KANSAS CITY, MO

PREP: 15 MIN. • **COOK:** 4 HOURS • **MAKES:** 10 SERVINGS

- 10 **boneless skinless chicken thighs (about 2½ pounds)**
- 1 **cup sliced peeled fresh or frozen peaches**
- 1 **cup golden raisins**
- 1 **cup peach preserves**
- ⅓ **cup chili sauce**
- 2 **tablespoons minced crystallized ginger**
- 1 **tablespoon reduced-sodium soy sauce**
- 1 **tablespoon minced garlic**
  Hot cooked rice, optional

1. Place chicken in a 4-qt. slow cooker coated with the cooking spray. Top with peaches and raisins. In a small bowl, combine the preserves, chili sauce, ginger, soy sauce and garlic. Spoon over top.
2. Cover and cook on low for 4-5 hours or until chicken is tender. Serve with rice if desired.

Black-Eyed Peas & Ham

We have these slow-cooked black-eyed peas often at our house. Ham and bacon make them extra delicious.

—DAWN FRIHAUF FORT MORGAN, CO

PREP: 20 MIN. + SOAKING • **COOK:** 5 HOURS
MAKES: 12 SERVINGS (¾ CUP EACH)

- 1 **package (16 ounces) dried black-eyed peas, rinsed and sorted**
- ½ **pound fully cooked boneless ham, finely chopped**
- 1 **medium onion, finely chopped**
- 1 **medium sweet red pepper, finely chopped**
- 5 **bacon strips, cooked and crumbled**
- 1 **large jalapeno pepper, seeded and finely chopped**
- 2 **garlic cloves, minced**
- 1½ **teaspoons ground cumin**
- 1 **teaspoon reduced-sodium chicken bouillon granules**
- ½ **teaspoon salt**
- ½ **teaspoon cayenne pepper**
- ¼ **teaspoon pepper**
- 6 **cups water**
  Minced fresh cilantro, optional
  Hot cooked rice

1. Rinse black-eyed peas. Place in a Dutch oven; add water to cover by 2 in. Bring to a boil; boil 2 minutes. Remove from heat; let soak, covered, 1-4 hours. Drain and rinse peas, discarding liquid.
2. Transfer peas to a 6-qt. slow cooker, add the next 12 ingredients. Cover and cook on low for 5-7 hours or until peas are tender. Sprinkle with cilantro if desired. Serve with rice.
NOTE *Wear disposable gloves when cutting hot peppers; the oils can burn skin. Avoid touching your face.*

Contest Winner

Saucy Pork Chops

I don't always have a lot of time to cook, so I've come to rely on my slow cooker a lot. I fix these tangy chops at least once a week. The meat's so tender, you can cut it with a fork.

—JENNIFER RUBERG TWO HARBORS, MN

PREP: 15 MIN. • **COOK:** 4 HOURS • **MAKES:** 4 SERVINGS

- 4 **bone-in pork loin chops (8 ounces each)**
- 1 **teaspoon garlic powder**
- ½ **teaspoon salt**
- ¼ **teaspoon pepper**
- 2 **tablespoons canola oil**
- 2 **cups ketchup**
- ½ **cup packed brown sugar**
- 1 **teaspoon liquid smoke, optional**

1. Sprinkle pork chops with garlic powder, salt and pepper. In a large skillet, brown chops in oil on both sides; drain.
2. In a small bowl, combine the ketchup, brown sugar and the liquid smoke if desired. Pour half of the sauce into a 3-qt. slow cooker. Top with pork chops and remaining sauce. Cover and cook on low for 4-5 hours or until the meat is tender.

Warm Crab Dip

Slow-cooked dips are ideal for parties since they free up the oven. Leftovers—if you have any—are great served over a baked potato the next day.
—**SUSAN D'AMORE** WEST CHESTER, PA

PREP: 20 MIN. • **COOK:** 2 HOURS
MAKES: 2⅓ CUPS

- 1 package (8 ounces) cream cheese, softened
- 2 green onions, chopped
- ¼ cup chopped sweet red pepper
- 2 tablespoons minced fresh parsley
- 2 tablespoons mayonnaise
- 1 tablespoon Dijon mustard
- 1 teaspoon Worcestershire sauce
- ¼ teaspoon salt
- ¼ teaspoon pepper
- 2 cans (6 ounces each) lump crabmeat, drained
- 2 tablespoons capers, drained
  Dash hot pepper sauce
  Assorted crackers

1. In a 1½-qt. slow cooker, combine the first nine ingredients; stir in crab.
2. Cover and cook mixture on low for 1-2 hours. Stir in capers and pepper sauce; cook 30 minutes longer to allow flavors to blend. Serve with crackers.

Cheddar Creamed Corn

I brought this super-simple recipe to a school potluck once and it was gone in no time. I've been asked to bring it to every function since.
—**JESSICA MAXWELL** ENGLEWOOD, NJ

PREP: 10 MIN. • **COOK:** 3 HOURS
MAKES: 9 SERVINGS

- 2 packages (one 16 ounces, one 12 ounces) frozen corn, thawed
- 1 package (8 ounces) cream cheese, cubed
- ¾ cup shredded cheddar cheese
- ¼ cup butter, melted
- ¼ cup heavy whipping cream
- ½ teaspoon salt
- ¼ teaspoon pepper

In a 3- or 4-qt. slow cooker, combine all ingredients. Cook, covered, on low 3-3½ hours or until cheese is melted and corn is tender. Stir mixture just before serving.

Contest Winner

Louisiana Red Beans and Rice

Smoked turkey sausage and red pepper flakes add zip to this slow-cooked version of the New Orleans classic. For more heat, add red pepper sauce at the table.
—**JULIA BUSHREE** COMMERCE CITY, CO

PREP: 20 MIN. • **COOK:** 8 HOURS
MAKES: 8 SERVINGS

- 4 cans (16 ounces each) kidney beans, rinsed and drained
- 1 can (14½ ounces) diced tomatoes, undrained
- 1 package (14 ounces) smoked turkey sausage, sliced
- 3 celery ribs, chopped
- 1 large onion, chopped
- 1 cup chicken broth
- 1 medium green pepper, chopped
- 1 small sweet red pepper, chopped
- 6 garlic cloves, minced
- 1 bay leaf
- ½ teaspoon crushed red pepper flakes
- 2 green onions, chopped
  Hot cooked rice

1. In a 4- or 5-qt. slow cooker, combine the first 11 ingredients. Cook, covered, on low 8-10 hours or until the vegetables are tender.
2. Stir before serving. Remove bay leaf. Serve with green onions and rice.
FREEZE OPTION *Discard bay leaf and freeze cooled bean mixture in freezer containers. To use, partially thaw in refrigerator overnight. Heat through in a saucepan, stirring occasionally and adding a little broth or water if necessary. Serve as directed.*

Slow-Cooked Turkey with Berry Compote

We love to eat turkey, and this delicious dish allows us to enjoy it without heating up the house. The berries make the perfect accompaniment.

—MARGARET BRACHER ROBERTSDALE, AL

PREP: 35 MIN. • **COOK:** 3 HOURS
MAKES: 12 SERVINGS (3¼ CUP COMPOTE)

- 1 teaspoon salt
- ½ teaspoon garlic powder
- ½ teaspoon dried thyme
- ½ teaspoon pepper
- 2 boneless turkey breast halves (2 pounds each)
- ⅓ cup water

COMPOTE
- 2 medium apples, peeled and finely chopped
- 2 cups fresh raspberries
- 2 cups fresh blueberries
- 1 cup white grape juice
- ¼ teaspoon crushed red pepper flakes
- ¼ teaspoon ground ginger

1. Mix salt, garlic powder, thyme and pepper; rub over turkey breasts. Place in a 5- or 6-qt. slow cooker. Pour water around turkey. Cook, covered, on low 3-4 hours (a thermometer inserted in turkey should read at least 165°).
2. Remove turkey from slow cooker; tent with foil. Let stand 10 minutes before slicing.
3. Meanwhile, in a large saucepan, combine compote ingredients. Bring to a boil. Reduce heat to medium; cook, uncovered, 15-20 minutes or until slightly thickened and apples are tender, stirring occasionally. Serve turkey with compote.

Beef & Veggie Sloppy Joes

I came up with this veggie-filled recipe, and now my three kids often request it. It's a new take on sloppy joes that reminds me of my own childhood.

—MEGAN NIEBUHR YAKIMA, WA

PREP: 35 MIN. • **COOK:** 5 HOURS
MAKES: 12 SERVINGS

- 4 medium carrots, shredded (about 3½ cups)
- 1 medium yellow summer squash, shredded (about 2 cups)
- 1 medium zucchini, shredded (about 2 cups)
- 1 medium sweet red pepper, finely chopped
- 2 medium tomatoes, seeded and chopped
- 1 small red onion, finely chopped
- ½ cup ketchup
- 3 tablespoons minced fresh basil or 3 teaspoons dried basil
- 3 tablespoons molasses
- 2 tablespoons cider vinegar
- 2 garlic cloves, minced
- ½ teaspoon salt
- ½ teaspoon pepper
- 2 pounds lean ground beef (90% lean)
- 12 whole wheat hamburger buns, split

1. In a 5- or 6-qt. slow cooker, combine the first 13 ingredients. In a large skillet, cook beef over medium heat 8-10 minutes or until no longer pink, breaking into crumbles. Drain; transfer beef to the slow cooker. Stir to combine.
2. Cook, covered, on low 5-6 hours or until heated through and vegetables are tender. Using a slotted spoon, serve beef mixture on buns.

SLOPPY JOE OMELET

Next time you have leftover sloppy joe meat, make an omelet. Spread reheated meat on top, sprinkle with shredded cheese, fold half the omelet over and enjoy!

—JIM B. PORTAGE, MI

COOKIES, BARS & CANDIES

Sometimes you need a little pick-me-up to get through the day, and these sweet treats can do the trick! Turn here for midday munchies, late-night snacks, coffee-break bites, bake-sale favorites and so much more!

Blueberry Crumb Bars

Think of these bars as blueberry crisp turned into a hand-held treat. Oats and blueberries come together in a sweet, no-fuss dish that's perfect anytime.

—**BLAIR LONERGAN** ROCHELLE, VA

PREP: 20 MIN. • **BAKE:** 20 MIN. + COOLING
MAKES: 1 DOZEN

- 1 **package yellow cake mix (regular size)**
- 2½ **cups old-fashioned oats**
- ¾ **cup butter, melted**
- 1 **jar (12 ounces) blueberry preserves**
- ⅓ **cup fresh blueberries**
- 1 **tablespoon lemon juice**
- ⅓ **cup finely chopped pecans**
- 1 **teaspoon ground cinnamon**

1. Preheat oven to 350°. In a large bowl, combine cake mix, oats and butter until crumbly. Press 3 cups into a greased 9-in. square baking pan. Bake 15 minutes. Cool on a wire rack for 5 minutes.

2. Meanwhile, in a small bowl, combine preserves, blueberries and lemon juice. Spread over crust. Stir pecans and cinnamon into remaining crumb mixture. Sprinkle over top.

3. Bake 18-20 minutes or until lightly browned. Cool on a wire rack before cutting into bars.

Contest Winner

Creamy Caramels

I found a recipe for soft, buttery caramels in a local newspaper several years ago and have been making them ever since. They beat the store-bought version!

—**MARCIE WOLFE** WILLIAMSBURG, VA

PREP: 10 MIN. • **COOK:** 30 MIN. + COOLING
MAKES: 2½ POUNDS

- 1 **teaspoon plus 1 cup butter, divided**
- 1 **cup sugar**
- 1 **cup dark corn syrup**
- 1 **can (14 ounces) sweetened condensed milk**
- 1 **teaspoon vanilla extract**

1. Line an 8-in. square pan with foil; grease the foil with 1 teaspoon butter and set aside.

2. In a large heavy saucepan, combine the sugar, corn syrup and remaining butter; bring to a boil over medium heat, stirring constantly. Boil slowly for 4 minutes without stirring.

3. Remove from the heat; stir in the milk. Reduce heat to medium-low and cook until a candy thermometer reads 238° (soft-ball stage), stirring constantly. Remove from the heat; stir in vanilla.

4. Pour into prepared pan (do not scrape saucepan). Cool. Using foil, lift candy out of pan. Discard foil; cut candy into 1-in. squares. Wrap individually in waxed paper; twist the ends.

NOTE *We recommend that you test your candy thermometer before each use by bringing water to a boil; the thermometer should read 212°. Adjust your recipe temperature up or down based on your test.*

No-Bake Fudgy Coconut Cookies

My daughter works at a summer camp, so I send her these for the kids. They ask for them every year. Instead of a cookie jar she keeps the treats in a coffee can called "The Wrangler Feeding Trough."

—**SUE KLEMM** RHINELANDER, WI

PREP: 30 MIN. + CHILLING
MAKES: 3½ DOZEN

- 1½ cups sugar
- ⅔ cup 2% milk
- ½ cup baking cocoa
- ½ cup butter, cubed
- ½ teaspoon salt
- ⅓ cup creamy peanut butter
- 1 teaspoon vanilla extract
- 2 cups quick-cooking oats
- 1 cup flaked coconut
- ½ cup white baking chips
- 1 teaspoon shortening

1. In a large saucepan, combine the first five ingredients. Bring to a boil, stirring constantly. Cook and stir 3 minutes.

2. Remove from heat; stir in peanut butter and vanilla until blended. Stir in oats and coconut. Drop mixture by tablespoonfuls onto waxed paper-lined baking sheets.

3. In a microwave, melt baking chips and shortening; stir until smooth. Drizzle over cookies; refrigerate until set. Store in airtight containers.

Vanilla Crescents

These crescent cookies are especially cozy at Christmastime, but they are truly wonderful all year long. Try them dunked into milk, tea or coffee.

—**CARA MCDONALD** WINTER PARK, CO

PREP: 20 MIN. • **BAKE:** 10 MIN./BATCH
MAKES: 4 DOZEN

- 1 cup unsalted butter, softened
- ½ cup sugar
- 1 teaspoon vanilla extract
- ⅛ teaspoon almond extract
- 2 cups all-purpose flour
- 1¼ cups ground almonds
- ½ teaspoon salt
  Confectioners' sugar

1. Preheat oven to 350°. In a large bowl, cream butter and sugar until light and fluffy. Beat in extracts. In another bowl, whisk flour, almonds and salt; gradually beat into creamed mixture.

2. Divide dough into four portions. On a lightly floured surface, roll each portion into a 24-in. rope. Cut ropes crosswise into twelve 2-in. logs; shape each into a crescent. Place 1½ in. apart on ungreased baking sheets.

3. Bake 10-12 minutes or until set. Cool on pans 2 minutes before removing to a wire rack. Dust warm cookies with confectioners' sugar.

Raspberry Cheesecake Bars

My family's love of raspberries and cheesecake make this a perfect dessert for us. The creamy, buttery treat is best eaten with a fork.

—JILL COX LINCOLN, NE

PREP: 30 MIN. • **BAKE:** 35 MIN. + CHILLING • **MAKES:** 2 DOZEN

- 1 cup all-purpose flour
- 1 cup finely chopped pecans
- ⅓ cup packed brown sugar
- ¼ teaspoon ground cinnamon
- ¼ teaspoon salt
- ⅓ cup cold butter
- 1 jar (12 ounces) seedless raspberry jam, divided
- 2 packages (8 ounces each) cream cheese, softened
- ¾ cup sugar
- ½ teaspoon grated lemon peel
- ½ teaspoon vanilla extract
- 3 large eggs, lightly beaten

TOPPING
- 1½ cups (12 ounces) sour cream
- 3 tablespoons sugar
- 1 teaspoon vanilla extract

1. In a small bowl, combine the flour, pecans, brown sugar, cinnamon and salt. Cut in butter until crumbly. Press onto the bottom of a greased 13x9-in. baking dish. Bake at 350° for 10-12 minutes or until lightly browned. Cool on a wire rack for 5 minutes.

2. Set aside 3 tablespoons jam; spread remaining jam over crust. In a large bowl, beat cream cheese and sugar until smooth. Beat in lemon peel and vanilla. Add eggs; beat on low speed just until combined. Spread evenly over jam. Bake for 20-25 minutes or until almost set.

3. In another bowl, combine the sour cream, sugar and vanilla; spread over cheesecake. Warm remaining jam and swirl over top. Bake 5-7 minutes or just until set.

4. Cool on a wire rack for 1 hour. Refrigerate for at least 2 hours. Cut into bars.

Fudgy Brownies with Peanut Butter Pudding Frosting

Rich brownies, topped with a peanut butter pudding frosting, make this a recipe the whole family will love. They're ideal for a potluck, bake sale or yummy after-dinner treat.

—AMY CROOK SYRACUSE, UT

PREP: 20 MIN. • **BAKE:** 25 MIN. + CHILLING • **MAKES:** 2½ DOZEN

- 1 package fudge brownie mix (13x9-inch pan size)
- 1½ cups confectioners' sugar
- ½ cup butter, softened
- 2 to 3 tablespoons peanut butter
- 2 tablespoons cold 2% milk
- 4½ teaspoons instant vanilla pudding mix
- 1 can (16 ounces) chocolate fudge frosting

1. Prepare and bake brownies according to package directions. Cool on a wire rack.

2. Meanwhile, in a small bowl, beat the confectioners' sugar, butter, peanut butter, milk and pudding mix until smooth. Spread over brownies. Refrigerate for 30 minutes or until firm. Frost with the chocolate fudge frosting just before cutting.

2. Preheat oven to 375°. On a lightly floured surface, roll dough to ½-in. thickness. Cut with a floured 2-in. cookie cutter. Place 1 in. apart on ungreased baking sheets.
3. Bake 10-12 minutes or until edges begin to brown. Cool on pans 5 minutes. Remove to wire racks to cool completely.
4. For frosting, in a large bowl, beat confectioners' sugar, butter, shortening, extracts and enough milk to reach desired consistency. Spread over the cookies. If desired, sprinkle with nonpareils.

Macadamia-Coconut Candy Clusters

My creamy candies are bake sale winners, though they're also great for cookie platters or gift-giving. They're a nice change from milk- or dark-chocolate clusters.
—**LORI BONDURANT** PADUCAH, KY

PREP: 25 MIN. + STANDING • **MAKES:** 3½ DOZEN

- 1 **package (10 to 12 ounces) white baking chips**
- 2 **teaspoons shortening**
- 1 **cup flaked coconut, toasted**
- ½ **cup crisp rice cereal**
- ½ **cup chopped macadamia nuts, toasted**

1. In a microwave, melt baking chips and shortening; stir until smooth. Add the coconut, cereal and nuts.
2. Drop by teaspoonfuls onto waxed paper; let stand until set. Store in an airtight container at room temperature.

Thick Sugar Cookies

Thicker than the norm, this sugar cookie is like one you might find at a good bakery. My children often request these for their birthdays and are always happy to help decorate.
—**HEATHER BIEDLER** MARTINSBURG, WV

PREP: 25 MIN. + CHILLING • **BAKE:** 10 MIN./BATCH + COOLING
MAKES: ABOUT 3 DOZEN

- 1 **cup butter, softened**
- 1 **cup sugar**
- 2 **large eggs**
- 3 **large egg yolks**
- 1½ **teaspoons vanilla extract**
- ¾ **teaspoon almond extract**
- 3½ **cups all-purpose flour**
- 1½ **teaspoons baking powder**
- ¼ **teaspoon salt**

FROSTING
- 4 **cups confectioners' sugar**
- ½ **cup butter, softened**
- ½ **cup shortening**
- 1 **teaspoon vanilla extract**
- ½ **teaspoon almond extract**
- 2 **to 3 tablespoons 2% milk**
  Assorted colored nonpareils, optional

1. In a large bowl, cream butter and sugar until light and fluffy. Beat in eggs, egg yolks and extracts. In another bowl, whisk flour, baking powder and salt; gradually beat into creamed mixture. Shape into a disk; wrap in plastic wrap. Refrigerate 1 hour or until firm enough to roll.

Glazed Maple Shortbread Cookies

While visiting friends in the United States, I make sure to purchase maple syrup and maple sugar, because it's the best I've ever had. These delicious cookies can be decorated with sprinkles, but their shape makes them fancy just as is.

—LORRAINE CALAND SHUNIAH, ON

PREP: 25 MIN. + CHILLING
BAKE: 20 MIN. + COOLING
MAKES: 1½ DOZEN

- 1 **cup butter, softened**
- ¼ **cup sugar**
- 3 **tablespoons cornstarch**
- 1 **teaspoon maple flavoring**
- 1¾ **cups all-purpose flour**
GLAZE
- ¾ **cup plus 1 tablespoon confectioners' sugar**
- ⅓ **cup maple syrup**

1. In a large bowl, beat butter, sugar and cornstarch until blended. Beat in flavoring. Gradually beat in flour.
2. Shape dough into a disk; wrap in plastic wrap. Refrigerate 45 minutes or until firm enough to roll.
3. Preheat oven to 325°. On a lightly floured surface, roll out dough to ¼-in. thickness. Cut with a floured 2¾-in. leaf-shaped cookie cutter. Place cookies 1 in. apart on parchment paper-lined baking sheets.
4. Bake 20-25 minutes or until edges are light brown. Remove from pans to wire racks to cool completely.
5. In a small bowl, mix confectioners' sugar and maple syrup until smooth. Spread over the cookies. Let stand until set.

Mini Cinnamon Roll Cookies

Intense cinnamon flavor fills this luscious cross between a snickerdoodle and a cinnamon roll. They taste best with a cup of freshly-brewed coffee.

—MARY GAUNTT DENTON, TX

PREP: 1 HOUR
BAKE: 10 MIN./BATCH + COOLING
MAKES: ABOUT 2½ DOZEN

- 1 **cup butter, softened**
- 1¾ **cups sugar, divided**
- 3 **large egg yolks**
- 1 **tablespoon plus 1 teaspoon honey, divided**
- 1 **teaspoon vanilla extract**
- 2½ **cups all-purpose flour**
- 1 **teaspoon baking powder**
- ½ **teaspoon salt**
- ½ **teaspoon cream of tartar**
- 1 **tablespoon ground cinnamon**
- 8 **ounces white baking chocolate, chopped**

1. In a large bowl, cream butter and 1¼ cups sugar until light and fluffy. Beat in the egg yolks, 1 tablespoon honey and vanilla. Combine the flour, baking powder, salt and cream of tartar; gradually add to creamed mixture and mix well.
2. Shape a heaping tablespoonful of dough into a 6-in. log. In a shallow bowl, combine the cinnamon and remaining sugar; roll the log in cinnamon-sugar. Loosely coil log into a spiral shape; place on a greased baking sheet. Repeat, placing cookies 1 in. apart. Sprinkle with remaining cinnamon-sugar.
3. Bake at 350° for 8-10 minutes or until set. Remove to wire racks to cool completely. In a small bowl, melt the baking chocolate with the remaining honey; stir until smooth. Drizzle over cookies. Let stand until set. Store in an airtight container.

Brown Sugar Cutout Cookies

Our neighbor made these for me when I was little, and now I make them for my kids, grandkids and for the children at school. Serve them with milk for the kids and tea for the grown-ups.

—NANCY LYNCH SOMERSET, PA

PREP: 55 MIN. + CHILLING
BAKE: 10 MIN./BATCH + COOLING
MAKES: 7½ DOZEN

- 1 cup butter, softened
- 2 cups packed dark brown sugar
- 3 large eggs
- 6 tablespoons cold water
- 3 tablespoons canola oil
- 1 teaspoon vanilla extract
- 6 cups all-purpose flour
- 1 teaspoon cream of tartar
- 1 teaspoon baking soda
- ½ teaspoon salt

ICING

- 1 cup butter, softened
- 4 teaspoons meringue powder
- 3 teaspoons cream of tartar
- ½ teaspoon salt
- 4 cups confectioners' sugar
- 4 to 6 tablespoons water

1. In a large bowl, cream the butter and brown sugar until light and fluffy. Beat in eggs, water, oil and vanilla. In another bowl, whisk flour, cream of tartar, baking soda and salt; gradually beat into creamed mixture.

2. Divide dough into four portions. Shape each into a disk; wrap in plastic wrap. Refrigerate 2 hours or until firm enough to roll.

3. Preheat oven to 350°. On a lightly floured surface, roll each portion of dough to ⅛-in. thickness. Cut with a floured 2¼-in. fluted square cookie cutter. Place 1 in. apart on greased baking sheets.

4. Bake 7-9 minutes or until bottoms are light brown. Remove from pans to wire racks to cool completely.

5. For icing, in a small bowl, beat the butter, meringue powder, cream of tartar and salt until blended. Beat in confectioners' sugar alternately with enough water to reach a spreading consistency. Spread over cookies. Let stand until set.

NOTE *Meringue powder is available from Wilton Industries. Call 800-794-5866 or visit* wilton.com.

Caramel Pretzel Bites

I created this recipe because I wanted to make my own version of a pretzel log dipped in caramel, chocolate and nuts from a popular candy store.

—MICHILENE KLAVER GRAND RAPIDS, MI

PREP: 45 MIN. + COOLING
MAKES: 6 DOZEN

- 2 teaspoons butter, softened
- 4 cups pretzel sticks
- 2½ cups pecan halves, toasted
- 2¼ cups packed brown sugar
- 1 cup butter, cubed
- 1 cup corn syrup
- 1 can (14 ounces) sweetened condensed milk
- ⅛ teaspoon salt
- 1 teaspoon vanilla extract
- 1 package (11½ ounces) milk chocolate chips
- 1 tablespoon plus 1 teaspoon shortening, divided
- ⅓ cup white baking chips

1. Line a 13x9-in. pan with foil; grease the foil with softened butter. Spread pretzels and pecans on bottom of the prepared pan.

2. In a large heavy saucepan, combine the brown sugar, cubed butter, corn syrup, milk and salt; cook and stir over medium heat until a candy thermometer reads 240°(soft-ball stage). Remove from heat. Stir in the vanilla. Pour over pretzel mixture.

3. In a microwave, melt chocolate chips and 1 tablespoon shortening; stir until smooth. Spread over caramel layer. In microwave, melt baking chips and remaining shortening; stir until smooth. Drizzle over top. Let stand until set.

4. Using foil, lift candy out of pan; remove foil. Using a buttered knife, cut candy into bite-size pieces.

CANDY-MAKING PREP

Making candy is about precision, so be sure to have your ingredients set out and ready before you start making the recipe. Also, for best results, don't substitute or alter the ingredients.

LOADED WITH NUTS

Looking to add a little crunch to your dessert spread? Almonds, peanuts, pistachios and more are here to help. Your crew will go nuts for these sweets!

Spiced Almond Brittle

I like sending homemade goodies to family and friends. When I couldn't decide between brittle and spiced nuts, I combined the two into one treat. One batch fills up about six gift tins.

—**LESLIE DIXON** BOISE, ID

PREP: 15 MIN. • **COOK:** 15 MIN. + COOLING • **MAKES:** 1¼ POUNDS

- 1 **cup sugar**
- ½ **cup light corn syrup**
- ¼ **cup water**
- ¼ **teaspoon salt**
- 1½ **cups unblanched almonds**
- 2 **tablespoons butter**
- ½ **teaspoon pumpkin pie spice**
- ¼ **teaspoon cayenne pepper**
- ¼ **teaspoon dried rosemary, crushed**
- ⅛ **teaspoon ground nutmeg**
- 1 **teaspoon baking soda**

1. Line 15x10x1-in. pan with parchment paper. (Do not spray or grease.)

2. In a large heavy saucepan, combine sugar, corn syrup, water and salt. Bring to a boil, stirring constantly to dissolve sugar. Using a pastry brush dipped in water, wash down the sides of the pan to eliminate sugar crystals. Cook, without stirring, over medium heat until a candy thermometer reads 260° (hard-ball stage).

3. Stir in almonds, butter and seasonings; cook until thermometer reads 300° (hard-crack stage), stirring frequently, about 8 minutes longer.

4. Remove from heat; stir in baking soda. (Mixture will foam.) Immediately pour onto prepared pan, spreading as thin as possible. Cool completely.

5. Break brittle into pieces. Store pieces between layers of waxed paper in an airtight container.

Chocolate Peanut-Butter Crunch Bars

My twist on the classic Rice Krispie bars brings in a salty-sweet twist. The bars feature a peanut butter layer underneath a rich chocolate topping—garnished with peanuts and pretzels.

—**SHERRI MELOTIK** OAK CREEK, WI

PREP: 20 MIN. + CHILLING • **MAKES:** 3 DOZEN

- 3 **cups miniature pretzels, coarsely chopped**
- 10 **tablespoons butter, divided**
- 1 **package (10½ ounces) miniature marshmallows**
- 3 **cups Rice Krispies**
- ½ **cup light corn syrup, divided**
- ¾ **cup peanut butter chips**
- 1 **cup (6 ounces) semisweet chocolate chips**
- ¼ **cup dry roasted peanuts, chopped**

1. Reserve ⅓ cup chopped pretzels. In a large microwave-safe bowl, microwave 6 tablespoons butter on high for 45-60 seconds or until melted. Stir in marshmallows; cook 1 to 1½ minutes or until marshmallows are melted, stirring every 30 seconds. Stir in the Rice Krispies and remaining chopped pretzels. Immediately press into a greased 13x9-in. baking pan.

2. In another microwave-safe bowl, combine 2 tablespoons butter and ¼ cup corn syrup. Microwave, uncovered, on high for 45-60 seconds or until butter is melted, stirring once. Add peanut butter chips; cook 30-40 seconds or until chips are melted, stirring once. Spread over cereal layer.

3. In a microwave-safe bowl, combine the remaining corn syrup and remaining butter. Cook on high for 45-60 seconds or until butter is melted, stirring once. Add chocolate chips; cook 30-40 seconds longer or until chips are melted, stirring once. Spread over top.

4. Sprinkle with peanuts and reserved pretzels; press down gently. Cover and refrigerate 30 minutes or until set. Cut into bars. Store in airtight containers.

NOTE *This recipe was tested in a 1,100-watt microwave.*

Pistachio-Walnut Cookies

I've had this cookie in my baking rotation for many years, and it never fails to please. I prefer pistachio nuts and black walnuts for sprinkling over the cookie cutouts, but get creative and try out whatever nuts you prefer.

—**LORRAINE CALAND** SHUNIAH, ON

PREP: 35 MIN. + CHILLING • **BAKE:** 10 MIN./BATCH + COOLING
MAKES: 4 DOZEN

- ¾ **cup butter, softened**
- ¾ **cup sugar**
- 1 **large egg**
- 1 **teaspoon vanilla extract**
- 2 **cups all-purpose flour**
- 1½ **teaspoons baking powder**
- ¼ **teaspoon ground nutmeg**

TOPPINGS

- 1 **large egg white**
- 1 **teaspoon water**
- ⅔ **cup chopped pistachios**
- ⅔ **cup chopped black walnuts**
  Melted dark chocolate chips, optional

1. In a large bowl, cream butter and sugar until light and fluffy. Beat in egg and vanilla. In another bowl, whisk the flour, baking powder and nutmeg; gradually beat into creamed mixture.

2. Divide dough in half. Shape each into a disk; wrap in plastic wrap. Refrigerate 2 hours or until firm enough to roll.

3. Preheat oven to 375°. On a lightly floured surface, roll each portion of dough to ⅛-in. thickness. Cut with a floured 2½-in. flower-shaped cookie cutter. Using a floured 1-in. flower-shaped cookie cutter, cut and remove the center of each. Reroll removed centers and scraps. Place the cookies 1 in. apart on greased baking sheets.

4. In a small bowl, whisk the egg white and water until blended; brush lightly over tops. Sprinkle with pistachios and walnuts.

5. Bake 8-10 minutes or until edges are golden brown. Cool on pans 2 minutes. Remove to wire racks to cool completely.

6. If desired, drizzle tops with melted chocolate. Let stand until set.

Cherry Kiss Cookies

Chocolate-covered-cherry lovers, get ready for this delectable dessert. It's a playful variation on thumbprint cookies that will be your new favorite treat.

—JOY YURK GRAFTON, WI

PREP: 20 MIN.
BAKE: 10 MIN./BATCH + COOLING
MAKES: 4½ DOZEN

- 1 **cup butter, softened**
- 1 **cup confectioners' sugar**
- ½ **teaspoon salt**
- 2 **teaspoons maraschino cherry juice**
- ½ **teaspoon almond extract**
- 6 **drops red food coloring, optional**
- 2¼ **cups all-purpose flour**
- ½ **cup chopped maraschino cherries**
- 54 **milk chocolate kisses, unwrapped**

1. Preheat oven to 350°. In a large bowl, beat butter, confectioners' sugar and salt until blended. Beat in the cherry juice, extract and, if desired, food coloring. Gradually beat in flour. Stir in cherries.

2. Shape dough into 1-in. balls. Place 1 in. apart on greased baking sheets.

3. Bake 8-10 minutes or until bottoms are light brown. Immediately press a chocolate kiss into the center of each cookie (cookie will crack around edges). Cool on pans for 2 minutes. Remove to wire racks to cool.

Chocolate Toffee Delights

I combined my best cookie recipe with some ingredients I had on hand and came up with these wonderful bars. The taste always reminds me of my favorite Girl Scout cookies.

—SHANNON KOENE BLACKSBURG, VA

PREP: 15 MIN. • **BAKE:** 30 MIN. + COOLING
MAKES: 3 DOZEN

- 1 **cup butter, softened**
- ½ **cup plus 2 tablespoons sugar, divided**
- ¾ **teaspoon almond extract**
- ½ **teaspoon coconut extract**
- 2 **cups all-purpose flour**
- ¼ **teaspoon salt**
- ¼ **teaspoon baking powder**
- ½ **cup flaked coconut**
- ½ **cup sliced almonds, toasted and cooled**
- 1 **jar (12¼ ounces) caramel ice cream topping**
- ¾ **cup dark chocolate chips**

1. Preheat oven to 350°. In a small bowl, cream butter and ½ cup sugar until light and fluffy. Beat in extracts. Combine the flour, salt and baking powder; gradually add to creamed mixture and mix well.

2. Press into a greased 13x9-in. baking pan. Bake 10 minutes. Prick crust with a fork; sprinkle with remaining sugar. Bake 15 minutes longer or until set.

3. Meanwhile, place the coconut and almonds in a food processor; cover and process until finely chopped. Transfer to a small bowl; stir in ice cream topping. Spread over crust. Bake 5-10 minutes or until edges are bubbly. Cool on a wire rack.

4. In a microwave, melt chocolate chips; stir until smooth. Drizzle over caramel mixture. Let stand until the chocolate is set. Cut into bars. Store in an airtight container.

Pumpkin Pie Spiced Blondies

My family loves pumpkin pie at holiday time and craves brownies all year long. So everyone's doubly happy when I bring out a platter of my spiced blondies.
—AMY ANDREWS MAPLE VALLEY, WA

PREP: 25 MIN. • **BAKE:** 25 MIN. + COOLING
MAKES: 16 SERVINGS

- ¾ cup butter, softened
- ¾ cup packed brown sugar
- 2 large eggs
- 4 teaspoons light corn syrup
- 1½ teaspoons rum extract
- 1⅓ cups all-purpose flour
- 2 teaspoons pumpkin pie spice
- ½ teaspoon baking powder
- ¼ teaspoon salt
- 1 cup white baking chips
- ¾ cup chopped pecans, optional

FROSTING
- 1¼ cups confectioners' sugar
- 3 tablespoons cream cheese, softened
- ⅛ teaspoon vanilla extract
- 1½ to 2 teaspoons orange juice

1. Preheat oven to 350°. In a large bowl, cream butter and brown sugar until light and fluffy. Beat in eggs, corn syrup and extract. In another bowl, whisk flour, pie spice, baking powder and salt; gradually beat into creamed mixture. Stir in baking chips and, if desired, pecans.

2. Spread into a greased 8-in. square baking pan. Bake 25-30 minutes or until a toothpick inserted in center comes out clean (do not overbake). Cool completely in pan on a wire rack.

3. In a small bowl, beat confectioners' sugar, cream cheese, vanilla and enough orange juice to reach a spreading consistency. Spread over blondies; cut into bars. Refrigerate any leftovers.

Old-Fashioned Oatmeal Raisin Cookies

I've been making these cookies for nearly 30 years. The spice cake mix provides a delicious backdrop to the oat and raisins. They're an all-time favorite with my family.
—NANCY HORTON GREENBRIER, TN

PREP: 10 MIN. • **BAKE:** 10 MIN./BATCH
MAKES: 7 DOZEN

- ¾ cup canola oil
- ¼ cup packed brown sugar
- 2 large eggs
- ½ cup 2% milk
- 1 package spice cake mix (regular size)
- 2 cups old-fashioned oats
- 2½ cups raisins
- 1 cup chopped pecans

1. In a large bowl, beat the oil and brown sugar until blended. Beat in eggs, then milk. Combine cake mix and oats; gradually add to brown sugar mixture and mix well. Fold in raisins and pecans.

2. Drop by tablespoonfuls 2 in. apart onto greased baking sheets. Bake at 350° for 10-12 minutes or until golden brown. Cool the cookies for 1 minute before removing to wire racks.

Quick & Easy Gumdrops

These homemade candies are softer than ones from the store. They've got that classic chewy appeal that people really love.

—LEAH REKAU MILWAUKEE, WI

PREP: 25 MIN. + CHILLING • **MAKES:** 1 POUND (64 PIECES)

- 3 envelopes unflavored gelatin
- ½ cup plus ¾ cup water, divided
- 1½ cups sugar
- ¼ to ½ teaspoon raspberry extract
  Red food coloring
  Additional sugar

1. In a small bowl, sprinkle gelatin over ½ cup water; let stand 5 minutes. In a small saucepan, bring sugar and remaining water to a boil over medium heat, stirring constantly. Add gelatin; reduce heat. Simmer 5 minutes, stirring frequently. Remove from heat; stir in extract and food coloring as desired.

2. Pour into a greased 8-in. square pan. Refrigerate, covered, 3 hours or until firm.

3. Loosen edges of candy from pan with a knife; turn onto a sugared work surface. Cut into 1-in. squares; roll in sugar. Let stand, uncovered, at room temperature for 3-4 hours or until all sides are dry, turning every hour. Store candy between layers of waxed paper in an airtight container in the refrigerator.

NOTE *For lemon gumdrops, use lemon extract and yellow food coloring. For orange gumdrops, use orange extract, yellow food coloring and a drop of red food coloring.*

Cherry-Chocolate Oatmeal Cookies

My kids love making these home-style cookies. They're so wonderful to eat when they are still warm!

—JAYE BEELER GRAND RAPIDS, MI

PREP: 25 MIN. • **BAKE:** 10 MIN./BATCH • **MAKES:** 6 DOZEN

- 1 cup butter, softened
- 1½ cups packed brown sugar
- 2 large eggs
- 1 teaspoon vanilla extract
- 1½ cups all-purpose flour
- 1 teaspoon ground cinnamon
- ½ teaspoon baking powder
- ½ teaspoon baking soda
- ½ teaspoon salt
- 2 cups old-fashioned oats
- 1 cup dried tart cherries
- 1 cup dark chocolate chips

1. Preheat oven to 350°. In a large bowl, cream the butter and brown sugar until light and fluffy. Beat in eggs and vanilla. In another bowl, whisk flour, cinnamon, baking powder, baking soda and salt; gradually beat into creamed mixture. Stir in oats, cherries and chocolate chips.

2. Drop by tablespoonfuls 2 in. apart onto ungreased baking sheets. Bake 9-11 minutes or until edges are golden brown. Cool on pans 1 minute. Remove to wire racks to cool.

Dark Chocolate Raspberry Fudge

Something about the combination of dark chocolate and raspberry is just so appealing. This fudge is a homemade treat that's always worth sharing. It makes a truly heartfelt gift.

—BARBARA LENTO HOUSTON, PA

PREP: 15 MIN. + FREEZING • **COOK:** 5 MIN. + CHILLING
MAKES: 3 POUNDS (81 PIECES)

- 1 package (10 to 12 ounces) white baking chips
- 1 teaspoon butter, softened
- 3 cups dark chocolate chips
- 1 can (14 ounces) sweetened condensed milk
- ¼ cup raspberry liqueur
- ⅛ teaspoon salt

1. Place baking chips in a single layer on a small baking sheet. Freeze 30 minutes. Line a 9-in. square pan with foil; grease foil with butter.

2. In a large microwave-safe bowl, combine the dark chocolate chips and milk. Microwave, uncovered, on high for 2 minutes; stir. Microwave in additional 30-second intervals, stirring until smooth. Stir in liqueur and salt. Add white baking chips; stir just until partially melted. Spread into prepared pan. Refrigerate 1 hour or until firm.

3. Using foil, lift fudge out of pan. Remove foil; cut the fudge into 1-in. squares. Store in an airtight container in the refrigerator.

NOTE *This recipe was tested in a 1,100-watt microwave.*

Quadruple Chocolate Chunk Cookies

Of all my recipes, I knew my Quadruple Chocolate Chunk Cookies would have the best shot at winning a cookie contest I entered. When your cookies feature Oreos, candy bars and all the other goodies that go into these treats, you can't go wrong.
—**JEFF KING** DULUTH, MN

PREP: 25 MIN. • **BAKE:** 10 MIN./BATCH • **MAKES:** 8 DOZEN

- 1 **cup butter, softened**
- 1 **cup sugar**
- 1 **cup packed brown sugar**
- 2 **large eggs**
- 2 **teaspoons vanilla extract**
- 2½ **cups all-purpose flour**
- ¾ **cup Dutch-processed cocoa**
- 1 **teaspoon baking soda**
- ¼ **teaspoon salt**
- 1 **cup white baking chips, chopped**
- 1 **cup semisweet chocolate chips, chopped**
- 1 **cup chopped Oreo cookies (about 10 cookies)**
- 1 **Hershey's cookies and cream candy bar (1.55 ounces), chopped**

1. Preheat oven to 375°. In a large bowl, cream the butter, sugar and brown sugar until light and fluffy. Beat in eggs and vanilla. In another bowl, whisk flour, cocoa, baking soda and salt; gradually beat into creamed mixture. Stir in the remaining ingredients.
2. Drop by tablespoonfuls 2 in. apart onto greased baking sheets. Bake 6-8 minutes or until set. Cool on pans 1 minute. Remove to wire racks to cool completely. Store cookies in an airtight container.

Butterscotch-Toffee Cheesecake Bars

I'd been making lemon cheesecake bars for years and wanted to switch things up. Using the original bar as a starting point, I decided to try a butterscotch and toffee version. The results were wonderful!
—**PAMELA SHANK** PARKERSBURG, WV

PREP: 15 MIN. • **BAKE:** 30 MIN. + CHILLING • **MAKES:** 2 DOZEN

- 1 **package yellow cake mix (regular size)**
- 1 **package (3.4 ounces) instant butterscotch pudding mix**
- ⅓ **cup canola oil**
- 2 **large eggs**
- 1 **package (8 ounces) cream cheese, softened**
- ⅓ **cup sugar**
- 1 **cup brickle toffee bits, divided**
- ½ **cup butterscotch chips**

1. Preheat oven to 350°. In a large bowl, combine cake mix, pudding mix, oil and 1 egg; mix until crumbly. Reserve 1 cup for topping. Press remaining mixture into an ungreased 13x9-in. baking pan. Bake 10 minutes. Cool completely on a wire rack.
2. In a small bowl, beat cream cheese and sugar until smooth. Add remaining egg; beat on low speed just until combined. Fold in ½ cup toffee bits. Spread over crust. Sprinkle with reserved crumb mixture. Bake 15-20 minutes or until filling is set.
3. Sprinkle with butterscotch chips and remaining toffee bits. Return to oven; bake 1 minute longer. Cool on a wire rack 1 hour. Refrigerate 2 hours or until cold. Cut into bars.

Snickerdoodles

My cookies get coated with sugar, spice and everything nice! They turn out soft on the inside and a little crunchy on the outside, the dough is easy to work with and they taste fantastic. What more could you ask for in a cookie?

—**ASHLEY WISNIEWSKI** CHAMPAIGN, IL

PREP: 30 MIN. • **BAKE:** 10 MIN./BATCH
MAKES: 3 DOZEN

- ¼ cup butter, softened
- 1 cup plus 2 tablespoons sugar, divided
- 1 large egg
- 1 tablespoon agave nectar
- 1 teaspoon vanilla extract
- 1¾ cups white whole wheat flour
- ½ teaspoon baking soda
- ½ teaspoon cream of tartar
- 2 teaspoons ground cinnamon

1. In a large bowl, cream butter and 1 cup sugar until blended. Beat in the egg, agave nectar and vanilla. Combine flour, baking soda and cream of tartar; gradually add to creamed mixture and mix well. In a small bowl, combine cinnamon and remaining sugar.
2. Shape dough into 1-in. balls; roll in cinnamon-sugar. Place 2 in. apart on baking sheets coated with cooking spray. Bake at 375° for 9-11 minutes or until lightly browned. Cool 2 minutes before removing cookies from pans to wire racks.

Contest Winner

Double-Decker Fudge

Microwave-quick and extra peanut buttery, this fudge is just the thing to have on hand for after-school treats or dessert. The best part? You need only five ingredients to make it!

—**SHERRI MELOTIK** OAK CREEK, WI

PREP: 15 MIN. + CHILLING
MAKES: ABOUT 1½ POUNDS

- 1 teaspoon butter
- 1 cup peanut butter chips
- 1 can (14 ounces) sweetened condensed milk, divided
- 1 teaspoon vanilla extract, divided
- 1 cup (6 ounces) semisweet chocolate chips

1. Line an 8-in. square pan with foil; butter foil and set aside.
2. In a microwave-safe bowl, combine the peanut butter chips and ⅔ cup milk. Microwave mixture on high for 1 minute; stir. Microwave at additional 15-second intervals, stirring until smooth. Stir in ½ teaspoon vanilla. Pour into prepared pan. Refrigerate for 10 minutes.
3. Meanwhile, in a microwave-safe bowl, combine chocolate chips and remaining milk. Microwave on high for 1 minute; stir. Microwave for additional 15-second intervals, stirring until smooth. Stir in the remaining vanilla. Spread over the peanut butter layer.
4. Refrigerate for 1 hour or until firm. Using foil, remove fudge from the pan. Cut into 1-in. squares.

Strawberry Shortcake Cookies

Strawberry shortcake is one of my favorite desserts. I thought it would be great to use it as inspiration for a cookie recipe. The pastry-like cookie is topped with pink strawberry frosting.

—ALLISON ANDERSON AVONDALE, AZ

PREP: 35 MIN. + CHILLING
BAKE: 15 MIN./BATCH + COOLING
MAKES: 2 DOZEN

- 2 cups all-purpose flour
- ½ cup sugar
- Dash salt
- ⅔ cup cold butter
- 2 tablespoons water
- 1 teaspoon vanilla extract

FROSTING
- ½ cup butter, softened
- ¾ cup fresh strawberries, sliced
- 2 tablespoons 2% milk
- 5 cups confectioners' sugar
- Additional sliced fresh strawberries, optional

1. In a large bowl, combine the flour, sugar and salt. Cut in butter until mixture resembles coarse crumbs. Combine water and vanilla; stir into crumb mixture just until moistened. Cover and refrigerate for 1-2 hours or until firm.

2. On a lightly floured surface, roll dough out to ¼-in. thickness; cut with a floured 3-in. round cookie cutter. Place 1 in. apart on greased baking sheets.

3. Bake at 325° for 15-18 minutes or until lightly browned. Cool for 2 minutes before removing to wire racks to cool completely.

4. In a large bowl, beat the butter, strawberries and milk until combined. Gradually add confectioners' sugar; beat until blended. Spread over the cookies; garnish with additional sliced strawberries if desired.

French Toast Cookies

I created these soft, sparkly cookies because my sister loves cinnamon French toast covered in maple syrup. In the case of these cookies, bigger is definitely better! I like to use white whole wheat flour, but any whole wheat flour will work.

—MARY SHENK DEKALB, IL

PREP: 25 MIN. + CHILLING • **BAKE:** 15 MIN.
MAKES: 1½ DOZEN

- ¾ cup butter, softened
- ¾ cup sugar, divided
- ½ cup packed brown sugar
- 1 large egg
- ⅓ cup corn syrup
- 2 teaspoons vanilla extract
- 2 teaspoons maple flavoring
- 1¼ cups all-purpose flour
- 1 cup whole wheat flour
- 2 teaspoons ground cinnamon
- 1 teaspoon baking soda
- ½ teaspoon salt

1. In a large bowl, cream butter, ½ cup sugar and brown sugar until light and fluffy. Beat in egg, corn syrup, vanilla and flavoring. In another bowl, whisk the remaining ingredients; gradually beat into creamed mixture. Refrigerate, covered, 1 hour or until firm enough to shape.

2. Preheat oven to 375°. Place the remaining sugar in a shallow bowl. Shape dough into 1¾-in. balls; roll in sugar. Place 2 in. apart on parchment paper-lined baking sheets.

3. Bake 11-13 minutes or until edges are golden brown. Remove from pans to wire racks to cool.

DAZZLING DESSERTS

It's time for the grand finale: dessert! Whether you're in the mood for tarts, cheesecakes, pies, cupcakes, pudding, cakes or something in between, these recipes will make your home crowd *ooh* and *aah!*

Grilled Stone Fruits with Balsamic Syrup

Get ready to experience another side of stone fruits. Hot off the grill, this summertime dessert practically melts in your mouth.

—**SONYA LABBE** WEST HOLLYWOOD, CA

START TO FINISH: 20 MIN.
MAKES: 4 SERVINGS

- ½ cup balsamic vinegar
- 2 tablespoons brown sugar
- 2 medium peaches, peeled and halved
- 2 medium nectarines, peeled and halved
- 2 medium plums, peeled and halved

1. In a small saucepan, combine the vinegar and brown sugar. Bring to a boil; cook until liquid is reduced by half.

2. Moisten a paper towel with cooking oil; using long-handled tongs, lightly coat the grill rack. Grill the peaches, nectarines and plums, covered, over medium heat or broil 4 in. from the heat for 3-4 minutes on each side or until tender.

3. Slice fruits; arrange on a serving plate. Drizzle with sauce.

Contest Winner

Blueberry-Blackberry Rustic Tart

My dad would often stop the car on the side of the road in Maine and say, "I smell blueberries." He always had a pail ready for picking! Mom would then bake up the wild berries in a cornmeal crust.

—**PRISCILLA GILBERT**

INDIAN HARBOUR BEACH, FL

PREP: 20 MIN. + CHILLING • **BAKE:** 55 MIN.
MAKES: 8 SERVINGS

- 2 cups all-purpose flour
- ⅓ cup sugar
- ¼ cup yellow cornmeal
- ⅔ cup cold butter, cubed
- ½ cup buttermilk

FILLING
- 4 cups fresh blueberries
- 2 cups fresh blackberries
- ⅔ cup sugar
- ⅓ cup all-purpose flour
- 2 tablespoons lemon juice
- 1 large egg, beaten
- 2 tablespoons turbinado (washed raw) sugar or coarse sugar
  Whipped cream, optional

1. In a large bowl, mix the flour, sugar and cornmeal; cut in the butter until crumbly. Gradually add buttermilk, tossing with a fork until dough holds together when pressed. Shape into a disk; wrap in plastic wrap. Refrigerate 30 minutes or overnight.

2. Preheat the oven to 375°. On a lightly floured surface, roll dough into a 14-in. circle. Transfer to a parchment paper-lined baking sheet.

3. In a large bowl, combine berries, sugar, flour and lemon juice; spoon over pastry to within 2 in. of edges. Fold pastry edge over filling, leaving center uncovered. Brush the folded pastry with beaten egg; sprinkle with turbinado sugar.

4. Bake 55-60 minutes or until crust is golden brown and filling is bubbly. Using parchment paper, slide tart onto a wire rack to cool. If desired, serve with whipped cream.

Triple Berry No-Bake Cheesecake

I've made many cheesecakes and enjoyed them all, but they're usually very time-consuming to create. When I first tried this no-bake recipe, my husband said it was better than the baked ones, and that was a big plus for me!

—JOYCE MUMMAU SUGARCREEK, OH

PREP: 20 MIN. + CHILLING
MAKES: 12 SERVINGS (3⅓ CUPS TOPPING)

- 1½ **cups graham cracker crumbs**
- ⅓ **cup packed brown sugar**
- ½ **teaspoon ground cinnamon**
- ⅓ **cup butter, melted**

FILLING

- 2 **packages (8 ounces each) cream cheese, softened**
- ⅓ **cup sugar**
- 2 **teaspoons lemon juice**
- 2 **cups heavy whipping cream**

TOPPING

- 2 **cups sliced fresh strawberries**
- 1 **cup fresh blueberries**
- 1 **cup fresh raspberries**
- 2 **tablespoons sugar**

1. In a small bowl, mix the cracker crumbs, brown sugar and cinnamon; stir in butter. Press onto the bottom and 1 in. up sides of an ungreased 9-in. springform pan. Refrigerate 30 minutes.
2. In a large bowl, beat cream cheese, sugar and lemon juice until smooth. Gradually add cream; beat until stiff peaks form. Transfer to prepared crust. Refrigerate, covered, overnight.
3. In a bowl, gently toss berries with sugar. Let stand 15-30 minutes or until juices are released from berries.
4. With a knife, loosen the sides of cheesecake from pan; remove rim. Serve cheesecake with topping.

Sunrise Pops

Bright, beautiful, cool, sweet, delicious and full of fresh fruits—what's not to like about these frozen treats?

—COLLEEN LUDOVICE MILWAUKEE, WI

PREP: 20 MIN. + FREEZING
MAKES: 10 POPS

- 1 **cup fresh strawberries, sliced**
- 1 **cup water, divided**
- 2 **tablespoons sugar, divided**
- 1 **cup clementine segments (about 5 medium), seeded if necessary**
- ½ **cup orange juice**
- 1 **cup cubed fresh pineapple**
- 10 **plastic or paper cups (3 ounces each) and wooden pop sticks**

1. Place strawberries, ½ cup water and 1 tablespoon sugar in a food processor; pulse until combined. Divide among cups. Top the cups with foil and insert sticks through foil. Freeze until firm, about 2 hours.
2. Wipe food processor clean. Add the clementines and orange juice; pulse until combined. Spoon over strawberry layer. Freeze, covered, until firm, about 2 hours.
3. Repeat with pineapple and the remaining water and sugar. Spoon over the clementine layer. Freeze, covered, until firm.

Rhubarb Fool with Strawberries

A fool is a classic British dessert made with whipped cream and cooked fruit. Try my quick version with rhubarb and berries.

—**CHERYL MILLER** FORT COLLINS, CO

PREP: 30 MIN. + CHILLING • **MAKES:** 6 SERVINGS

- 3 cups sliced fresh or frozen rhubarb (1-inch pieces)
- ⅓ cup sugar
- ¼ cup orange juice
  - Dash salt
- 1 cup heavy whipping cream
- 2 cups fresh strawberries, halved

1. In a large saucepan, combine rhubarb, sugar, orange juice and salt. Bring to a boil. Reduce heat; simmer, covered, 6-8 minutes or until rhubarb is tender. Cool slightly.

2. Process rhubarb mixture in a blender until smooth. Transfer to a bowl; refrigerate, covered, until cold.

3. Just before serving, in a large bowl, whip cream until soft peaks form. Lightly fold in pureed rhubarb and strawberries.

Skillet Blueberry Slump

My mother-in-law made a slump of wild blueberries with dumplings and served it warm with a pitcher of farm cream. We've been eating slumps for nearly 60 years!

—**ELEANORE EBELING** BREWSTER, MN

PREP: 25 MIN. • **BAKE:** 20 MIN. • **MAKES:** 6 SERVINGS

- 4 cups fresh or frozen blueberries
- ½ cup sugar
- ½ cup water
- 1 teaspoon grated lemon peel
- 1 tablespoon lemon juice
- 1 cup all-purpose flour
- 2 tablespoons sugar
- 2 teaspoons baking powder
- ½ teaspoon salt
- 1 tablespoon butter
- ½ cup 2% milk
  - Vanilla ice cream

1. Preheat oven to 400°. In a 10-in. ovenproof skillet, combine the first five ingredients; bring to a boil. Reduce heat; simmer, uncovered, 9-11 minutes or until slightly thickened, stirring occasionally.

2. Meanwhile, in a small bowl, whisk flour, sugar, baking powder and salt. Cut in butter until mixture resembles coarse crumbs. Add milk; stir just until moistened.

3. Drop batter in six portions on top of the simmering blueberry mixture. Transfer to oven. Bake, uncovered, 17-20 minutes or until dumplings are golden brown. Serve warm with ice cream.

1. In a large bowl, combine flour and salt; cut in shortening until crumbly. Gradually add water, tossing with a fork until dough forms a ball. Divide dough in half so that one portion is slightly larger than the other; wrap each in plastic wrap. Refrigerate 30 minutes or until easy to handle.

2. Preheat oven to 400°. On a lightly floured surface, roll out larger portion of dough to fit a 9-in. deep-dish pie plate. Transfer pastry to pie plate.

3. In a large bowl, toss apples with lemon juice and vanilla; add berries and rhubarb. Combine flour, allspice, cinnamon and 1½ cups sugar; add to apple mixture and toss gently to coat. Spoon into crust; dot with butter.

4. Roll out remaining pastry; make a lattice crust. Trim, seal and flute edges. Brush milk over lattice top. Sprinkle with remaining sugar.

5. Bake 15 minutes. Reduce the heat to 350°; bake 50-60 minutes longer or until crust is golden brown and filling is bubbly. Cover edges with foil during the last 15 minutes to prevent overbrowning if necessary. Cool on a wire rack.

NOTE *If using frozen rhubarb, measure rhubarb while still frozen, then thaw completely. Drain in a colander, but do not press liquid out.*

Frozen Chocolate Monkey Treats

These bites make it fun and easy for the little ones to get a little playful with their food. Let them choose between dipping the snacks into peanuts, sprinkles or coconut, and if they're old enough, let them lend a hand with slicing the bananas.
—**SUSAN HEIN** BURLINGTON, WI

PREP: 15 MIN. + FREEZING • **COOK:** 5 MIN. • **MAKES:** 1½ DOZEN

- 3 **medium bananas**
- 1 **cup (6 ounces) dark chocolate chips**
- 2 **teaspoons shortening**
   Toppings: chopped peanuts, toasted flaked coconut and/or colored jimmies

1. Cut each banana into six pieces (about 1 in.). Insert a toothpick into each piece; transfer to a waxed paper-lined baking sheet. Freeze until completely firm, about 1 hour.

2. In a microwave, melt chocolate and shortening; stir until smooth. Dip the banana pieces in chocolate mixture; allow excess to drip off. Dip in toppings as desired; return to baking sheet. Freeze at least 30 minutes before serving.

NOTE *To toast coconut, bake in a shallow pan in a 350° oven for 5-10 minutes or cook in a skillet over low heat until golden brown, stirring occasionally.*

Berry-Apple-Rhubarb Pie

I bake this family favorite every year for a get-together at my sister's home, where the dessert is known as "Uncle Mike's pie." The berries, apples and rhubarb I use are all home-grown.
—**MICHAEL POWERS** NEW BALTIMORE, VA

PREP: 30 MIN. + CHILLING • **BAKE:** 65 MIN. + COOLING
MAKES: 8 SERVINGS

- 2⅔ **cups all-purpose flour**
- 1 **teaspoon salt**
- 1 **cup butter-flavored shortening**
- 6 **to 8 tablespoons cold water**

FILLING

- 2 **cups thinly sliced peeled tart apples**
- 1 **tablespoon lemon juice**
- 1 **teaspoon vanilla extract**
- 1 **cup halved fresh strawberries**
- 1 **cup fresh blueberries**
- 1 **cup fresh raspberries**
- 1 **cup fresh blackberries**
- 1 **cup sliced fresh or frozen rhubarb**
- ⅓ **cup all-purpose flour**
- 1 **teaspoon ground allspice**
- 1 **teaspoon ground cinnamon**
- 1½ **cups plus 1 teaspoon sugar, divided**
- 2 **tablespoons butter**
- 1 **tablespoon 2% milk**

GET THE KIDS INVOLVED!

My girls compile a list of dishes we don't get a chance to make during a busy week. They also take turns looking for new recipes for me to try. It's so wonderful to have them in the kitchen with me!
—**KRISTIN K.** LETHBRIDGE, AB

Red Velvet Cake Bites

Any cake mix can work for this recipe, but red velvet is my usual go-to. I've rolled chopped macadamia nuts into pineapple cake and dipped the balls into white chocolate. Whatever you do, have fun!

—**ANNE POWERS** MUNFORD, AL

PREP: 45 MIN. + CHILLING
BAKE: 25 MIN. + COOLING
MAKES: 5 DOZEN

- 1 **package red velvet cake mix (regular size)**
- 1 **can (16 ounces) cream cheese frosting**
- 1 **pound each white, milk chocolate and dark chocolate candy coating**

1. Prepare and bake the cake mix according to package directions, using a 13x9-in. baking pan. Cool cake completely.

2. Crumble cake into a large bowl. Add frosting; beat well. Refrigerate 1 hour or until easy to handle. Shape into 1-in. balls; transfer to waxed paper-lined baking sheets. Refrigerate at least 1 hour.

3. In a microwave, melt the white candy coating; stir until smooth. Dip 20 cake balls in coating; allow excess to drip off. Return to baking sheets; let stand until set. Repeat with milk chocolate and dark chocolate coatings and remaining cake balls. Store in airtight containers.

FREEZE OPTION *Freeze uncoated cake balls in freezer containers, layered between waxed paper. To use, thaw in covered containers. Dip in coatings as directed.*

Contest Winner

Lemon-Berry Shortcake

Bake a simple cake using lovely, fresh strawberries, and enjoy this summertime classic with a generous layer of whipped topping and berries.

—**MERYL HERR** GRAND RAPIDS, MI

PREP: 30 MIN. • **BAKE:** 20 MIN. + COOLING
MAKES: 8 SERVINGS

- 1⅓ **cups all-purpose flour**
- ½ **cup sugar**
- 2 **teaspoons baking powder**
- ¼ **teaspoon salt**
- 1 **large egg**
- ⅔ **cup buttermilk**
- ¼ **cup butter, melted**
- 1 **tablespoon lemon juice**
- 1 **teaspoon grated lemon peel**
- 1 **teaspoon vanilla extract**
- 1 **cup sliced fresh strawberries**

TOPPING
- 1½ **cups sliced fresh strawberries**
- 1 **tablespoon lemon juice**
- 1 **teaspoon sugar**
- 2 **cups reduced-fat whipped topping**

1. In a large bowl, combine the flour, sugar, baking powder and salt. In another bowl, combine the egg, buttermilk, butter, lemon juice, lemon peel and vanilla. Stir into dry ingredients just until moistened. Fold in strawberries. Pour into a greased and floured 9-in. round baking pan.

2. Bake at 350° for 20-25 minutes or until a toothpick inserted near center comes out clean. Cool for 10 minutes before removing from pan to a wire rack to cool completely.

3. For the topping, in a large bowl, combine the strawberries, lemon juice and sugar. Cover and refrigerate until serving. Spread whipped topping over cake. Drain the strawberries; arrange over the top.

Gingersnap Pumpkin Cake

On the first day we had cool weather following all of the summer heat, we were getting together with friends. I baked this pumpkin cake because I could feel fall in the air.

—KONI BREWER WOODWAY, TX

PREP: 20 MIN. • **BAKE:** 50 MIN. + COOLING
MAKES: 12 SERVINGS

- 1 can (15 ounces) solid-pack pumpkin
- 2 cups sugar
- 4 large eggs
- 1 cup canola oil
- 2 cups all-purpose flour
- 2 teaspoons baking soda
- 2 teaspoons pumpkin pie spice
- ½ teaspoon salt

ICING

- 4 ounces cream cheese, softened
- ¼ cup butter, softened
- ½ teaspoon vanilla extract
- 1¾ cups confectioners' sugar
- 5 gingersnap cookies, crushed

1. Preheat oven to 350°. Grease and flour a 10-in. fluted tube pan.

2. In a large bowl, beat the pumpkin, sugar, eggs and oil until well blended. In another bowl, whisk flour, baking soda, pie spice and salt; gradually beat into pumpkin mixture.

3. Transfer the batter to prepared pan. Bake 50-55 minutes or until a toothpick inserted in center comes out clean. Cool in pan 10 minutes before removing to a wire rack to cool completely.

4. In a small bowl, beat the cream cheese, butter and vanilla until blended. Gradually beat in the confectioners' sugar until smooth. Frost cake; sprinkle with crushed cookies.

FREEZE OPTION *Wrap cooled cake in plastic wrap, then cover securely in foil; freeze. To use, thaw cake before unwrapping. Frost and decorate cake as directed.*

NOTE *To remove cake easily, use solid shortening to grease plain and fluted tube pans.*

German Apple Pie

Our babysitter shared her apple pie recipe with me, and I've baked it countless times since then, to everyone's delight.

—MRS. WOODROW TAYLOR
ADAMS CENTER, NY

PREP: 20 MIN. • **BAKE:** 65 MIN. + COOLING
MAKES: 8 SERVINGS

- 1½ cups all-purpose flour
- ½ teaspoon salt
- ½ cup shortening
- 1 teaspoon vanilla extract
- 2 to 3 tablespoons ice water

FILLING

- 1 cup sugar
- ¼ cup all-purpose flour
- 2 teaspoons ground cinnamon
- 6 cups sliced peeled tart apples
- 1 cup heavy whipping cream
  Whipped cream, optional

1. In a small bowl, combine flour and salt; cut in shortening until crumbly. Add vanilla. Gradually add the water, tossing with a fork until dough forms a ball. Roll out pastry to fit a 9-in. pie plate. Transfer pastry to pie plate. Trim pastry to ½ in. beyond edge of pie plate; flute edges.

2. For filling, combine sugar, flour and cinnamon; sprinkle 3 tablespoons into the crust. Layer with half of the apples; sprinkle with half of remaining sugar mixture. Repeat layers. Pour cream over all.

3. Bake at 450° for 10 minutes. Reduce the heat to 350° and bake for 55-60 minutes or until apples are tender. Cool on a wire rack. Store in the refrigerator. Serve with whipped cream if desired.

Contest Winner

When Christmas, Thanksgiving, Halloween or Independence Day rolls around, you'll be set when it comes to dessert. Whip up one of these delightful recipes to celebrate!

Contest Winner

one-fourth full with batter. Drop streusel by heaping teaspoonfuls into center of each cupcake. Cover with remaining batter.

3. Bake at 350° for 18-20 minutes or until a toothpick inserted in the cake portion comes out clean. Cool for 10 minutes before removing from pans to wire racks to cool completely.

4. In a small bowl, beat cream cheese and butter until fluffy. Add the confectioners' sugar and vanilla; beat until smooth. Frost cupcakes. Store in the refrigerator.

Chocolate-Drizzled Gingerbread

Although this cozy gingerbread has tasty chocolate and warm spices, it's even better with a dollop of whipped cream on top.
—**PRECI D'SILVA** DUBAI, UAE

PREP: 25 MIN. • **BAKE:** 40 MIN. + COOLING • **MAKES:** 9 SERVINGS

- ½ **cup butter, softened**
- ½ **cup packed brown sugar**
- 1 **large egg**
- ½ **cup molasses**
- 1¾ **cups all-purpose flour**
- 1 **teaspoon baking powder**
- ½ **teaspoon ground ginger**
- ¼ **teaspoon salt**
- ⅛ **teaspoon ground cloves**
- ½ **cup water**
- 4 **ounces bittersweet chocolate, melted and slightly cooled**

TOPPING
- ¾ **cup heavy whipping cream**
- 2 **tablespoons confectioners' sugar**
- ¼ **teaspoon ground ginger**
  Chopped crystallized ginger and chocolate shavings, optional

Pumpkin Streusel Cupcakes

A spiced streusel filling really dresses up these yummy cupcakes. No one will guess you used a boxed mix and canned pumpkin!
—**DONNA GISH** BLUE SPRINGS, MO

PREP: 25 MIN. • **BAKE:** 20 MIN. + COOLING • **MAKES:** 2 DOZEN

- 1 **package spice cake mix (regular size)**
- 1¼ **cups water**
- 3 **large eggs**
- ½ **cup canned pumpkin**

STREUSEL
- ½ **cup packed brown sugar**
- ½ **teaspoon ground cinnamon**
- 1 **tablespoon butter**

FROSTING
- 1 **package (8 ounces) cream cheese, softened**
- 2 **tablespoons butter**
- 2 **cups confectioners' sugar**
- ½ **teaspoon vanilla extract**

1. In a large bowl, combine the cake mix, water, eggs and pumpkin. Beat on low speed just until moistened. Beat on medium for 2 minutes.

2. In a small bowl, combine brown sugar and cinnamon; cut in butter until crumbly. Fill paper-lined muffin cups

1. Preheat oven to 325°. In a large bowl, cream butter and brown sugar until light and fluffy. Add egg, then molasses, beating well after each addition.

2. In another bowl, mix flour, baking powder, ground ginger, salt and cloves; gradually add to creamed mixture alternately with water, beating well after each addition.

3. Pour half of the batter into a greased 8-in. square baking dish. Drizzle with half of the melted chocolate. Top with remaining batter and chocolate. Bake 40-45 minutes or until a toothpick inserted in center comes out clean. Cool completely on a wire rack.

4. For topping, in a small bowl, beat cream until it begins to thicken. Add the confectioners' sugar and ginger; beat until soft peaks form. Serve with cake. If desired, sprinkle with crystallized ginger and chocolate shavings.

Red, White & Blue Berry Trifle

This luscious trifle tastes best if made the day before serving. Keep additional blueberries and raspberries on hand for decoration.
—**KAIA MCSHANE** MUNSTER, IN

PREP: 20 MIN. + CHILLING • **MAKES:** 12 SERVINGS

- 1 can (14 ounces) sweetened condensed milk
- 1½ cups 2% milk
- 2 packages (3.4 ounces each) instant lemon pudding mix
- ½ cup sour cream
- 2 cups fresh blueberries
- 2 cups fresh raspberries
- 1 tablespoon lemon juice
- 1 package (16 ounces) frozen pound cake, thawed and cubed
- 1 container (8 ounces) frozen whipped topping, thawed
  Additional blueberries and raspberries, optional

1. In a large bowl, whisk condensed milk, 2% milk and pudding mix for 2 minutes. Fold in sour cream. In another bowl, toss blueberries and raspberries with lemon juice.

2. In a greased 9-in. springform pan, layer half of each of the following: cake cubes, berry mixture and pudding mixture. Repeat. Refrigerate, covered, at least 2 hours before serving.

3. To serve, remove rim from pan. Serve with the whipped topping and, if desired, additional berries.

Gourmet Caramel Apples

Peanut butter and pretzels add a salty twist to these sweet harvest apples. They'll be the treats you can't wait to make every fall.
—*TASTE OF HOME* TEST KITCHEN

PREP: 20 MIN. + STANDING • **MAKES:** 4 SERVINGS

- 4 large tart apples
- 4 wooden pop sticks
- 1 cup milk chocolate chips
- 1 cup semisweet chocolate chips
- 4½ ounces white candy coating, coarsely chopped
- 1 teaspoon shortening
- 1 package (11 ounces) Kraft caramel bits
- 2 tablespoons water
- 4 pretzel rods, coarsely crushed
- ½ cup Reese's pieces

1. Line a baking sheet with waxed paper and grease the paper; set aside. Wash and thoroughly dry apples. Insert a pop stick into the top of each; set aside.

2. Place the chocolate chips in separate microwave-safe bowls. Heat in a microwave until melted; stir until smooth. In another microwave-safe bowl, melt candy coating and shortening; stir until smooth.

3. Combine caramels and water in another microwave-safe bowl. Heat in a microwave until melted; stir until smooth. Dip apples into caramel; turn to coat. Immediately press pretzels and Reese's pieces into sides of apples. Drizzle melted chocolate and candy coating over tops. Place on prepared pan; let stand until set.

Rosy Rhubarb Upside-Down Cake

Look no further if you're searching for a sunny dessert! This delightful, rosy-colored cake is moist on top and light as a feather on the bottom.

—DAWN LOWENSTEIN
HUNTINGDON VALLEY, PA

PREP: 35 MIN. • **BAKE:** 35 MIN. + COOLING
MAKES: 9 SERVINGS

- 3 cups cubed fresh or frozen rhubarb (1-inch, about 8 stalks)
- ¾ cup sugar
- ¾ cup water
- 1 tablespoon lemon juice
- ½ teaspoon ground cinnamon
- ¼ teaspoon ground nutmeg

CAKE
- 3 tablespoons butter, melted
- ¼ cup packed brown sugar
- 1 cup all-purpose flour
- 1 teaspoon baking powder
- ¼ teaspoon salt
- 2 large eggs
- ⅔ cup sugar
- 1 teaspoon lemon extract

1. Preheat the oven to 350°. In a large saucepan, combine the first six ingredients; bring to a boil. Reduce the heat; simmer, uncovered, 6-8 minutes or until the rhubarb is crisp-tender, stirring to dissolve the sugar. Drain, reserving 6 tablespoons of the cooking liquid.

2. Pour butter into an 8-in. square baking dish. Sprinkle with brown sugar; top with drained rhubarb. Sift the flour, baking powder and salt together twice.

3. In a large bowl, beat eggs on high speed 3 minutes. Gradually add sugar, beating until thick and lemon-colored. Beat in extract and reserved cooking liquid. Fold in flour mixture. Pour over rhubarb. Bake 35-40 minutes or until top springs back when lightly touched.

4. Cool 10 minutes before inverting onto a serving plate. Serve warm.

Chocolate Raspberry Cupcakes

These cupcake are so amazing that some people have been know to finish them in two bites. But most prefer to savor each decadent morsel. Keep the cupcakes in the fridge for about a week and in the freezer for a month.

—KIM BEJOT AINSWORTH, NE

PREP: 30 MIN. + CHILLING
BAKE: 20 MIN. + COOLING
MAKES: 2½ DOZEN

- 1 cup baking cocoa
- 2 cups boiling water
- 1 cup butter, softened
- 2½ cups sugar
- 4 large eggs
- 2 tablespoons cold strong brewed coffee
- 2 teaspoons vanilla extract
- 2¾ cups all-purpose flour
- 2 teaspoons baking soda
- ½ teaspoon baking powder
- ½ teaspoon salt
- 1 cup seedless raspberry jam

FROSTING
- 1 can (13.66 ounces) coconut milk
- 1 package (12 ounces) dark chocolate chips
- ½ cup butter, cubed
- ⅓ cup confectioners' sugar
- 2 tablespoons coffee liqueur
  Toasted coconut

1. In a small bowl, combine cocoa and water; set aside to cool.

2. In a large bowl, cream butter and sugar until light and fluffy. Add the eggs, one at a time, beating well after each addition. Beat in coffee and vanilla. Combine the flour, baking soda, baking powder and salt; add to creamed mixture alternately with cocoa mixture, beating well after each addition.

3. Fill paper-lined muffin cups two-thirds full. Drop the jam by teaspoonfuls into the center of each cupcake. Bake at 350° for 18-23 minutes or until a toothpick inserted in the cake portion comes out clean.

4. Cool cupcakes for 10 minutes before removing from pans to wire racks to cool completely. Spread ½ teaspoon jam over each cupcake.

5. For frosting, spoon 1 cup cream from top of coconut milk and place in a small saucepan. Bring just to a boil; remove from the heat. Add chocolate chips; whisk until smooth. Stir in the butter, confectioners' sugar and coffee liqueur. Refrigerate for 1½ hours or until chilled.

6. In a small bowl, beat chocolate mixture until soft peaks form, about 15 seconds. Frost cupcakes. Garnish with coconut.

Frozen Strawberry Delight

Simple, pretty and refreshing, this cool dessert will become a most-requested recipe in no time. Sprinkle in some fresh blueberries for a patriotic twist.

—BARBARA CHRISTENSEN

JACKSONVILLE, FL

PREP: 20 MIN + FREEZING
MAKES: 10 SERVINGS

- 1 **can (14 ounces) sweetened condensed milk**
- ¼ **cup lemon juice**
- 4 **cups sliced fresh strawberries, divided**
- 1 **carton (8 ounces) frozen whipped topping, thawed and divided**
- 8 **Oreo cookies, crushed**

1. Line an 8x4-in. loaf pan with foil, letting edges hang over sides; set aside.
2. In a large bowl, combine the milk and lemon juice; fold in 2 cups strawberries and 2 cups whipped topping. Transfer half of the mixture to the prepared pan. Sprinkle with cookie crumbs; top with remaining strawberry mixture. Cover and freeze for 6 hours or overnight.
3. To serve, using foil, lift the dessert out of pan. Invert onto a serving plate; discard foil. Spread the remaining whipped topping over top and sides of dessert; garnish with the remaining strawberries. Cut into slices.

Sparkling Cider Pound Cake

This pound cake is incredible and reminds me of fall with every bite. Using sparkling apple cider in the batter and the glaze gives it a deliciously unique flavor. I love everything about it!

—NIKKI BARTON PROVIDENCE, UT

PREP: 20 MIN. • **BAKE:** 40 MIN. + COOLING
MAKES: 12 SERVINGS

- ¾ **cup butter, softened**
- 1½ **cups sugar**
- 3 **large eggs**
- 1½ **cups all-purpose flour**
- ¼ **teaspoon baking powder**
- ¼ **teaspoon salt**
- ½ **cup sparkling apple cider**

GLAZE
- ¾ **cup confectioners' sugar**
- 3 **to 4 teaspoons sparkling apple cider**

1. Preheat oven to 350°. Line the bottom of a greased 9x5-in. loaf pan with parchment paper; grease paper.
2. In a large bowl, cream butter and sugar until light and fluffy. Add eggs, one at a time, beating well after each addition. In another bowl, whisk flour, baking powder and salt; add to the creamed mixture alternately with cider, beating well after each addition.
3. Transfer to prepared pan. Bake 40-50 minutes or until a toothpick inserted in center comes out clean. Cool in the pan 10 minutes before removing to a wire rack to cool the cake completely.
4. In a small bowl, mix the glaze ingredients until smooth; spoon over top of cake, allowing it to flow over sides.

Contest Winner

Raspberry Sugar Cream Tarts

My tarts bring back memories of baking with Mom when I was young. They're perfect for holidays, as well as for gifts.

—**CATHY BANKS** ENCINITAS, CA

PREP: 30 MIN. • **BAKE:** 15 MIN. + COOLING • **MAKES:** 3 DOZEN

- ¾ cup unsalted butter, softened
- ½ cup sugar
- 2 large egg yolks
- ¾ teaspoon almond or vanilla extract
- ⅛ teaspoon salt
- 1¾ cups all-purpose flour

FILLING
- 3 tablespoons seedless raspberry spreadable fruit
- ¾ cup sugar
- 3 tablespoons all-purpose flour
  Dash salt
- ¾ cup heavy whipping cream
- ⅓ cup half-and-half cream
- ½ teaspoon almond or vanilla extract
  Fresh raspberries, optional

1. In a large bowl, cream butter and sugar until light and fluffy. Beat in the egg yolks, extract and salt. Gradually beat in the flour.

2. Shape the dough into ¾-in. balls; place in greased mini-muffin cups. Press evenly onto the bottoms and up sides of cups. Bake at 350° for 10-12 minutes or until light brown. Cool in pans on wire racks.

3. Spread ¼ teaspoon spreadable fruit onto the bottom of each crust. In a small bowl, combine the sugar, flour and salt. Whisk in the whipping cream, half-and-half and extract just until blended (mixture will be thin). Spoon 2 teaspoons filling into each crust. Bake 12-14 minutes or until filling just begins to bubble.

4. Cool for 10 minutes before removing from pans; cool completely on wire racks. If desired, top with raspberries. Refrigerate leftovers.

Chocolate Lover's Custards

Just one spoonful of this custard, and you'll be hooked! Smooth and decadent, it's a dessert staple for anyone fond of chocolate.

—**LORRAINE CALAND** SHUNIAH, ON

PREP: 25 MIN. • **BAKE:** 30 MIN. + CHILLING • **MAKES:** 8 SERVINGS

- 2½ cups heavy whipping cream
- ½ cup sugar
- 5 ounces white baking chocolate, chopped
- 6 large egg yolks
- 1 teaspoon vanilla extract

TOPPING
- 3 ounces bittersweet chocolate, melted
- 1 ounce white baking chocolate, melted

1. In a small saucepan, heat cream and sugar until bubbles form around sides of pan. Add white chocolate; stir until smooth. Remove from the heat. In a small bowl, whisk the egg yolks; stir a small amount of hot cream mixture into egg yolks. Return all to the pan, stirring constantly. Stir in the vanilla.

2. Transfer to eight 6-oz. ramekins or custard cups. Place cups in a baking pan; add 1 in. of boiling water to pan. Bake, uncovered, at 325° for 30-35 minutes or until centers are just set (mixture will jiggle). Remove ramekins from water bath; cool for 10 minutes. Cover and refrigerate custard for at least 4 hours.

3. Working one at a time, spread bittersweet chocolate over each custard. Immediately place drops of white chocolate over the top and swirl with a toothpick. Refrigerate for 15 minutes or until chocolate is firm.

Peanut Butter-Chocolate Ice Cream Torte

One of the great taste combinations of all time: peanut butter, chocolate, ice cream and Oreo cookies. This frozen dessert is wonderful to have on hand for when unexpected guests drop by!

—**DANA SOUTHWICK** MANTON, CA

PREP: 30 MIN. + FREEZING • **MAKES:** 12 SERVINGS

24 **Oreo cookies**
⅓ **cup butter, melted**
FILLING
1 **quart chocolate ice cream, softened**
1½ **cups creamy peanut butter**
1 **quart peanut butter ice cream with peanut butter cup pieces, softened**
TOPPING
2 **cups (12 ounces) semisweet chocolate chips**
1 **cup heavy whipping cream**
1½ **cups coarsely chopped miniature peanut butter cups**

1. Place the cookies in a food processor. Cover and pulse until fine crumbs form. Transfer to a large bowl and stir in butter. Press onto the bottom and 1 in. up the sides of a greased 10-in. springform pan; cover and freeze for at least 15 minutes.

2. Spread chocolate ice cream into the crust; cover and freeze until firm. Spread peanut butter over the chocolate layer and top with peanut butter ice cream. Cover and freeze until firm.

3. Place the chocolate chips in a large bowl. In a small saucepan, bring cream just to a boil. Pour over chocolate; whisk until smooth. Cool to room temperature, stirring occasionally. Spread over top of dessert. Immediately sprinkle with peanut butter cups. Cover and freeze for 1 hour before serving.

Blood-Orange Pomegranate Sorbet

When guests set eyes on this ruby-red dessert, they'll know they're in for a treat. It's a lovely ending for a hearty meal.
—*TASTE OF HOME* TEST KITCHEN

PREP: 20 MIN. + FREEZING • **MAKES:** 7 SERVINGS (3½ CUPS)

8 **medium blood oranges**
1 **cup sugar**
1 **cup pomegranate juice**
2 **tablespoons orange liqueur**
Blood orange slices and pomegranate seeds

1. Grate 1 tablespoon orange peel; set aside. Squeeze juice from all of the oranges. Strain and discard pulp. In a small saucepan, combine the sugar, orange juice and peel. Cook and stir over medium heat until sugar is dissolved. Set aside to cool.

2. In a large bowl, combine the orange juice mixture, pomegranate juice and orange liqueur. Fill cylinder of ice cream freezer two-thirds full; freeze according to manufacturer's directions.

3. Transfer to a freezer container; freeze for 4 hours or until firm. Spoon into dessert dishes. Garnish with orange slices and pomegranate seeds.

Chocolate Brownie Waffle Sundaes

One of my best friends loves chocolate as much as I do, so I like to make this over-the-top treat for when we're playing board games or cards.

—VICKI DUBOIS MILLTOWN, IN

START TO FINISH: 30 MIN.
MAKES: 8 WAFFLES (4 SERVINGS)

- 2 ounces unsweetened chocolate, chopped
- 1¼ cups all-purpose flour
- 1 cup packed brown sugar
- ½ teaspoon salt
- ½ teaspoon baking soda
- ¼ teaspoon ground cinnamon
- 2 large eggs
- ½ cup 2% milk
- ¼ cup canola oil
- 1 teaspoon vanilla extract
- ¼ cup chopped pecans
- 4 scoops vanilla ice cream
- ¼ cup chopped pecans, toasted
  Hot caramel and/or fudge ice cream toppings

1. In a microwave, melt chocolate; stir until smooth. Cool slightly.
2. In a large bowl, combine the flour, brown sugar, salt, baking soda and cinnamon. In another bowl, whisk the eggs, milk, oil and vanilla; stir into the dry ingredients until smooth. Stir in pecans and melted chocolate (batter will be thick).
3. Bake in a preheated waffle iron according to the manufacturer's directions until golden brown. Serve with ice cream, toasted pecans and ice cream toppings.

Contest Winner

Berry Dream Cake

I use cherry gelatin to give a boxed cake mix an eye-appealing marbled effect. You can top it with whatever fruit you like.

—MARGARET MCNEIL GERMANTOWN, TN

PREP: 15 MIN. + CHILLING
BAKE: 30 MIN. + COOLING
MAKES: 15 SERVINGS

- 1 package white cake mix (regular size)
- 1½ cups boiling water
- 1 package (3 ounces) cherry gelatin
- 1 package (8 ounces) cream cheese, softened
- 2 cups whipped topping
- 4 cups fresh strawberries, coarsely chopped

1. Prepare and bake cake mix batter according to package directions, using a greased 13x9-in. baking pan.
2. In a small bowl, add boiling water to gelatin; stir 2 minutes to completely dissolve. Cool cake on a wire rack 3-5 minutes. Using a wooden skewer, pierce top of cake to within 1 in. of edge; twist skewer gently to make slightly larger holes. Gradually pour gelatin over the cake, being careful to fill each hole. Cool 15 minutes. Refrigerate, covered, 30 minutes.
3. In a large bowl, beat cream cheese until fluffy. Fold in whipped topping.

Carefully spread over cake. Top with strawberries. Cover and refrigerate for at least 2 hours before serving.

S'more Pie

I love desserts and was looking for a way to use hazelnut spread when I came up with this recipe. I wanted something that could be prepped quickly, too. This certainly delivered on both of my desires.

—KAREN BOWLDEN BOISE, ID

PREP: 10 MIN. + CHILLING • **BROIL:** 5 MIN.
MAKES: 8 SERVINGS

- 1 package (8 ounces) cream cheese, softened
- 1¼ cups heavy whipping cream
- 1 jar (13 ounces) Nutella
- 1 graham cracker crust (9 inches)
- 3 cups miniature marshmallows

1. In a large bowl, beat the cream cheese and cream until thickened. Add Nutella; beat just until combined. Spoon into the crust. Cover and refrigerate for at least 3 hours.
2. Just before serving, top with marshmallows; press gently into filling. Broil 6 in. from the heat for 1-2 minutes or until marshmallows are golden brown.

Cool Watermelon Pops

The kids are going to flip when they see these picture-perfect pops. They're almost too cute to eat (but you'll be glad you did!).

—TASTE OF HOME TEST KITCHEN

PREP: 20 MIN. + FREEZING
MAKES: 28 POPS

- 2 **cups boiling water**
- 1 **cup sugar**
- 1 **package (3 ounces) watermelon gelatin**
- 1 **envelope unsweetened watermelon cherry Kool-Aid mix**
- 2 **cups refrigerated watermelon juice blend**
- ⅓ **cup miniature semisweet chocolate chips**
- 2 **cups prepared limeade**
- 2 **to 3 teaspoons green food coloring, optional**

28 **freezer pop molds or 28 paper cups (3 ounces each) and wooden pop sticks**

1. In a large bowl, combine water, sugar, gelatin and Kool-Aid mix; stir until sugar is dissolved. Add the watermelon juice. Fill each mold or cup with 3 tablespoons watermelon mixture. Freeze until almost slushy, about 1 hour. Sprinkle with chocolate chips. Top molds with holders. If using cups, top with foil and insert sticks through foil. Freeze.

2. In a small bowl, combine limeade and food coloring if desired. If using freezer molds, remove holders. If using paper cups, remove foil. Pour limeade mixture over tops. Return holders or foil. Freeze until firm.

Maple Ricotta Mousse with Candied Pecans

Try not to sneak too many of the maple-flavored nuts while you make dessert. They're even better with the mousse.

—KATHLEEN GILL PAHRUMP, NV

PREP: 25 MIN. + COOLING
MAKES: 4 SERVINGS

- ⅔ **cup maple syrup**
- ¼ **cup chopped pecans**
- ½ **cup heavy whipping cream**
- 1¼ **cups whole-milk ricotta cheese**
- ½ **cup mascarpone cheese**

1. Place syrup in a small saucepan; bring to a boil. Reduce heat; simmer, uncovered, 5 minutes. Transfer to a bowl; cool completely.

2. In a small heavy skillet, cook and stir pecans over medium heat, about 3 minutes. Drizzle with 1 tablespoon cooked syrup; cook and stir 1 minute longer. Spread on foil to cool.

3. In a small bowl, beat cream until soft peaks form. In a large bowl, beat the ricotta and mascarpone cheeses until light and fluffy. Gradually beat in ⅓ cup cooled syrup; gently fold in whipped cream.

4. To serve, spoon the mousse into dessert dishes. Drizzle with remaining cooled syrup; top with candied pecans.

Chocolate-Cherry Ice Cream Cake

I make this ice cream cake ahead of time and keep it in the freezer, wrapped in foil, for a week or so before serving. Just make sure to let it sit out for 10 minutes or so before you cut into it.

—**SCARLETT ELROD** NEWNAN, GA

PREP: 30 MIN. + FREEZING • **MAKES:** 12 SERVINGS

- 1½ cups Oreo cookie crumbs (about 15 cookies)
- 2 tablespoons butter, melted
- 4 cups cherry ice cream, softened if necessary
- 8 Oreo cookies, coarsely chopped
- 1 cup (6 ounces) miniature semisweet chocolate chips, divided
- 4 cups fudge ripple ice cream, softened if necessary
  Sweetened whipped cream, optional
- 12 fresh sweet cherries

1. Preheat oven to 350°. In a small bowl, mix cookie crumbs and butter. Press onto bottom and 1 in. up sides of a greased 9-in. springform pan. Bake 8-10 minutes or until firm. Cool on a wire rack.

2. Spread cherry ice cream into crust; freeze, covered, until firm. Layer with chopped cookies and ½ cup chocolate chips. Spread fudge ripple ice cream over chocolate chips. Sprinkle with remaining chocolate chips. Freeze, covered, 8 hours or until firm.

3. Remove cake from freezer 10 minutes before serving; carefully loosen sides from pan with a knife. Remove rim from pan. If desired, serve with whipped cream. Top with the cherries.

Banana Pudding

I didn't see my son for more than two years after he enlisted in the Marines after high school. When he finally arrived back home, I just grabbed hold of him at the airport and burst out crying. And when we got to our house, the first thing he ate was two bowls of my banana pudding.

—**STEPHANIE HARRIS** MONTPELIER, VA

PREP: 35 MIN. + CHILLING • **MAKES:** 9 SERVINGS

- ¾ cup sugar
- ¼ cup all-purpose flour
- ¼ teaspoon salt
- 3 cups 2% milk
- 3 large eggs
- 1½ teaspoons vanilla extract
- 8 ounces vanilla wafers (about 60 cookies), divided
- 4 large ripe bananas, cut into ¼-inch slices

1. In a large saucepan, mix sugar, flour and salt. Whisk in milk. Cook and stir over medium heat until thickened and bubbly. Reduce heat to low; cook and stir 2 minutes longer. Remove from heat.

2. In a small bowl, whisk eggs. Whisk a small amount of hot mixture into eggs; return all to pan, whisking constantly. Bring to a gentle boil; cook and stir 2 minutes. Remove from heat. Stir in vanilla. Cool 15 minutes, stirring occasionally.

3. In an ungreased 8-in. square baking dish, layer 25 vanilla wafers, half of the banana slices and half of the pudding. Repeat layers.

4. Press plastic wrap onto surface of pudding. Refrigerate 4 hours or overnight. Just before serving, crush remaining wafers and sprinkle over top.

Never-Miss Apple Cake

I bake apple cake to officially usher in the fall season. The family just loves it, and it tastes so good that eating one piece is nearly impossible. You'll see!

—**JAMIE JONES** MADISON, GA

PREP: 40 MIN. • **BAKE:** 50 MIN. + COOLING • **MAKES:** 12 SERVINGS

- 1 package (8 ounces) cream cheese, softened
- ¼ cup sugar
- 1 large egg

CAKE

- 1¾ cups sugar
- 1 cup canola oil
- 3 large eggs
- 2 cups all-purpose flour
- 2 teaspoons baking powder
- 2 teaspoons ground cinnamon
- 1 teaspoon salt
- ¼ teaspoon baking soda
- 2 cups chopped peeled tart apples
- 1 cup shredded carrots
- ½ cup chopped pecans, toasted

PRALINE ICING

- ½ cup packed brown sugar
- ¼ cup butter, cubed
- 2 tablespoons 2% milk
- ½ cup confectioners' sugar
- ½ teaspoon vanilla extract
- ¼ cup chopped pecans, toasted

1. Preheat oven to 350°. Grease and flour a 10-in. fluted tube pan. In a small bowl, beat cream cheese and sugar until smooth; beat in egg.

2. For cake, in a large bowl, beat sugar, oil and eggs until well blended. In another bowl, whisk the flour, baking powder, cinnamon, salt and baking soda; gradually beat into sugar mixture. Stir in apples, carrots and pecans.

3. Transfer half of the batter to prepared pan; layer with cream cheese mixture, then the remaining batter. Bake 50-60 minutes or until a toothpick inserted in cake portion comes out clean. Cool 10 minutes before removing to a wire rack to cool completely.

4. For icing, in a large saucepan, combine brown sugar, butter and milk; bring to a boil. Cook and stir 1 minute. Remove from heat; whisk in confectioners' sugar and vanilla until smooth. Drizzle over cake. Sprinkle with pecans.

NOTES *To remove cakes easily, use solid shortening to grease plain and fluted tube pans. To toast nuts, bake in a shallow pan in a 350° oven for 5-10 minutes or cook in a skillet over low heat until lightly browned, stirring the nuts occasionally.*

Deconstructed Raspberry Pie

No need to go traditional when it comes to this fun graham cracker pie. Try it with fresh strawberries or blueberries, too.

—*TASTE OF HOME* TEST KITCHEN

PREP: 15 MIN. • **BAKE:** 5 MIN. + COOLING • **MAKES:** 4 SERVINGS

- 2⅔ cups fresh raspberries
- 2 teaspoons sugar
- ½ cup graham cracker crumbs
- 2 tablespoons butter, melted
- 4 tablespoons whipped cream in a can
- ¼ teaspoon baking cocoa

1. In a small bowl, combine raspberries and sugar; set aside.

2. In another small bowl, combine cracker crumbs and butter. Press the mixture into an 8x6-in. rectangle on an ungreased baking sheet. Bake at 350° for 5-6 minutes or until lightly browned. Cool completely on a wire rack. Break into large pieces.

3. To assemble, divide half of the graham cracker pieces among four dessert plates; top with ⅓ cup raspberries. Repeat the layers. Top each with 1 tablespoon whipped cream and dust with cocoa.

Substitutions & Equivalents

EQUIVALENT MEASURES

3 teaspoons	= 1 tablespoon		16 tablespoons	= 1 cup
4 tablespoons	= ¼ cup		2 cups	= 1 pint
5⅓ tablespoons	= ⅓ cup		4 cups	= 1 quart
8 tablespoons	= ½ cup		4 quarts	= 1 gallon

FOOD EQUIVALENTS

GRAINS

Macaroni	1 cup (3½ ounces) uncooked	= 2½ cups cooked
Noodles, Medium	3 cups (4 ounces) uncooked	= 4 cups cooked
Popcorn	⅓ - ½ cup unpopped	= 8 cups popped
Rice, Long Grain	1 cup uncooked	= 3 cups cooked
Rice, Quick-Cooking	1 cup uncooked	= 2 cups cooked
Spaghetti	8 ounces uncooked	= 4 cups cooked

CRUMBS

Bread	1 slice	= ¾ cup soft crumbs, ¼ cup fine dry crumbs
Graham Crackers	7 squares	= ½ cup finely crushed
Buttery Round Crackers	12 crackers	= ½ cup finely crushed
Saltine Crackers	14 crackers	= ½ cup finely crushed

FRUITS

Bananas	1 medium	= ⅓ cup mashed
Lemons	1 medium	= 3 tablespoons juice, 2 teaspoons grated peel
Limes	1 medium	= 2 tablespoons juice, 1½ teaspoons grated peel
Oranges	1 medium	= ¼ -⅓ cup juice, 4 teaspoons grated peel

VEGETABLES

Cabbage	1 head	= 5 cups shredded	Green Pepper	1 large	= 1 cup chopped
Carrots	1 pound	= 3 cups shredded	Mushrooms	½ pound	= 3 cups sliced
Celery	1 rib	= ½ cup chopped	Onions	1 medium	= ½ cup chopped
Corn	1 ear fresh	= ⅔ cup kernels	Potatoes	3 medium	= 2 cups cubed

NUTS

Almonds	1 pound	= 3 cups chopped	Pecan Halves	1 pound	= 4½ cups chopped
Ground Nuts	3¾ ounces	= 1 cup	Walnuts	1 pound	= 3¾ cups chopped

EASY SUBSTITUTIONS

When you need...		Use...
Baking Powder	1 teaspoon	½ teaspoon cream of tartar + ¼ teaspoon baking soda
Buttermilk	1 cup	1 tablespoon lemon juice or vinegar + enough milk to measure 1 cup (let stand 5 minutes before using)
Cornstarch	1 tablespoon	2 tablespoons all-purpose flour
Honey	1 cup	1¼ cups sugar + ¼ cup water
Half-and-Half Cream	1 cup	1 tablespoon melted butter + enough whole milk to measure 1 cup
Onion	1 small, chopped (⅓ cup)	1 teaspoon onion powder or 1 tablespoon dried minced onion
Tomato Juice	1 cup	½ cup tomato sauce + ½ cup water
Tomato Sauce	2 cups	¾ cup tomato paste + 1 cup water
Unsweetened Chocolate	1 square (1 ounce)	3 tablespoons baking cocoa + 1 tablespoon shortening or oil
Whole Milk	1 cup	½ cup evaporated milk + ½ cup water

Cooking Terms

Here's a quick reference for some of the most common cooking terms used in recipes:

BASTE To moisten food with melted butter, pan drippings, marinades or other liquid to add more flavor and juiciness.

BEAT A rapid movement to combine ingredients using a fork, spoon, wire whisk or electric mixer.

BLEND To combine ingredients until *just* mixed.

BOIL To heat liquids until bubbles form that cannot be "stirred down." In the case of water, the temperature will reach 212°.

BONE To remove all meat from the bone before cooking.

CREAM To beat ingredients together to a smooth consistency, usually in the case of butter and sugar for baking.

DASH A small amount of seasoning, less than ⅛ teaspoon. If using a shaker, a dash would comprise a quick flip of the container.

DREDGE To coat foods with flour or other dry ingredients. Most often done with pot roasts and stew meat before browning.

FOLD To incorporate several ingredients by careful and gentle turning with a spatula. Used generally with beaten egg whites or whipped cream when mixing into the rest of the ingredients to keep the batter light.

JULIENNE To cut foods into long thin strips much like matchsticks. Used most often for salads and stir-fry dishes.

MINCE To cut into very fine pieces. Used often for garlic or fresh herbs.

PARBOIL To cook partially, usually used in the case of chicken, sausages and vegetables.

PARTIALLY SET Describes the consistency of gelatin after it has been chilled for a short amount of time. Mixture should resemble the consistency of egg whites.

PUREE To process foods to a smooth mixture. Can be prepared in an electric blender, food processor, food mill or sieve.

SAUTE To fry quickly in a small amount of fat, stirring almost constantly. Most often done with onions, mushrooms and other chopped vegetables.

SCORE To cut slits partway through the outer surface of foods. Often used with ham or flank steak.

STIR-FRY To cook meats and/or vegetables with a constant stirring motion in a small amount of oil in a wok or skillet over high heat.

GENERAL RECIPE INDEX

ALPHABETICAL RECIPE INDEX